D0151764

The **New Deal** for Artists

Richard D. McKinzie

Princeton University Press

The **New Deal** for Artists

N8838
.M32

INDIANA
PURDUE
LIBRARY.
APR 1974
FORT WAYNE

for my Mother and Father

Copyright © 1973
by Princeton University Press

All Rights Reserved
LC: 70-39053
ISBN: 0-691-04613-1
This book has been set in Linotype Janson
Printed in the United States of America
by Princeton University Press
Princeton, New Jersey

Contents

List of Illustrations

Preface

Franklin D. Roosevelt frequently spoke of his desire for Americans to have "a more abundant life." Most people assumed the depression President's phrase meant greater material abundance and its obvious by-products, and to a large extent it did. Certainly Roosevelt endorsed an array of new federal activities in the hope of sparking an exhilarating upward spiral of production and consumption. But "a more abundant life" meant more to Roosevelt. It meant improvement in life style which was cerebral as well as physical. Roosevelt came by this desire honestly. His was an altruistic concern long held in America by the best of his class. Dutch patroons like the Roosevelts—old families of wealth, the patrician elite of America—inherited, and were taught at preparatory schools like Groton, a strong sense of noblesse oblige.

Since this elite also received a strong grounding in the traditional arts, it was natural—perhaps it was noblesse oblige in the best sense—that they wished to bestow upon others their feeling of respect and appreciation for the traditional arts. As President, Roosevelt was willing to do the noble thing, and support painting, theater, and other creative arts in the same way he supported them as the "lord" of Hyde Park manor. He would lend his name and limited financial support to the broad effort. He would *not* stoop to brawling in any controversies his support might generate, and he would not allow his patronage to jeopardize enterprises more beloved by him.

Roosevelt's paternalism made possible federal subsidies to the cultural arts. One must hasten to add, however, that other rationales had gained currency which justified national cultural up-lift. Political radicalism, which was strong throughout the depression decade, carried with it the idea of mass cultural awareness and of art forms which reflected a radical ideology and served its purposes. And, during the depression, America experienced an upsurge of nationalism accompanied by patriotic self-examination. This phenomenon included a new concern for locale, the vernacular, and the American scene—for a culture which was uniquely American. The radicals and new nationalists placed the cultural projects of the New Deal much higher in their schemes for the good life than did the President. Roosevelt seems to have been rather satisfied with most of the achievements of the ragtag art projects he appended to federal agencies. (Patricians never expected their patronage to be revolutionary.) The nationalists were appreciative, but wished for more. And the radicals considered the government effort a botched opportunity to provide Americans with their cultural rights.

The American government channeled its subsidies to artists through two agencies: the Section of Painting and Sculpture (later Section of Fine Arts) in the Treasury Department, and the Federal Art Project in the Works Progress Administration. Both could be justified on grounds that they kept the skills of artists from deteriorating at a time when there were few private commissions and sales. Both units also aspired to make art a larger part of American life and thereby improve the quality of that life. The Federal Art Project chief, Holger Cahill, operated under the assumption that large production and mass participation could bring the desired changes. He inclined to leave judgment of the quality of the work to posterity. The Treasury's champion of art for the people, Edward Bruce, held that exposing the public to consistently good art would achieve the goal. Bruce had strong convictions about what constituted "good" art, and artists who worked for the Treasury had to meet his technical and aesthetic standards.

Each art unit had its special successes and failures. The Treasury unit brought painting and sculpture to more than a thousand American towns, many of which formerly had no original art. The Federal Art Project returned to the taxpayers well over 2,500

murals, 17,000 sculptures, 108,000 easels, and 11,000 designs. In addition it operated over 100 Community Art Centers, compiled a 20,000 piece Index of American Design, made posters, models, photographs, and many other items. Neither the Treasury nor the Federal Art Project succeeded in convincing the representatives of the American people that federal art patronage was such an uplifting activity that it should be considered as a proper function of government and therefore be continued. The life of the Treasury art unit depended upon money siphoned from the public construction program of the depression—and that atrophied in the 1940s. When Bruce proved unable to find other financial support, his art unit withered away. The Federal Art Project was tainted by its affiliation with the more politically radical Federal Theatre Project and Federal Writers Project. All of Roosevelt's cultural projects became the focus of the powerful conservative coalition which the voters returned to Congress in 1938. While the art effort survived a few more years, new laws weakened central control and the quality of the work began to decline. The most important questions—about the criteria for "quality" art, the place of art in American life, and the compatibility of the creative temperament with the requirements of bureaucratic efficiency—were never resolved satisfactorily. True to his heritage and his sense of the proper, Roosevelt abandoned the art projects (with no feelings of betrayal) when he concluded that they added nothing significant to the most important task of his life—winning the Second World War.

This book is about an experiment. It is not an evaluation or explication of art work produced under government auspices. It is not an assessment of the effects of the government's largesse upon the psyches of artists during the depression. My focus is much more upon social and political forces than upon the creative urge and its result. Perhaps some who would have preferred a different emphasis will be moved to undertake their own studies. I can only hope that they will find the same sense of excitement in the thirties, and the personal fulfillment in the search, that I found in the course of my own work.

Few ideas or ambitions, it seems to me, are ever transformed into books without the generous assistance of librarians, archivists, participants in the events, colleagues, and friends. Clearly, this book could not exist were it not for the help extended to me by many people. For more than a year Robert M. Kvasnicka and Helen Finneran Ulibarri of the National Archives staff serviced my requests with good humor and competence. Garnett McCoy, archivist of the Archives of American Art, introduced me to the collections of his organization. And I owe thanks to the staffs of the Smithsonian Institution, Columbia Oral History Research Office, and the Library of Congress.

I am indebted to Belisario R. Contreras for long enthusiastic conversations about the Treasury art program. Francis V. O'Connor has bolstered me at many points—making available material from his own research on the Federal Art Project, sharing his thoughts on art and government patronage, and correcting several of my early errors. I am especially appreciative of his help in locating several of the illustrations for this book.

Two professors at Indiana University are largely responsible for the evolution of this book. By his kindly disposition, Professor Robert H. Ferrell helped me keep my enthusiasm high. Just as important, he gave freely of his very special talent with words, and made numerous suggestions for improving the flow and clarity of the prose. An account of my debts to Professor John E. Wiltz is too long to list here. His influence was highly significant in my decision to pursue an academic career; he guided me through initiation and apprenticeship in academe; and he criticized, prodded, and supported me in the writing of this book.

A number of other individuals have contributed to this work. I have been the beneficiary of the humane manner and grand talents of Lalor Cadley, Mary Laing, Marjorie Putney, and Russ Rollins of Princeton University Press. Dorothy C. Miller Cahill kindly permitted me access to the Holger Cahill Oral Reminiscence and volunteered corrections of sections of this manuscript which deal with Cahill. My colleague and friend Theodore A. Wilson asked probing questions and later helped eliminate the rough edges of my prose. Jane DeHart Mathews made useful suggestions based upon her studies of the Federal Theatre. Kathleen O'Connor McKinzie bore my fitful disposition during the long period of digestion and writing, and, because of her own expertise on the Federal Writers Project, saved me from numerous errors of fact and interpretation. For reading and criticizing the manuscript I also wish to acknowledge James T. Patterson, M. A. Robbins, Donald Lord, and Doris Chipman. I am also thankful for the financial support of the American Philosophical Society. With gratitude to all these, and others, who have helped, I reserve for myself the responsibility for any errors or inadequacies.

Kansas City, Missouri   RICHARD D. MCKINZIE
July 1972

The **New Deal** for Artists

1

The Entering Wedge

The museum director who, in the midst of the great depression, criticized murals recently completed and beloved by the artist Thomas Hart Benton withered in Benton's retaliatory blast. "If it were left to me," the Missouri artist growled, "I wouldn't have any museums. Museums don't buy enough of my paintings in an average year to pay for my boy's music lessons. Who looks at paintings in a museum? I'd rather sell mine to saloons, bawdy houses, Kiwanis and Rotary Clubs, Chambers of Commerce— even women's clubs. People go to saloons, but never to museums." To all that, which undoubtedly was true, Benton added: "The typical museum is a grave yard run by a pretty boy with delicate curving wrists and a swing in his gait." As if to add documentary proof to at least a part of his contention, Benton loaned band leader and nightclub owner Billy Rose his painting of "Persephone," mythical queen of Hades who returned to the surface of the earth part of each year. Prominently displayed in Rose's club, The Diamond Horseshoe, 43,000 people saw it in three weeks. In 1930 only two art museums in America—permitting them to count class and special-event attendance and vast herds of school children on escorted "field trips"—could claim that more people passed through their doors during the same length of time.[1]

The fine arts of painting and sculpture never had been an important or conscious force in the lives of the vast majority of Americans. Perhaps the crudities of the early frontiers had generated qualities of mind which were incompatible with the emo-

3

tional appeals of art. Perhaps the parochial disdain of European tastemakers for things American had prompted a retaliatory rejection of the aesthetic standards the continent had dictated. More likely, life for most people simply was too difficult to devote time and money to an enterprise which promised no amelioration of the daily struggle. It seemed natural to those who rose to relative affluence to admire and purchase goods which promised body comfort. Some of the things they coveted boasted extraneous ornaments, as if to testify to the affluence of the owner, but proper objets d'art seemed irrelevant to enjoying or understanding life.

In contrast, those few thousand families who comprised the national "aristocracy" nurtured art as a part of their loudly proclaimed European origins and heritage. Men of wealth in the eighteenth and early nineteenth centuries sent their sons to Europe to drink in education and culture at the fount. The very wealthy whose progeny remained at home demanded of educators strong doses of European "refinements." Thus, by definition, an upper-class American was interested in art, albeit European-style art. In time, this elite supported a substantial group of native-born artists, most of whom imitated French and Italian masters. A few American artists achieved international fame, and by the second decade of the twentieth century, many had abandoned sterile copying from continental models for the subject matter of their own country.

Emergence of a distinctively "American" style in the plastic arts was slow. The President's Research Committee on Social Trends, appointed by Herbert Hoover in 1929, reported in 1933 that American art still embodied strong foreign influence. The Committee found that conflict between native impulse, which was becoming stronger, and foreign influence resulted in art characterized by much uncertainty and experimentation. The Committee also placed the federal government's imprimatur upon what laymen and critics had been saying for years; that, sociologically, painting and sculpture were not important, that "for the overwhelming majority of the American people the fine arts of painting and sculpture, in their non-commercial, non-industrial forms, do not exist."[2]

Liberal intellectuals in these years, in some ways the philosophical if not the financial heirs of the earlier patrons, believed that art, especially in light of increased leisure, education, and abundance, could speak to all men, could enrich and give meaning to the lives of factory workers and farmhands. This uplifting ability of art would have been demonstrated much earlier, more than a few of them argued, had not the "robber barons" in the latter part of the nineteenth century corrupted American artists. Those gaudily rich scions of the industrial revolution who displaced the old aristocrats, conspicuous consumers to a man, asked artists to prove the virtue of property. They thereby brought false values into the studios and deflected artists from their legitimate goals. Acquisitive men bought only from "famous" artists. A name for its own sake became important, talent and the quality of individual paintings were often ignored, and prices of art works depended upon the artist's rank in the "star system." Hoping to win a place in this artificial hierarchy, lesser artists often quoted prices far higher than they would have accepted. The typical art salesman, a critic of the system said, behaved "as if he were a combination custom tailor and diamond merchant."[3]

Prices and quality became hopelessly confused; indeed, for most people the terms were synonymous. Even the collector-financier J. P. Morgan, when asked if he would look at an old master priced at $12,000, replied that he did not purchase cheap pictures. The average citizen came to revere art for its dollar value and thought of most everything above the level of religious lithographs as the exclusive enjoyment of the wealthy. As a result, artists developed affected mannerisms, unnecessarily erudite jargon, and social amenities for public consumption while further alienating and bewildering those Americans who liked "pretty things."

Feeling among intellectuals was that the depression was a blessing which saved art in the United States from permanent harm. Prices and sales had dropped precipitously. A 165 market price index for art in 1929 had shriveled to 50 by 1933. Art importation was down over 80 percent and the production of artists' materials was off by almost half. A more important point was that by curtailing art purchases by the wealthy the de-

depression good in some ways

pression did much to smash the snobbishness and artificiality which had characterized American art. The economic crisis, these observers admitted, also brought numbness and despair to the artistic community. It remained for a new force to provide impetus for a new art and for its reconciliation with society. Civic groups such as the National Recovery Council, a number of artists' organizations, and several artists saw government as the logical agent of reform. Most proponents of federal patronage glossed over the potential problems of censorship, regimentation, and obtaining public support. Most of them invoked the examples of European subsidies to artists, although few knew the details of the European programs or studied the results.

The artist George Biddle believed in 1933 that the federal government could produce "a real spurt in the arts." Biddle, who was to become the "father of federal art projects" and spokesman for influential artists organizations, had the artistic background and social credentials to make his voice heard. He was a member of an influential Philadelphia family, descended, the society pages noted frequently, from American heroes William and Edmond Randolph. He was the brother of future Solicitor General and New Deal adviser Francis Biddle, and he had attended Groton and Harvard with President Franklin D. Roosevelt. Having no taste for the career in law which family tradition dictated and for which he had prepared himself, Biddle sailed for France in 1911 and took up a new life as an artist. For all but one of the next 15 summers he traveled on the continent and in Latin America, meeting and learning from such famous artists as Mary Cassatt and Diego Rivera. He quickly proved himself as a painter, and the most casual observer of his work knew that he had a sensitive social conscience. Those better acquainted with him were aware of his belief that art had not functioned as a positive influence upon society for centuries; that it had been, "so to speak, a prostitute, well paid, sleeping in expensive beds, but divorced . . . from our program of life." They also knew of his conviction that American art could blossom by finding expression in the great social adjustments of the depression and New Deal.[4]

Biddle was convinced that since 1900 appreciation of art in America, however slightly, had been increasing. The number of visitors to art museums and the number of students in public school and college art classes had enlarged in the 1920s. Money invested in art museums had risen from $15,000,000 in 1910 to $58,000,000 in 1930. By the latter year the nation boasted 167 art museums, 56 percent more than in 1920, and art museums led scientific, industrial, and general museums in rate of growth and investment in buildings. Biddle believed the gains, small in terms of the potential audience, could be accelerated by placing easily understood art before more people.[5]

Biddle saw the mural as a particularly important art form of the future. His inspiration, clearly, was the experiment in the 1920s sponsored by Mexican President Alvaro Obregon in which young artists covered public buildings in Mexico City with murals expressing the ideas of the Mexican revolution. For this work the artists had received a small salary from the government—at low wages. The commitment of the Mexican muralists to the social ideals they depicted, the freedom given them to express their views, and the release from monetary worries enabled them to produce what some critics, then and since, have considered the greatest national school of mural painting since the Italian Renaissance. A similar achievement, Biddle believed, could be brought into being in the United States.

On May 9, 1933, Biddle addressed a letter to his old classmate, Franklin D. Roosevelt, then in his third month in the White House. Noting the grand achievements of the Mexican muralists, he portrayed young American artists, supporters of a Roosevelt-guided social revolution, as being eager to express the ideals of that revolution on the public walls of America. The work could help achieve Roosevelt's social ideals and would remain as monuments to them. The artistic community wanted only the government's cooperation. Biddle thought "a little impetus" could spark a wave of national expression in socially oriented mural art.[6]

As a beginning, Biddle wanted to organize a group of muralists who shared common social and aesthetic ideas, and to have this group, under government auspices, decorate one public building. After the group received its commission the artists would work together for a year, encouraging, criticizing, "gathering ideas from the community of thought." In this way no artist would

5

think only of his assigned space. The result would be a single, social, ordered theme "a little different from anything before." Biddle hoped the gesture by the government, and the paintings it produced, would receive wide publicity and encourage architects and the public to cooperate further with artists. He thought that it would stimulate younger artists and architectural sculptors across the country to organize, and that these groups would select the men to receive future work.[7]

Biddle's idea of public employment of artists during the depression was not new to the President. Artists had been on the New York state payroll while he was Governor. The state work relief director, Harry L. Hopkins, in 1932 had put to work several needy artists under supervision of New York City's College Art Association. Before Congress had passed the New Deal's first relief bill, more than 100 artists were teaching and painting murals in settlement houses in New York at state expense. However, Biddle was the first to win a sympathetic hearing from the President for the suggestion that the federal government subsidize artists.[8]

His idea struck a chord, and Roosevelt asked him to talk with Assistant Secretary of the Treasury Lawrence W. Robert, the custodian of federal buildings. Biddle said that his heart "beat with excitement" when he received the President's reply. "Here," he recalled, "was the entering wedge to the promotion of an idea."[9]

He set about bringing together American mural artists, who, in his opinion, were or might be kindred spirits, and quickly received tentative commitments from some of the most eminent: Thomas Hart Benton, Edward Laning, Reginald Marsh, Henry Varnum Poor, Boardman Robinson, and Maurice Sterne. Therefore, early in June 1933 Biddle drove to Washington from his country home in New York to confer with Assistant Secretary Robert. He learned that the Treasury Department, the builder and custodian of all federal buildings, had authority also to commission artists to decorate them. In practice the architect of a building usually picked the artists to decorate it, and because a handful of architects was responsible for the familiar "federal

classic" style, the equally small group of artists known to the architects decorated almost all federal buildings.

Robert told Biddle the new multimillion dollar Department of Justice building in Washington's federal triangle remained unembellished because the money which Congress had authorized for art in new buildings was not being spent during the depression. In effect the government had declared that art was a luxury. No doubt because Roosevelt had encouraged Biddle, Robert now indicated that the policy might be changed. To gain additional support, Biddle outlined his plan to Eleanor Roosevelt, Secretary of Labor Frances Perkins, Secretary of the Interior Harold L. Ickes, and Assistant Secretary of Agriculture Rexford G. Tugwell. To each he emphasized the eagerness of young, liberal artists to express, and to leave an artistic record of, "the ideas for which the present administration is fighting."[10]

He soon ran into trouble. Roosevelt had forwarded Biddle's proposal to the National Commission of Fine Arts, presidential advisers on art since its creation by Congress in 1910. The Commission by law and executive order advised upon the design and location of buildings in the national capital, upon selection and location of public monuments, fountains, and statues, and upon "questions involving art . . . with which the federal government is concerned."[11] Charles Moore, chairman of the Commission since 1915, and six other presidential appointees comprising the body held more conservative views of art and politics than did Biddle and his group. The men who guarded Pierre L'Enfant's plan for the capital opposed all that smacked of the twentieth century and a good part of that which belonged to the nineteenth. They demanded that art in Washington be "classical." One member, Egerton Swartwout, an architect, revealed something of the Commission's outlook when he wrote to chairman Moore that he hated the word "functionalism," for "with this wretched concrete anything is possible, and to my way of thinking architecture as such has really ceased to exist; that is, architecture meaning beautified construction."[12]

Classical architecture, of course, demanded art in a classical spirit. It went without saying that unseemly poverty generated by the depression, and the inclination of those who gathered around Biddle to exploit it in art, was inconsistent with the Commission's idea of the classical spirit. In time Moore was to pronounce, in behalf of the Commission, any government promotion of contemporary art "fundamentally unsound" because ephemeral conditions influenced it and it lacked "those elements of stability consonant with the stability of the Nation itself." Art worthy of a federal building, in a word, must possess universality, beauty, and must promote American patriotism.[13]

Eugene F. Savage, a painter of note and also a member of the Commission, wrote a long criticism of Biddle's plan which Moore endorsed and sent to the President on July 28. The Commission's report reminded Roosevelt that the beauty of the capital was in no sense the result of experiment. It was the result of work by men of proved dependability. Biddle's band of muralists, "painters of easel pictures of an incidental nature," irresponsibly demanded such freedom as would negate the traditional collaboration between architect, sculptor, painter, and landscape architect. Worse, the profession had condemned the work of members of the group for "chaotic composition"; their work professed a social faith abhorrent to the general public; and the work of some members had embarrassed those who commissioned it. "I would think," Savage reported, "the government would be glad to avoid such experiences."[14]

This incident reflected the bitterness of long standing between conservative (or "academic") artists and modernists. Essentially, the conservatives based their art on the past, taking a great many of their models, although certainly not all, from classical Greece and Rome. They respected traditional notions about form and space and color. They saw art as noble and scholarly, and, if it were good, slightly mystical. The modernists wanted to be free of the past, to express the spirit and idiom of the day—power, speed, misery, brotherhood, Ford cars, pinstripe suits. They were less interested in timeless virtues and passions than in the awesome present of the 1930s. Some modernists focused on personal feelings which they could best express in nonrepresentational patterns.

Of course, the meanings of "conservative" and "modernist" were constantly changing. Many modernists of the early 1920s were comfortably conservative by definitions accepted in 1933. The issue between conservatives and modernists was not, at base, whether artistic modes should change, but how rapidly and in what manner, and what continuity, or lack of it, there should be with the past. Biddle's proposal that the government commission his group of avowed modernists raised the factional squabbling to new heat.

Roosevelt was interested in Biddle's idea, but he obviously did not wish to embroil himself in a controversy over aesthetics. In forwarding the Commission's report to Biddle, he remarked only that it did "not sound very encouraging for the mural paintings." Biddle was not easily defeated. He was determined to decorate the Department of Justice building and continued to work for his plan through other channels. He won the support of Louis Simon, supervising architect for the Treasury Department, and of Charles L. Borie, architect of the Department of Justice building. Robert began to show initiative, writing that despite the report of the Commission of Fine Arts the Treasury could probably work out an agreeable program.

Biddle made a serious effort to conciliate the Commission of Fine Arts. He sent in testimonials to prove that members of his group were more than "mediocre easel painters" and that the profession, by and large, respected their work. Eugene Savage eventually modified his first damning assessment of the group, contending that many of the statements in his report stemmed from misunderstanding. But aesthetic and political differences were too great for the Commission to condone Biddle's scheme.[15]

Meantime, Robert had turned for advice to a fellow Treasury Department official, Edward Bruce, who had recently come to the Treasury Department as an expert on silver and had accompanied the American delegation to the London Economic Conference in June 1933. Expertise in monetary policy was only a peripheral talent for Bruce. As a young man, he had attended Columbia Law School, but after a short practice in New York migrated to the Philippines where he managed to borrow enough

1 Edward Bruce in the late 1920s, before he became chief of the Public Works of Art Project and the Section of Fine Arts

money to buy the *Manila Times*. Bruce later entered the China trade and became president of the Pacific Development Company. When this venture failed, he decided to develop artistic talents discovered at Columbia and took up painting as a profession. At forty-four Bruce turned down attractive opportunities in both business and law and went to Italy where for six years he studied painting under the American artist Maurice Sterne. For ten years Bruce painted successfully, holding numerous exhibitions and selling some pieces for as much as $5,000. He came to Washington in 1932 to represent the West Coast Chambers of Commerce on the issue of Philippine independence and, perhaps ironically, was recruited by the Treasury Department as an expert on international monetary matters.[16] Knowing Bruce's background, Robert asked his opinion of Biddle's proposal, indicating that the Treasury was willing to consider a new method of securing art for federal buildings.

Bruce was enthusiastic about the prospect of government patronage. In autumn 1933 he arranged a series of "working dinners" in his spacious Northwest Washington home at which ranking government personages, many of whom he had met as a lobbyist and Treasury adviser, were recruited to the idea of more public art. Assistant Secretary Robert, Justice Harlan Stone of the Supreme Court, Jerome Frank of the Department of Agriculture, Jacob Baker of the Emergency Relief Commission, and Ralph Renault of the *Washington Post* attended the first dinner on October 31. All recognized the plight of artists and the virtue of "doing something for art." Robert stated that he could ignore the Commission of Fine Arts and place mural decorations in public buildings if he had a sponsoring committee representing "a sufficient variety of art interests so that he would be protected in acting on their advice." Bruce's collaborators agreed that about 25 leading artists, critics, and museum directors ought to sponsor and lend prestige to any program that might evolve. At this same meeting Robert asked Bruce to see Biddle, who, he said, "had independently been active" on the subject of government employment of artists.[17]

Early in November, Biddle and Bruce combined forces. They talked with Charles L. Borie, architect of the Department of Jus-

8

2 Edward Bruce, *San Francisco*, 1928, oil commissioned for the Governing Board Room of the San Francisco Stock Exchange

tice building, who, according to usual practice, would select artists for the building's embellishments. Borie was enthusiastic about murals and thought "nobody could handle it better than ... Mr. George Biddle." However, the Treasury refused to release funds for the project. Bruce and Biddle next confronted Public Works Administrator Harold L. Ickes, who could, if he so decided, set aside a certain amount of money for artists from the $400,000,000 being transferred from PWA to the relief administration.

The search for a patron in the bureaucracy was at an end. After listening for twenty minutes, Ickes expressed "entire approval" of the principle of work for artists financed from relief funds. Ickes fancied himself a friend of art, but some have speculated that he wanted to prevent Assistant Secretary Robert, whom he disliked for political reasons, from enhancing his image as the depression patron of artists. In any case, the next day, Ickes's general counsel, Henry Hunt, sent a memorandum to Relief Administrator Harry L. Hopkins recommending transfer of part of the relief allotment to the Treasury Department for a project to employ artists.[18]

With money on the way, Bruce and Biddle had second thoughts about its administration. They concluded that the factionalism prevalent in the art community would make undesirable an advisory committee of artists and sculptors. Bruce suggested to Robert, and got, an advisory committee of New Dealers and the chairman of the Commission of Fine Arts, with himself as secretary of the committee and overlord of the project. The advisory committee never exercised real influence over the project; Edward Bruce certainly did.[19]

George Biddle preferred painting murals to administering a grant for a project. He relaxed his efforts in expectation that the money promised by Ickes would enable him to begin work soon in the Department of Justice building. Edward Bruce thus emerged as chief promoter for government employment of artists. Aggressive and dedicated, he also had the advantages of being an insider in the bureaucracy and of having a legal and business background. Bruce's guidance meant a shift in rationale and goals. Biddle hoped to receive government patronage for a self-appointed group of socially concerned artists; Bruce leaned toward subsidizing as many "good" artists as possible in the hope of arousing national enthusiasm for art. To launch the program Bruce talked of using Biddle's group, "with perhaps three or four additions," to decorate the Justice building, but there would be no other self-appointed groups. Biddle stressed portrayal in pigment and silica of the ideals of the Roosevelt administration. Bruce lectured dinner guests on the theme of federal art patronage as a pump-priming investment. He argued that good art created desire which in turn created demand. "If we can create the demand for beauty in our lives," he promised, "our slums will go. The ugliness will be torn down and beauty will take its place." Even Charles Moore of the Commission of Fine Arts, whom Biddle had called an "old dodo" among other things, found enthusiasm for such reasoning.[20]

Bruce devised a scheme in which a decentralized organization would aid artists and carry beauty to the people. The country would be divided into regions, each with a regional chairman and advisory committee selected by the central office. The regional groups would select and supervise artists. These regional committees, according to the plan, would organize subcommittees "to foster local initiative." The Public Works of Art Project (PWAP), as Bruce named the proposed appendage of the Treasury Department, should receive enough money to support 1,500 artists at $35 to $45 weekly, 1,000 artists at $20 to $30, and 500 laborers at $15 weekly. Biddle, on reading the details of the large project which his modest proposal had precipitated, said he experienced the same "generous feeling" he had had at the 1913 Armory Show, the alleged birthplace of modern art in America.[21]

Harry Hopkins agreed to allocate to PWAP $1,039,000 for artists' relief. The money came from the new Civil Works Administration, the agency created to administer the $400,000,000 transferred from Ickes's PWA. To help unemployed workers through the winter, Hopkins's CWA intended to employ 4,000,000 people within 30 days, to pay them "a going rate," and to exempt them from "embarrassing certifications by relief officials." In announcing the inclusion of artists, Hopkins explained that they had been "hit just as hard by unemployment as any other producing worker." Government and art both had a service to render the people of the country, and it was common sense to let them do it together.[22] Of course, in handling the art project the Treasury subsidiary would be bound by all CWA policies and regulations.

Now that financing was assured and Robert had approved the organizational plan for the PWAP, Bruce turned to enlisting people who could make his idea work. With Robert's consent and the blessing of his highly placed collaborators, Bruce sent invitations to over a dozen prominent museum directors to meet in Washington.

The museum directors and advisory committee met at Bruce's home in Northwest Washington on December 8, 1933. Eleanor Roosevelt was a special guest. Her knitting punctuating her comments, the First Lady told the gathering it was "unbelievable that a great nation could fail to utilize . . . its creative talents to the fullest." Although the museum directors all spoke in favor of government aid to art, some were slow to comprehend the plan before them. One director asked if he could use government money to purchase a mural panel from a local "genius." "You can't," Bruce put in, "but you can set the genius to work next week to paint another, at $35 a week." A director from New Orleans asked if he could use his artists to record "the dying scenes of the Old South, the Negro shanties, the wooden plows, the stills." Without denying the request, Bruce reminded his questioner that the Eighteenth Amendment had been repealed and that there was "a new deal in art and liquor." "Why not get your boys," he asked in turn, "to depict the grand new high power, mass production stills that are turning out good liquor for the new administration?" After lengthy discussion Bruce's plan won approval and, before the afternoon ended, the group organized a regional PWAP committee in each of the 16 geographic divisions set up by the Civil Works Administration. The museum directors present became chairmen with the understanding that they and their appointed committees would hire artists and supervise their work.[23] Bruce personally selected chairmen and committees for the few regions not represented.

It was necessary to spend the allotment from the CWA before

3 Washington, 1933: initiating the Public Works of Art Project. From left to right, Edward Bruce, Eleanor Roosevelt, Lawrence W. ("Chip") Robert, assistant secretary of the Treasury, and Forbes Watson, technical director of PWAP, with a map of the regions into which artists would be organized

11

February 15, 1934, although there was talk of an additional grant for the art project if it proved successful. The first item of business was to hire artists, and to that end the regional chairmen dispersed to spread the word and to set up their payrolls. Regional committees met in seemingly endless sessions; and Bruce at one stage did not sleep for three nights. These efforts produced immediate results. Not sure to whom they owed their sudden good fortune, artists all over the nation happily abandoned idleness or stopgap employment to face blank canvas with new hope. Eight days after the organizational meeting 86 artists received their first checks.[24]

The idea of government employment electrified lovers of art. Many people proclaimed the end of the alienation of the American artist. Homer St. Gaudens, director of the Carnegie Institute of Art, exulted that at last artists would feel they had been "taken into the national soul." Caught up in the enthusiasm he had helped to create, Edward Bruce encouraged the notion that the artist was like any other artisan who paid rent, ate, and had a family—not a remote aesthete who lived in an attic and existed on inspiration. The fact that government had taken such a realistic position, Bruce contended, made the PWAP more than an employment program; it could not help but stimulate the creative juices of grateful American artists.[25]

Forbes Watson, who was appointed the $300-a-month technical director of the project, became its chief philosopher and spokesman. Bruce had approached this former art critic of the *Brooklyn Eagle* and editor of *The Arts* on a busy street in New York City, had reminded him of his duty to the country, art, and American artists, and invited him to join the PWAP. Watson, who was respected by artists even if they disagreed with him, turned out scores of articles and speeches proclaiming the artist's new status. He believed the government program could effect a "complete change in the economic and social relationship between the artist and his fellow citizens." Emancipated from dependence on the plutocracy, the artist could develop a larger, simpler, and more natural commerce in art and come into closer contact with American life. The new circumstances hardly could fail to inspire a deeper interpretation of that life. The influence of the artist on the community would be inestimable. Watson foresaw "new and . . . superior social structures." He wrote that the artist, "happily installed in the simple life," would tend to "devulgarize the community and to raise its social level to the higher spiritual plane on which the artist normally exists."[26]

Not all artists or art organizations so understood their new status. Some individuals expressed what Watson called "morning-coated horror" at the idea of employing artists at $40 a week. More specific criticism focused on the program's leadership. From New York City, home of the nation's most influential art organizations, came sharp protest regarding the Treasury's choice for PWAP regional chairman, Mrs. Juliana Force, director of the Whitney Museum of American Art. The protesters, mostly conservative artists, feared that Mrs. Force would deliver the program to the modernists. The presidents of the National Sculptors Society, the Society of Mural Painters, the Architectural League, the American Artists Professional League and others—eight in all—charged that Mrs. Force and a regional committee "identified with a definite art movement" would favor "a very small percentage of those artists professionally engaged." There was talk in traditional circles of carrying an appeal to the President.[27]

The American Artists Professional League drew up an alternate plan wherein representatives of leading art societies would comprise a "Board of Control and Award of Art Commissions for the CWA Fund." According to the League, these organizations knew the abilities and needs of artists better than a government agency and would be more representative of prevailing tastes.[28]

Mrs. Force retorted that the Treasury Department barred artists and art critics from regional committees and, therefore, she could not placate her detractors by appointing them. In truth, the Washington administrators were vague about qualifications for regional committeemen and some regional committees did include artists. At any rate, Mrs. Force denied the charges, pointed to members of her group who were associated with the academic tradition, and withdrew from the controversy. "I will work to the limit," she told the press, "but I won't waste time fighting."[29]

Neither Bruce nor Watson seriously considered offering palliatives to the New York clubs. For political reasons they claimed from the beginning that the Treasury Department was inalterably catholic in taste; but they were no friends of the hand-in-vest portrait or gods-and-slain-dragons academic school. Watson's attitude toward the clubs was distaste bordering on contempt; he thought of them as exclusive, self-serving coteries that had judiciously inserted the words "national" or "American" in their titles to enable them to solicit funds for fine-sounding prizes—plums for the adroit in art politics. Now PWAP had come along and threatened the system. Watson could understand that a "good president of a plum-picking club would be remiss in his duties if he did not protest the indignity to such beautiful objects as plums of putting them out of reach of his fellow club members." Much of the criticism over control of the federal grant was the result of honest differences on aesthetics. However, the most accurate characterization of the infighting was probably that of the artist John Sloan; it was: "the natural result of throwing corn in the chicken coop. There are bound to be feathers flying."[30]

The regional chairmen and their committees faced large problems when they began to employ artists. The CWA was an employment program, Assistant Secretary Robert admonished the chairmen. PWAP could choose from among all artists who met the single qualification of current unemployment. Bruce and Robert expected the chairmen to enroll the best of the unemployed. In a larger sense, Harry Hopkins made clear, CWA was a relief program to provide unemployed workers with "a decent American standard." Should an artist's ability or his need weigh heaviest with PWAP regional committees? If it were ability, then there was the matter of recognizing it. The search for merit, Robert announced, would not be dominated by any particular school or group.[31] Bruce insisted that the subject of the art produced be "the American scene." Did prescribing the American scene give academic, modern, and abstract artists equal opportunity, and could the committees be sufficiently impartial and competent to admit and compare the merits of work from each school? The Treasury plan called for dividing artists into two classes. "Class A" artists, the best ones, would draw about $38 a week; "Class B" at least $10 less. Could committees presume to rank members of

a profession in which there were so few universally accepted standards? The inconsistency with which regional committees reacted to these problems, and the haste in which they employed the first artists, left many disenchanted with what had seemed, initially, such a noble gesture.

Aspiring government artists came in droves to PWAP offices. The first applicant in Los Angeles was a plumber who "did a little painting." He was followed by a flood of little old ladies who painted little scenes from nature, art students, and down-at-the-heel commercial artists. Fully three-fourths of Southern California's applicants were not bona fide artists. From the District of Columbia-Maryland-Virginia region came the report that the bulk of the work of applicants was so obviously unsuitable that it wasted the time of the full committee to review all of it. Artists were waiting in line at the Chicago office before the newspapers announced the project. Of the large number who presented themselves after the newspaper announcement, the committee permitted about 700 to register and employed about 145. Despite the number of amateurs and incompetents, each committee needed a larger quota than that assigned it by Bruce's office.[32] To legitimate artists who thought of the PWAP as a relief agency with special sympathy for their profession, it was particularly humiliating to flunk a relief "quality" test and be rejected.

Nowhere was the reaction to rejection more vociferous than in New York City, the center of art in the United States. Mrs. Force had 600 jobs to dispense. To help make the selections she included on her committee, among others, the director of the Museum of Modern Art, the curator of paintings for the Metropolitan Museum of Art, and the director of the Brooklyn Museum. She announced the program in a confused statement of its relief purpose. To charges that she would promote only modern art she retorted: "This is a relief measure. We are interested in knowing only one thing about any artist, that is 'Is he in need of employment'?"[33] In the next three months 4,000 artists and pseudo-artists indicated by their registration that they were.

To get the project off to a speedy start Mrs. Force hired a few artists she knew through her work as director of the Whitney Museum. Later, she registered a few more at her office in the

Whitney; but when it became obvious that there would be an overwhelming response, she turned over registration to the New York CWA office. Artists found these procedural shifts confusing and frustrating.

During the first week of the PWAP, Mrs. Force sent a form letter to every art organization in the city—except one—requesting lists of unemployed artists. As work became available the regional committee sifted through the cards and lists and called in for review the work of artists they thought might fit into the jobs available.[34]

The notable omission among these organizations, the one which did not receive the form letter, was the Unemployed Artists Group. The Unemployed Artists Group had organized in September 1933, when New York state's Emergency Work Bureau phased out its art project. The impetus for its formation was the desire of ex-project workers for further state assistance for artists. The Group soon gained a reputation for radicalism. When the College Art Association of New York called a meeting between unemployed artists and representatives of the state Temporary Emergency Relief Administration, Philip Bard, leader of the Unemployed Artists Group, demanded from the floor that the state develop a new art project. In the meantime, he asserted, it should pay all artists a living wage, allowing them to work in their own studios, or buy their completed pictures in lieu of salary. The demand created such a sensation that the meeting broke up in confusion. Members of New York City's art establishment who were present at the meeting recognized few of the 300 individuals who so overwhelmingly supported Bard. They concluded that the meeting was "packed with undesirable radicals."[35] Indeed, many of the Unemployed Artists Group had connections with the left-wing John Reed Club, anathema to patricians such as Juliana Force.

Ostensibly, Mrs. Force omitted the Unemployed Artists from her mailing because it had no known address. The organization nonetheless sent in a list of unemployed artists. When the regional committee invited practically no one from the Group to display work, the militants concluded that Mrs. Force and the committee had discriminated in favor of better known artists. As if in anticipation of this charge, Mrs. Force modified her stand on the project's relief purpose, announcing that Washington had ordered elimination of the words "Needy" and "Relief" in connection with PWAP artists and employment of the "best material available."[36]

The Unemployed Artists refused to accept the new interpretation, and on December 28, 1933 a delegation of about 50 members appeared at the Whitney Museum. Their spokesman, Bernarda Bryson, demanded to know why artists who had registered first remained uncalled while some unregistered artists had commissions, and why artists in dire need remained hungry while

4 Bernarda Bryson (PWAP), *Union Square*

5 Phil Bard (FAP), *Aftermath*

some unemployed but solvent artists had commissions. Mrs. Force tried to explain the initial confusion about registration. She pointed out that work for city buildings had to win the approval of the New York City Art Commission and in some cases of city officials. Securing approved projects was a slow process and the committee then selected the best artists for approved projects, regardless of the order of their registration. Miss Bryson, who was soon to become Mrs. Ben Shahn, insisted that many artists were in great need. "Need," Mrs. Force brought her up short, "is not in my vocabulary." While a Whitney Museum stenographer wrote feverishly, Miss Bryson, the poor, young radical, and Mrs.

Force, the comfortable, middle-aged aristocrat, exchanged charge for countercharge. Presently Mrs. Force turned to her accusers: "You admit that you came with a preconceived idea that I play favorites. . . . I tell you that is an accusation I will not tolerate and I will answer no more questions."[37] In effect, the Unemployed Artists Group had been thrown out of the office.

Two weeks later the militants, renamed the Unemployed Artists Association, marched 100 strong from the Garibaldi statue in Washington Square to the Whitney. When Mrs. Force learned they were coming she called the police. Plainclothesmen from Manhattan's eighth precinct arrived to protect museum property

15

and control the crowd in the street. Philip Bard and four other marchers were permitted inside. They entered, while protesting criminal treatment and police intimidation. An altercation followed in which Mrs. Force refused to proceed until Bard retracted the word "intimidation." He did so, according to the hastily resummoned stenographer, only when the police lieutenant present "placed hands" on him as a prelude to removal. Outside the museum, police stood as a protective barrier between the museum and the milling artists who carried banners and placards reading: "THE WORD 'NEED' IS NOT IN MY VOCABULARY, SAYS MRS. FORCE," "I REGISTERED THREE WEEKS AGO—WHEN WILL I GET A CARD?," "WE PROTEST AGAINST THE 'MERIT' SYSTEM," and "WE DEMAND SUMMONS FOR ALL ARTISTS IN ORDER OF REGISTRATION."[38]

Inside, Bard insisted once again that Mrs. Force fill her quota, employ hungry artists, and permit Unemployed Artists to serve on the selection committee. "I am sorry you can't insist with me," Mrs. Force interrupted, "I am an appointee of the government. . . . This was an autocratic appointment. The government told me to select the artists and I am selecting them and that is that." Emboldened by the presence of the police, Mrs. Force made her own demands: insisting that the artists cease marching on the Whitney and that they submit their complaints in writing. When Bard retorted that artists' democratic rights included being hired when in need or at least being a part of the selection committee and that the protests would continue, Mrs. Force snapped, "I can't waste my time any longer."[39] The interview abruptly ended.

The following week in a room above Stewart's Restaurant on West 4th Street, two of Mrs. Force's employees—spies for an evening—mingled with the Unemployed Artists who had met to reaffirm their position that all artists had a right to be employed and to demand that government continue and expand the art project, end classification of artists, and that officials cease issuing misleading statements. The organization leaders stressed the importance of group protests and assured the artists that their marches on the Whitney were a small part of the greater mass action which was needed to secure justice for workers in all the crafts. While the radicals planned further picketing of the Whitney, Mrs. Force was compiling a brief for the District Attorney to discredit or establish the disloyalty or criminality of the Unemployed Artists Association.[40]

Meanwhile, two well-meaning New Yorkers provoked an incident which embittered the Unemployed Artists even more toward Mrs. Force. The artist John Sloan and the sculptor William Zorach, both so eminent that money was not a main consideration, took PWAP jobs in New York paying $38.25 a week to show their appreciation for the federal gesture toward art. Both technically qualified by signing PWAP application statements that their regular incomes were less than $60 a month. Sloan, whose predepression paintings had sold for $2,000 to $50,000, admitted in good humor that he paid $175 a month for his studio apartment and could get along without the $38.25. But the news "flabbergasted" the New York deputy CWA chairman, and a hundred artists demonstrated outside Mrs. Force's office demanding that needy artists receive preference.[41] Their good intentions frustrated, Sloan and Zorach resigned.

When quota cuts in February affected the entire CWA and reduced the number of PWAP artists, the Unemployed Artists joined 5,000 fellow militants who marched on the Madison Avenue CWA headquarters, encircled the building, and sang the "Internationale" while a committee presented demands inside. The sizable minority of artists who believed with the 5,000 marchers that government had the obligation to sustain them in their occupations during the depression descended on Mrs. Force with demands and ominous delegations eight times before the end of March. Concerned for the safety of art objects during the demonstrations and perhaps for her own safety, Mrs. Force abruptly closed the Whitney and moved her office to CWA headquarters.

Mrs. Force was incredibly abrasive and her procedures were both unimaginative and autocratic, but her equivocal position on the precedence of talent over need merely reflected the confusion on that point in Washington. In the rush to make use of available funds before the February 15, 1934 deadline, regional committees in many cases hired the first unemployed artists who appeared and hired, thereafter, those who seemed in greatest need. The greater attention to need than to quality caught Bruce and Watson off guard. Their goal was to advance art, and they knew the public would judge the project more by the quality of the work than by the number of artists saved.

Some weeks passed before the PWAP administrators obtained appropriate assurances from CWA officials. They then ordered regional chairmen to "eliminate the drones" and to advise dissidents to "see the local relief or their pastor." To demands that artists be provided jobs because of need, the official reaction now became: "We have nothing to do with relief."[42]

In addition to obtaining public recognition of the quality of the work produced by project artists, Bruce knew he must demonstrate that he had run a taut ship and had managed the million dollar grant wisely if PWAP was to continue past the February 15 terminal date. Art patrons had been so joyful at the news of government subsidy that museums, art schools, and universities gladly donated office space for the regional directors, and in some places work space for the artists. Throughout the existence of PWAP the project spent no money for rent. Low overhead enabled Bruce to spend more than 90 percent of his money on salaries for artists.[43]

Vouchers and requisitions for travel, office equipment and supplies, and unusually expensive materials for artists, of course, had to be drawn "exactly to meet Government regulations." The lumbering, cantankerous Procurement Division of the Treasury Department, responsible for supplying government agencies, could not work nearly fast enough to supply the special demands of artists. To get around the problem Bruce asked the artists to furnish their own canvas, brushes, and paints. Only when the materials cost 5 or 6 percent of the artist's salary did the PWAP business manager accept material requisitions. Still, there were obstructions. Congress had prohibited the purchase of foreign products. This was a difficult problem, business manager Cecil Jones admitted, since "there is no linen grown [sic] in the United States." The purchase of superior European pigments or oils, of course, was out of the question.[44]

6 Symeon Shimin (Section of Fine Arts), *Contemporary Justice and the Child* (detail), mural in the Justice Department building, Washington, D.C.

Bruce systematically favored each cabinet department with some product from federal artists and attempted to win congressional support. By the time the request for an additional grant was under consideration, PWAP artists were designing murals for the United States Military Academy at West Point and recording Civilian Conservation Corps activities for the War Department; negotiating for murals at Annapolis with the Navy Department; painting a portrait of ex-Postmaster General Albert S. Burleson for the Post Office Department; planning or painting murals in the cafeterias of the Departments of Agriculture and Commerce; preparing portraits for embassies; employing Indian artists with the blessing of the Interior Department; and awaiting permission to begin work on the walls of the Justice Department. When the Republican National Committee charged that the Treasury had wasted public money by employing "hundreds of individuals belonging to the belly-ache school of artists to daub our public schools with so-called murals," Bruce moved to offset the possible effect by asking all artists on the project to write personal letters to their congressmen and senators. Although Republican Representative Charles Tabor feared some public buildings might be "very much damaged" by PWAP art, Bruce remained confident. The "yappers," he wrote, "aren't going to get very far. The best crowd in Washington is back of us and howls that come into any portion of the government are automatically referred to us."[45]

His confidence was not misplaced. In two months the PWAP had demonstrated its bureaucratic orthodoxy, mobilized more than 2,400 artists, and made influential friends. Assistant Secretary of the Treasury Robert, spared embarrassing administrative and fiscal questions, confidently asked that the experiment be continued. The further knowledge about American artists would be "invaluable" to the Treasury, he said, in its search for talent to decorate federal buildings.[46]

CWA granted additional funds to extend the program two and a half months, although the amount made it necessary to cut the payroll in half before May 1. The cut represented no particular chastening of the PWAP; rather, it reflected the problems of the parent CWA. Criticism of government employment at "the going rate" of people who took no means test had increased. Director of the Budget Lewis W. Douglas was but one high official who feared that CWA created political forces which might become uncontrollable later. Like others, Douglas abhorred the idea of a government "employment" project and regarded CWA workers as "simply beneficiaries of the bounty of the government."[47]

Roosevelt determined to continue CWA through the winter, but on a reduced scale. In the weeks remaining to them PWAP artists produced hundreds of art items, more people learned of the experiment, and Bruce laid the foundation for future programs. Ironically, George Biddle, who had fathered the program of federal patronage, never painted for the PWAP. The murals he wanted to create for the Justice Department building could not be paid for with PWAP money, government lawyers ruled, because funds for decoration of that building had been included in the construction cost figures already approved by Congress. Convincing the Supervising Architect of the Treasury and a jelly-like bureaucracy of accountants to release the money required continuous agitation from Biddle and Bruce for another 9 months. In the spring of 1934 Biddle, now behind the scenes, was learning something of the frustrations of trying to move the obstinate machinery of government. At the same time, Bruce was learning something of the problems and promise of organized projects for artists, and of dealing with those who had paid for them.

[1] Benton quoted in Edwin C. McReynolds, *Missouri: A History of the Crossroads State* (Norman, Okla., 1962), 447-48; Frederick P. Keppel and R. L. Duffus, *The Arts in American Life* (New York, 1933), 67.

[2] Keppel and Duffus, *The Arts in American Life*, 15, 122.

[3] See unpublished manuscripts in [Forbes] "Watson file," Record Group 121 (Records of the Public Building Service), Preliminary Inventory Entry 105 (National Archives, Washington, D.C.). Hereafter records in the National Archives cited by Record Group and Preliminary Inventory Entry Number, thus, RG121/105.

[4] See scrapbooks in George Biddle Papers (Manuscript Division, Library of Congress); George Biddle Diary [summer 1933], on Archives of American Art (Washington, D.C.) Microfilm Reel D127. Hereafter all microfilms of the Archives of American Art cited as AAA Reel.

[5] Keppel and Duffus, *The Arts in American Life*, 65-66; George Biddle, *An American Artist's Story* (Boston, 1939), 259-68.

[6] Biddle, *American Artist's Story*, 265, 268; Biddle to Franklin D. Roosevelt, May 9, 1933, Franklin D. Roosevelt Papers (Franklin D. Roosevelt Library, Hyde Park) on AAA Reel NDA/HP1. Most of the materials in the Roosevelt Library pertaining to the federal art projects have been placed on AAA Reels NDA/HP1 and NDA/HP4.

[7] Biddle, *American Artist's Story*, 269-70; George Biddle Diary, May 30, 1933.

[8] *American Magazine of Art*, XXVI (Dec. 1933), 521; William F. McDonald, *Federal Relief Administration and the Arts* (Columbus, 1969), 248-50, 357-59.

[9] Biddle, *American Artist's Story*, 269.

[10] *Ibid.*, 271-72; Biddle to Eleanor Roosevelt, June 28, 1933, Biddle to Frances Perkins, June 28, 1933, Biddle Papers.

[11] H. Paul Caemmerer, *The Commission of Fine Arts, 1911-1963: A Brief History* (Washington, 1964), 2-4, 7.

[12] Egerton Swartwout to Charles Moore, July 15, 1936, Charles Moore Papers (Manuscript Division, Library of Congress).

[13] Moore to Christian J. Peoples, Jan. 3, 1936, RG121/118.

[14] Moore to Roosevelt, July 28, 1933, copy in Biddle Papers.

[15] Biddle, *American Artist's Story*, 272-73; Memorandum by Biddle [Sept. 1933], with penciled notation: "Pres. has seen and on file," Biddle Papers.

[16] See Olin Dows, "The New Deal's Treasury Art Programs: A Memoir," *Arts in Society*, II (No. 4), 54-55. Some materials on Bruce's career prior to his affiliation with the Treasury Department may be found in the Edward Bruce Papers (Archives of American Art), AAA Reels D82 and D83.

[17] Memorandum: "Government Support of Arts and Crafts" [by Edward Bruce], nd, Biddle Papers.

[18] *Ibid.*; Henry T. Hunt to Harry Hopkins, Nov. 9, 1933, Biddle Papers; George Biddle Diary, June 23, 1933; Biddle, *American Artist's Story*, 275.

[19] George Biddle Diary, Nov. 9, 1933; Memorandum: "Federal Support of Fine Arts," Bruce to Roberts [sic] Nov. 13, 1933, Biddle Papers; *Report of the Assistant Secretary of the Treasury to Federal Emergency Relief Administrator—Public Works of Art Project: Dec. 8, 1933 to June 30, 1934* (Washington, 1934), 2. Hereafter cited as *PWAP Report*. The members of the Advisory Committee were Lawrence W. Robert, Frederick A. Delano, Charles Moore, Rexford Tugwell, Harry Hopkins, Henry T. Hunt, and Edward Bruce.

[20] Memorandum: "Federal Support of Fine Arts," Biddle to Bruce, Nov. 16, 1933, Bruce to Biddle, Nov. 22, 1933, Biddle Papers; Bruce's typed draft of remarks, nd, RG121/124.

[21] "Preliminary Plan on Public Works of Art Project" [by Edward Bruce, Nov. 1933], mimeographed copy in Biddle Papers; Biddle, *American Artist's Story*, 258.

[22] CWA Press Release #446, Dec. 11, 1933, RG121/105; *Art Digest*, VIII (Dec. 15, 1933), 6.

[23] *PWAP Report*, 3; Dows, "The New Deal's Treasury Art Programs," 55; *Congressional Record*, 76 Cong., 3 Sess. (1939), 1476; George Biddle Diary, Dec. 8, 1933.

[24] *PWAP Report*, 4; Bruce to Charles Bittinger, Dec. 12, 1933, RG121/105.

[25] *New York Times*, Dec. 12, 1933.

[26] Undated manuscript in "Watson file," RG121/105; Memorandum, Watson to Bruce, June 3, 1934, RG121/106; Forbes Watson, "Steady Job," *American Magazine of Art*, XXVII (April 1934), 168-70.

[27] *New York Times*, Dec. 13, 14, 1933.

[28] *Art Digest*, VIII (Dec. 15, 1933), 31.

[29] *New York Times*, Dec. 14, 1933.

[30] Undated manuscript in "Watson file," RG121/105; *New York Times*, Dec. 14, 1933, March 11, 1934.

[31] Treasury Department Press Release, "Statement by L. W. Robert Jr.," Nov. 29, 1933, in Biddle Papers.

[32] Clipping from *Honolulu Advertiser*, March 6, 1934, RG121/110; clipping from *Chicago Daily News*, Dec. 23, 1933, RG121/111; George H. Code to Duncan Phillips, Jan. 9, 1934, RG121/116. Quotas were assigned on the basis of estimated artist population in each region.

[33] *New York Times*, Dec. 13, 1933.

[34] Report in "District Attorney's File," RG121/116.

[35] *Ibid.* For a full account of the evolution from John Reed Club through Unemployed Artists Group to Artists Union, see Gerald M. Monroe, "The Artists Union of New York," unpublished Ed.D. dissertation, New York University, 1971, 33ff.

[36] *Ibid.*; *New York Times*, Dec. 22, 1933.

[37] "District Attorney's File" (Exhibit G), RG121/116.

[38] *Ibid.*

[39] *Ibid.* (Exhibit K).

[40] *Ibid.* (Exhibits R and S). No legal action was forthcoming.

[41] Clipping from *New York Herald Tribune*, March 18, 1934, RG121/111.

[42] Memorandum, Watson to Bruce, Feb. 2, 1934, RG121/105; Watson to Duncan Phillips, Dec. 10, 1933, Bruce to Robert, Feb. 8, 1934, RG 121/106; Forbes Watson, "The Public Works of Art Project: Federal, Republican, or Democratic?" *American Magazine of Art*, XXVII (Jan. 1934), 7.

[43] *PWAP Report*, 5; Edward Bruce, "Implications of the Public Works of Art Project," *American Magazine of Art*, XXVII (April 1934), 114.

[44] Minutes of Meeting of Regional Chairmen of Public Works of Art Project [Feb. 20, 1934], RG121/102.

[45] Bruce to [PWAP artists], Jan. 22, 1934, clipping from *New York American*, Feb. 9, 1934, RG121/105; memorandum, Bruce to Robert, Jan. 25, 1934, Bruce to Arthur Millier, Jan., 1934, RG121/106; clipping from *Washington Star*, Jan. 25, 1934, RG121/110.

[46] Memorandum, Robert to Julius F. Stone, Jan. 29, 1934, RG121/106.

[47] Lewis W. Douglas to Roosevelt, Jan. 24, 1934, Douglas to Mrs. Jewell W. Swafford, May 28, 1934, RG51 (Records of the Bureau of the Budget). Additional allocations to PWAP approximated $273,000, bringing the total federal outlay to $1,312,000.

2

Bid for Survival

Edward Bruce understood how tenuous federal patronage of art was. When the CWA expired in the spring of 1934, PWAP would also die. Future patronage depended on pleasing the patron. That, in short, meant encouraging art with the widest popular appeal and thwarting art which might bring awkward public outbursts that would embarrass or anger Congress and the President. Bruce had to make artists feel free and, at the same time, extract from them a quantity and quality of production that representatives of the people and watchdogs of the purse could appreciate. When conflict occurred, and it was inherent in the system, Bruce resolved it with the goals of public acceptance and efficiency more in mind than artistic freedom. PWAP officials encouraged a wide variety of art forms to broaden the ap-

peal of the project and deftly managed the allocation and display of some of the better pieces to win influential friends. By the time PWAP ended Bruce had established a claim to some sort of further subsidy. A part of the price of this claim was the stunned sensibilities of a few artists who felt little inspiration from the American scene or interpreted it in ways unacceptable to PWAP administrators.

Soon after PWAP began a journalist asked: "Must art be C.W.A.'d into Rooseveltianism?" Others wondered what would happen when an artist who did not share the ideals of the administration caricatured American society, the New Deal, Harry Hopkins, or Roosevelt. In short, would the artist be free? "The answer," PWAP administrators said, "unhesitatingly, unanimously

21

and without qualification is Yes!"[1] But the extent to which censorship and freedom existed depended of course on how one defined those eternally vague words. No region escaped recommendations by leaders in Washington concerning individual artists and unconventional art. When the subcommittee for the Minneapolis program hired only two of the eight artists recommended by Forbes Watson, the technical director inquired in a letter to the regional chairman whether the Minneapolis group was "thoroughly in touch with the artists." It was not surprising when Edward B. Rowan, the assistant director of the PWAP and former director of The Little Gallery in Cedar Rapids, charged a Pittsburgh artist who painted storybook characters for a local elementary schoolroom with poor judgment and technical incompetence. The many-lipped "Beast" paired with "Beauty," Rowan wrote, was a "grotesque most certainly inexcusable" as a decoration for the schoolroom.[2] Such interventions were infrequent and certainly of less import than Bruce's prescription of proper subject matter for government art. Whether from desire to please the federal patron, or from aesthetic or philosophic conviction, Bruce insisted that artists interpret the "American scene." "We

7 Peter Blume (PWAP),
Beatty's Barn (detail), water-
color now in the National
Collection of Fine Arts,
Smithsonian Institution

8 Detail of an oil by Burgoyne
Diller (PWAP). Later chief
of the mural division of the
WPA's Federal Art Project in
New York City, Diller was one
of the few non-representational
artists on the PWAP rolls

definitely want to achieve this," a directive said, and it urged every regional director to check carefully the subject of each project. Rowan announced that any artist who found only foreign subjects sufficiently picturesque and worthy of painting "had better be dropped and an opportunity given to the man or woman with enough imagination and vision to use the beauty and possibility for aesthetic expression in the subject matter of his own country." The goal of the PWAP was a permanent record of the aspirations and achievements of the American people. In light of that goal, the leaders in Washington informed regional chairmen, "any artist who paints a nude for the Public Works of Art Project should have his head examined." If an artist accepted employment from the federal government, he should be willing to make certain concessions to his employer.[3]

Without raising the question of what, exactly, the "American scene" might include, the regional chairmen and committees imposed their own views. The committee in northern California gave assurance that it had always "frowned upon imaginative and picturesque work which has seemed irrelevant to the American scene." John S. Ankeny, chairman of the Texas-Oklahoma region, soothed conservative southwesterners with a promise that no grammarschool child would be sent home to have nightmares and no embryonic engineer's sense of proportion would suffer violence from exposure to "the distorted forms of modernistic art." Nor would anything "communistic" adorn Texas or Oklahoma walls, nor Greek goddesses or blind-folded justices or scenes of ancient history, since none of that was any part of the American scene. Ankeny promised to give artists the opportunity to submit their own ideas; but if they were not approved, his committee would dictate new ones. At the art colony in Westport, Connecticut, PWAP artists were expressly forbidden to experiment with "cubism, futurism, and all forms of modernism." Thus, the American scene, with minor variations, took form on canvases across the country. The reaction from one faction of artists was predictable: "Preposterous! Unbelievable! Conservative idiocy!"[4]

Perhaps the most publicized clash between artists and their new patron occurred over alleged communist propaganda in a new memorial tower to volunteer firemen on San Francisco's Telegraph Hill. About 25 PWAP artists received wall space in stair wells and lobbies of Coit Tower, named for Miss Lillie M. Coit, onetime mascot of the Knickerbocker Volunteer Firemen and donor of $125,000 for the beautification of San Francisco. A month before the tower's scheduled opening, newspaper editors touring the building discovered a miner in one panel reading the *Western Worker*, a communist weekly. Other irregularities turned up. There were shocking headlines on newspapers and books by Karl Marx, Erskine Caldwell, and other proletarian writers in a library fresco. The *San Francisco Chronicle* was missing from a newsstand in another panel, and a hammer and sickle and motto, "Workers of the World Unite," appeared in one of three panels by the artist Clifford Wight. Unless there were changes, the editors warned, they would take a hostile attitude toward the whole project. Walter Heil, the regional chairman, insisted that the objectionable details were not present in the original designs approved by his committee and the San Francisco Art Commission. Heil led the commissioners through the tower. They emerged and pronounced what they saw "in opposition to

9 Bernard Zakheim (PWAP), *Library*, mural in the Coit Tower, San Francisco

10 Detail of Bernard Zakheim's *Library*. The *Western Worker*, a communist weekly, and the volume by Karl Marx were among elements in the Coit Tower murals which aroused contemporary protest

24

the generally accepted tradition of native Americanism," whereupon the San Francisco Park Commission locked the great doors. Edward Bruce advised Heil to insist on completion of the murals according to the approved design. If the wayward artists refused to do the work, Bruce telegraphed, "get others of the group" to do it. The PWAP chief considered the work propaganda, detrimental to the best interests of American art, and "likely to discourage further government patronage."[5]

Of the three artists accused of propaganda, the commission discovered that the worst offender had not submitted sketches. The project already was under way when Clifford Wight began his three panels depicting "Rugged Individualism," "The New Deal," and "Communism"—the last of which, Wight explained, was "another alternative which exists in the current American scene." Victor Arnautoff, technical director and art chief of the project, had approved Wight's sketches on the job. Wight failed to understand why he should remove his mural. The Communist Party was perfectly legal and it regularly nominated candidates for the highest offices. That his panel appealed to only one section of the community was no reason for removing it. How could artists truly record the American scene if the PWAP discarded fringe and minority ideas as propaganda? No one censored the press for admitting the existence of communism; Wight failed to understand why artists had not the same freedom. To aid Wight and prevent disfigurement of the murals, the San Francisco Artists' and Writers' Union set up pickets around Coit Tower. The Union, describing its position as "firm and irrevocable," declared that creative artists had complete and untrammeled liberty to depict life and all manifestations of society, "whether capitalist, communist, or what not," as they saw fit.[6] Bruce saw it differently. "They are welcome to all the propaganda they want," he wrote, "but I don't see why they should do it on our money." He forwarded to director Heil the opinion of legal advisers that, while alteration of the murals might be cause for legal action, complete obliteration could not, since the artists had no property claims to the murals. "I hope they don't fool around with this Socialistic thing any longer," he wrote impatiently, "and wipe the damn painting out of the Tower."[7]

25

After reconsideration, the San Francisco Art Commission dropped demands that artists Victor Arnautoff and Bernard Zakheim change headlines and book titles in their paintings. The dispute soon was reduced to the fate of one Soviet emblem painted by Wight over a window. When the tower opened several months later, Wight's emblem had disappeared.[8]

Clifford Wight and other artists whose work was censored represented the exception to the PWAP's dealings with artists. The large majority who received PWAP checks did not feel compromised by conforming with PWAP's definition of the American scene. Most of these artists voluntarily put in more than the 30 hours a week required by CWA regulations, and considered the quantity of work expected of them entirely reasonable. Murals went up on location without publicity and most graphics, watercolors, and oils took form routinely in the artists' homes and studios. Occasionally an appreciative and serious artist returned a payroll check to the government with the explanation that the art he produced for the money did not measure up to his own standards. Most artists, in truth, echoed the sentiment of Dorothy Houts, a competent but by no means great easel painter: "When all this started, I felt as low as a worm—you might hardly know me now!" A few artists, mostly in the largest cities where supervision was constant and bureaucrats touchy, complained of regimentation and the amount of work their supervisors demanded. John B. Flannagan, New York sculptor who later achieved renown, claimed to have worked 90 hours on a statuary group in one week and attracted attention by not working at all the next two weeks. The inspector who began visiting him daily reported too little progress, reprimanded him, and finally, for not working the required 30 hours, dismissed him. In Washington, D.C., another sculptor applied for an extension after the expiration of the PWAP to finish what he claimed to be the best piece of his career. The supervisor thought the sculptor merely wanted to "extort more money." A Treasury agent confiscated the sculpture and locked it in a government warehouse despite the sculptor's protests to Mrs. Roosevelt and statements by Harry Hopkins that it was "ridiculous" to impose time limits on a sculptor.[9] The issue, never resolved, was whether these persons and a few other artists

11 Victor Arnautoff (PWAP), detail of mural in the Coit Tower, San Francisco. Arnautoff's picture of street life in the city was criticized for its unpleasant details

12 Victor Arnautoff (PWAP), detail of mural in the Coit Tower, San Francisco. The San Francisco *Chronicle* was missing from the newsstands, while a radical paper was prominently displayed

were lazy, extortionists, naturally slow, or at a creative impasse.

The 3,749 artists who received checks during the four and a half months of PWAP turned out 15,663 pieces of art and craft. Never, Bruce reported to his superiors, were more American artists constantly at work at one time. Any sculpture, painting, design, or product of a craft which the directors thought constituted an embellishment to public property came within the project's scope. The result ranged from murals to Indian blankets. Oils, 3,821 of them, 2,938 watercolors, and 1,518 prints headed the list. There were 1,076 etchings, 889 wood blocks, 706 murals and mural sketches, 647 sculptures, over 500 drawings, 490 poster panels, and 99 carvings. Project artists contributed bas reliefs, batiks, habitat groups, decorative maps, portraits, Pueblo pottery, stage sets, tapestries, lighting fixtures, and mosaics. An additional 700 to 800 items could only be described as "Miscellaneous."[10]

Numerically, some 400 completed murals comprised less than 3 percent of the items produced, but they commanded disproportionate attention. Government art became chiefly mural art in the public mind. PWAP rules permitted artists to decorate post offices, courthouses, community centers, municipal auditoriums—any building supported wholly or in part by taxes, federal, state, or local. The great demand and the limited number of experienced muralists encouraged the development of the cooperative or "team" mural.

In a cooperative mural one artist designed the work and the others helped him carry it out. The arrangement had the advantage of using the best talent for design and gave experience to artists who had not worked with murals. Cleveland, New Haven, Dallas, San Francisco, and Iowa City all received cooperative murals. Grant Wood, working at the University of Iowa, supervised what was probably the most successful project. Wood became an assistant professor and his artists received university credit for their work. When the 22 artists first descended to their workshop—a revamped swimming pool—Wood discovered equal numbers of artistic conservatives and radicals. The original polite tolerance between the factions, Wood reported, grew into such strong community feeling that eventually each man was willing to subordinate his own personal mannerisms to make a harmonious whole. They were proud that their panels looked as if one man had done all the work. When the PWAP reduced regional quotas, Wood's artists decided to pool and reallocate their checks rather than have the group broken up. Later, to finish the work, the group made plans to live in tents, have the wives cook army style, and pay group expenses by sending a few members elsewhere to work. An additional grant made this unnecessary, but Wood believed they would have carried on. The result of Wood's teamwork, while frustrating to critics accustomed to praising or blaming individuals, won considerable renown.[11]

Not everyone who wanted a mural accepted the aesthetic judgment of the artists or the PWAP administrators. Events at the national military and naval academies illustrated the problem. The artist T. Loftin Johnson designed a mural for the end wall of West Point's Cadet Mess Hall showing three rows of figures—ancient, medieval, and modern posed according to Lord Creasy's *Fifteen Decisive Battles of the World*. Johnson and the generals wrangled over details until PWAP expired. Only later, under the Works Progress Administration, was Johnson able to execute the 2,459 square-foot panel—the largest in America, so he said. The team mural, "The Battle of Santiago," for Annapolis' hallowed Memorial Hall occasioned even more controversy. From the beginning Rear Admiral Thomas C. Hart, superintendent of the Academy, insisted on quite literal reproduction. Washington PWAP administrators, believing Assistant Secretary of the Navy Harry L. Roosevelt was their strong ally, announced bluntly that "the literalness demanded by the Admiral . . . will not be carried out." The admiral continued to insist that all sketches be approved by naval authorities and that only the Navy could interpret proper policies for Memorial Hall. Privately, PWAP officials came to refer to the admiral as "a peanut." Meanwhile, the Navy destroyer *MacFarland* transported to Santiago on the southeastern coast of Cuba the three artists appointed to execute the mural and obligingly took positions off the harbor so that the artists could make studies from different angles. In the spirit of the Good Neighbor the mayor of Santiago declared the artists public guests and detailed an English-speaking policeman to help them interview witnesses of the battle. The PWAP ended shortly after the artists returned, and only through intricate manipulations did Bruce obtain funds to complete the work. Admiral Hart, however, refused to have it in Memorial Hall. The battleship *Brooklyn*, he thought, was too prominent in the mural—dominating the canvas far more than it did the actual Battle of Santiago. A year later the artists received permission to install the mural in a less important building at the naval academy.[12]

The PWAP employed about 70 southwestern and Plains Indian artists in a unique program. In Oklahoma, Kiowas, taking the subject matter from their festivals and religious rites, erected murals at two state colleges and in the building of the state historical society. In New Mexico, at Santa Fe and Albuquerque, Indian artists and craftsmen painted murals, manufactured rugs, blankets, pottery, and jewelry for the Indian Service Buildings to stimulate the native crafts. Part of the work went to new schools, hospitals, and community centers in the area. Mrs. Nina Collier, daughter-in-law of the Indian Commissioner, supplied much of the pressure in behalf of the Indian artists. Forbes Watson came away from a conference with her convinced that he saw a great Indian artist on every reservation and wanted to put the work of decorating the Indian buildings by Indian artists over PWAP "like a tent." PWAP administrators asked regional chairmen to treat Indian artists "just exactly as they would treat white artists from the point of view of their quality as artists and a just and fair quota."[13] All indications are that they did.

During the first week of the PWAP, Bruce asked Secretary of War George H. Dern, General Douglas A. MacArthur, and Civilian Conservation Corps (CCC) director Robert Fechner to put PWAP artists in CCC camps. In early January the CCC agreed to take about 30 artists. Salaries and matters of art came under PWAP jurisdiction while the CCC provided free quarters, cheap meals, and privileges granted the supervisory staff. Artists' instructions charged them to make a pictorial record of CCC work and "such subjects as appeal" within a reasonable radius of the camp. Whatever the artists felt about the vigorous life, their special status spared them its worst rigors and they seemed to value the assignment as "experience." The CCC artists' work intrigued

PWAP officials, and the CCC hierarchy, who also liked the favorable publicity, wanted the art to embellish the unusually stark walls of the CCC buildings. When the PWAP ended in April the atmosphere was conducive to retaining artists in residence. Fechner finally put the question to Roosevelt in a CCC Executive Council meeting. The CCC would begin paying up to 100 artists, the Council decided, with the Treasury Department's art agency monitoring the art. Roosevelt approved, but reduced the artists to the level of CCC enrollees; that is, a cash allowance of $30 a month, subsistence, shelter, clothing, medical attention, and the discipline of lower ranks. The artist provided his own materials, spent 40 hours a week on his art, and, in theory, was relieved from ordinary work in camp.[14] Edward Rowan presided over CCC art until the late 1930s; but the poverty, restrictions, and crudity of the CCC enrollee's world made the artists' lot less happy than in the early days under the PWAP.

"Miscellaneous" art reported by regional chairmen defied more specific classification. PWAP work most nearly approached manual labor in New York where Mrs. Force arranged with Mayor Fiorello LaGuardia for artists to clean and repair the statues and monuments in the city. The work was most scientific at the Army Medical Museum in Washington where artists constructed models of skin diseases and bas-reliefs of the conductive system of the heart—all in natural color. The work was most amusing in Nebraska where the head of the state committee, described by the regional chairman as a "doddery old gentleman . . . who knows nothing about painting," thought he had discovered a genius, and commissioned her to draw a nice valentine to send President Roosevelt on February 14.[15]

When the Civil Works Administration expired in the spring of 1934, a source of art patronage went with it. To continue the good work Bruce had to find another benevolent agency or request funds from Congress. In either case, he reasoned, the future depended upon enthusiasm in Washington. He relied heavily on the success of an exhibition in the Corcoran Gallery of Art from April 24 to May 20.

Bruce had planned a national exhibition from the end of the PWAP's first month. By the end of the third month he was ex-

horting the regional chairmen to send their best products to Washington. Before the end of the fourth month he forbade regional chairmen to let any local exhibition interfere with the national. "The perpetuation of the whole program of the project," he telegraphed them, "will be affected by the results of this exhibition."[16]

Bruce and Watson arranged and selected the work for exhibition. They chose more than 500 items from the thousands sent, and bragged that they could have assembled five more exhibitions of equal quality. Both believed government patronage had sparked a major development in American art. Bruce waxed eloquent that Roosevelt's desire to give people "a more abundant life" had inspired artists to their finest efforts. At a Washington party the weekend before the opening, Watson announced: "This will be the greatest art event in this country since the Armory Show, and very much in the same fashion, will probably be praised by critics and ridiculed by reporters." In the revolutionary spirit of the Armory Show, he continued, hitherto unknown American artists now "cut themselves loose from foreign influence" to find inspiration in the American scene. Most of the work, Watson believed, showed "courage, truth, and a real spirit of adventure."[17]

There was at least one similarity between the Armory Show and the Corcoran Exhibition—the public sensation created by one of the pieces. Most Americans knew the Armory Show through Marcel Duchamp's controversial, cubistic painting "Nude Descending a Staircase," and if they were aware of the Corcoran Exhibition it was through Paul Cadmus's "The Fleet's In." The difference was that the controversy over "Nude Descending a Staircase" was purely a matter of art, while that over "The Fleet's In" involved both art and censorship. "The Fleet's In" showed several sailors engaged in highly informal interchanges with curvaceous damsels of obviously insecure reputation. The New York regional committee and Bruce and Watson selected it for exhibition, but, somehow, it got sidetracked into the salons of the Navy Department where all enjoyed it until retired Admiral Hugh L. Rodman spied it. The Admiral failed to see the humor. The "disgraceful, sordid, disreputable, drunken

13 Paul Cadmus (PWAP), *The Fleet's In*. Withdrawn by government request from the exhibition of PWAP art at the Corcoran Gallery, Washington, April-May 1934

brawl" gave the public the wrong idea about sailors, among whom, the Admiral insisted, it was "the rare exception to find a man who would stoop to such a disgraceful orgy." Other naval leaders supported Admiral Rodman. "Right artistic," pronounced Secretary of the Navy Claude A. Swanson, but "not true of the Navy." Those who felt unqualified to discuss the merit of Cadmus's work questioned whether government should subsidize libels on the national defense. Finally, Swanson's assistant secretary, Harry Roosevelt, phoned Bruce and asked him to withdraw the picture from the forthcoming exhibition. Bruce complied.[18]

Pre-event press releases of the Corcoran Exhibition portended a stuffy opening: ceremony involving the First Family, admission by card only of social and official Washington, music by the Navy Band Orchestra. The five o'clock starting hour raised the question as to whether tuxedo or business suit was correct. Not many tuxedos appeared. Mrs. Roosevelt made a few remarks about art being a necessity, the crowd cheered and moved about the galleries, filling them with such earthy descriptives, as "swell" and "lousy."[19]

Critics noted the absence of nudes, night club subjects, pretty women, aristocratic-looking men, and genteel houses. They noted a predominance of machinery, locomotives, steamships, workers, and common subjects of village and farm life. One reporter calculated that at least 192 of the 498 subjects were of labor and industrial character. Most critics seemed surprised that the canvases displayed so little rebellion or despair. They agreed with the President that the art revealed "hope and courage," was "robust and American," and lacked "both slavery to classical standards and decadence common to much European art." Even the picture "Unemployed Boy," called by Mrs. Roosevelt "almost the swellest thing in the exhibit," showed a face, the First Lady and critics said, more baffled than resentful. No major critic suggested the government's money had been ill spent. Most agreed that government had provided new impetus for American art. The Corcoran's attendance figures during the exhibition—26,537 compared with 11,632 during the corresponding period the year before—seemed to bear out that contention.[20]

Outside Washington, where the public viewed less carefully selected art, reactions varied. When the Los Angeles Museum of Art exhibited local PWAP work, 33,000 visitors turned out for the opening, breaking all attendance records for a California art exhibition, and overshadowing the Corcoran's month-long statistics. In other regional centers only a few people knew about the existence of local art work. Such was the case in New Orleans, the regional director complained, because he could stir no interest in the local press. The *St. Louis Globe Democrat*'s critic insisted that local art lacked the hope and courage applauded in Washington; instead, "social unrest, discontent, envy, hatred, and class consciousness" characterized it. Yet the newspaper writers of New Haven, Connecticut, to cite an opposite example, could only praise the artists for leaving what local critics estimated as $25,000 worth of art in their town which would "endure for hundreds of years."

The aesthetic and political orientation of the critics partly accounted for the diverse reception. In addition, there were vast differences in the art resources of the 16 regions. According to Forbes Watson the southeastern United States and the Dakotas were barren of artistic talent. The Pacific coast abounded in enthusiasm but suffered from "artiness" and considerable uncertainty in taste. Some of the Northwest's few artists showed vigor, but many still belonged to the "Kiss Mamma" school. Most of the artists in the Southwest seemed to have immigrated from other parts of the country, producing mixed results. The Midwest impressed Watson as "definitely stronger than the average observer of New York exhibitions would have suspected." The most sophisticated work, he hastened to add, "came from exactly where one would expect," namely, the New York region.[21] New York artists, of course, had been more carefully selected; had benefited by virtue of their numbers from mutual criticism and a sense of artistic community; and their residence in the nation's cultural capital had made them more sensitive to the prejudices of critics like Watson.

As art resources and public reaction varied from region to region so did the assessment of the project by regional chairmen. Ellsworth Woodward, chairman of the New Orleans region, voiced doubts about the efficacy of committee selection of artists. Committees chose safe artists and rejected the mass, among whom a few younger and more teachable ones might be brought into eminence. Choosing a few reasonably successful artists ran the risk of establishing a complacent favored group. Most vehement was Merle Armitage, regional chairman of southern California, who felt his artists deserved more acclaim than they received. He pronounced most of the work created under the PWAP "so much paint, mere illustrations by hacks and students repeating over again endlessly problems which were solved by better men years ago." Eventually Armitage abandoned all schemes to help artists through organized efforts. "Only mediocre artists run in packs," he said. "The creative artist is always the lone wolf." Most regional chairmen, nonetheless, shared Juliana Force's view that PWAP advanced public art appreciation at least ten years and helped to convince the average person he could afford works of art.[22]

Bruce sought to build on his success by liberally dispensing PWAP art through Washington. The Roosevelts chose 32 items from the Corcoran Exhibition for the White House and an envoy of Mrs. Roosevelt later selected 10 more. Secretary of Labor Frances Perkins took 130 oil paintings from the Corcoran on a year's loan to brighten the new Department of Labor building. The largest allocation, 451 framed oils and watercolors, went to the House of Representatives Office Building. The demand for free pictures became so great that Bruce ordered all oils and watercolors reserved for members of Congress and "higher government officials." Lesser bureaucrats had to choose among etchings and lithographs. While most PWAP work found its way to local schools and government buildings, Bruce knew how to engender friendly support when additional pieces arrived. He bestowed art on such unlikely admirers as the experimental homesteads of the Resettlement Administration and four of the Navy's destroyers. To assure that no "rejects or discards" circulated in Washington and marred the image, PWAP chiefs destroyed what they considered to be the worst products of project artists. Other mediocre or poor art, minus the PWAP brass tags or any other identification, ended up as posters on dreary walls of the D.C. Transient Shelters and waiting rooms of the D.C. Board of Public Assistance. Watson prophesied that the government could sell the PWAP art in a hundred years and realize a "net profit of something more than $5,000,000." But the government would have to find the art first. In the frenzied closing days no one kept accurate records. Even Bruce, who was rarely self-critical, later admitted that keeping tabs on the paintings was a job "we did not do well."[23]

Few artists had other jobs when PWAP released them on April 28, and many projects, especially mural projects, remained half completed. The Federal Emergency Relief Administration, reactivated with the demise of the CWA, agreed to employ artists to finish the work they had begun if they could qualify for relief. The FERA also urged its state offices to organize work for artists using the members of the PWAP regional committees as unpaid advisers and supervisors. Not many artists were optimistic about staying on a government project because work under FERA was uncertain. Even if an artist submitted to the humiliation of going on relief, the number of work days permitted him depended on his "budget deficiency" as determined by FERA's monthly examination of his assets and liabilities. And many state relief administrators simply did not accept "painting pictures" as legitimate relief "work."

PWAP brought to light no genius, but many artists gained national recognition through the project and several held their first successful exhibitions. The artists and the public still suspected each other, but many in both groups sensed that a healthy movement was under way. Bruce failed to prove that he could reconcile bureaucratic restrictions with the occasionally erratic, free, and creative spirit. Still, he appeared to have obtained the artists' best efforts while proving himself an able administrator. The idea that CWA was a general employment program, rather than a restricted relief measure, enabled Bruce to make quality, whatever the difficulties in defining it, the first consideration in embellishing public property; to focus on developing American art as much as aiding American artists.

At the time of the dissolution of CWA and the constriction of relief activities there seemed no possibility for another program for artists as broad as the PWAP. But this was 1934. The confidence and enthusiasm and willingness to experiment that early New Dealers had brought to the national capital were not yet dulled. Bruce believed he would find other support. As many people saw it, the idea of subsidy to art was liberal, the method worked out by Bruce democratic, the result enlightening. If some questions remained unresolved, what program ever was perfect? By October 1934 Bruce would have a new project, one even more to his liking than the PWAP.

[1] Forbes Watson, "The Public Works of Art Project," *American Magazine of Art*, XXVII (Jan. 1934), 6.

[2] Edward B. Rowan to John O'Connor, Jr., RG121/105; Watson to Walter S. Brewster, Jan. 20, 1934, RG121/116.

[3] Rowan to [Regional Chairmen], March 5, 1934, RG121/105; Rowan to Walter Heil, March 6, 1934, RG121/116.

[4] Clippings from *Washington Post*, March 9, 1934, *Dallas Times Herald*, Dec. 20, 1934, RG121/105.

[5] *Literary Digest*, CXVIII (Aug. 15, 1934), 24, 31; clipping from *San Francisco News*, July 4, 1934, RG121/111; telegram, Watson to Bruce, June 2, 1934, telegram, Bruce to Heil, June 2, 1934, RG121/105.

[6] Clifford Wight to Walter Heil and San Francisco Art Commission, nd, "Statement of the Executive Committee of the Artists' and Writers' Union on the Threatened Disfigurement of Paintings in the Coit Memorial Tower . . . ," RG121/105.

[7] Bruce to Rowan, July 27, 1934, RG121/114; Bruce to Cecil Jones, July 21, 1934, RG121/124; telegram, Rowan to Heil, July 21, 1934, RG121/105.

[8] Telegram, Heil to PWAP, July 11, 1934, RG121/116.

[9] Clipping from *New York Evening Journal*, May 17, 1934, in Edward Bruce Papers (Archives of American Art), AAA Reel D91; Dorothy Houts to Rowan, Jan. 27, 1934, "John B. Flannagan" folder, RG121/105; clipping from *Washington Post*, June 19, 1934, RG121/109.

[10] *PWAP Report*, 5. At its peak PWAP employed a few more than 2,500. The 3,749 cited above indicates considerable turnover during the four and a half months.

[11] *PWAP Report*, 7; Grant Wood to Edward Alden Jewell, quoted in *New York Times*, May 27, 1934.

[12] Major General William D. Connor to James N. Rosenberg, Oct. 20, 1934, T. Loftin Johnson to Bruce, March 10, 1935, clipping from *New York Herald Tribune*, July 9, 1936, RG121/123; Watson to Theodore Sizer, Feb. 8, May 4, 1934, Sizer to Watson, April 23, 1934, Thomas C. Hart to Harry L. Roosevelt, March 1, 1934, RG121/106; Arthur Goldschmidt to Eleanor H. Little, Aug. 22, 1934, RG121/114; Rowan to Goldschmidt, April 22, 1935, RG121/123.

[13] *New York Times*, Jan. 21, 1934; clipping from *Washington Daily News*, April 27, 1934, RG121/111; *Indians at Work: A News Sheet for Indians and the Indian Service*, mimeographed, 1 (Jan. 15, 1934), 20 (Feb. 15, 1934), 38 (April 1, 1934), 37, copies in RG121/110; Watson to John S. Ankeny, Jan. 3, 15, 1934, RG121/116.

[14] Bruce to Robert Fechner, Dec. 12, 1933, memorandum, na, Jan. 4, 1934, RG121/105; Fechner to Bruce, May 22, June 4, 1934, RG121/106; clipping from *Happy Days* (June 1, 1935), Edward Rowan Papers (Archives of American Art), AAA Reel D142; Treasury Department Art Projects *Bulletin*, No. 9 (March–May 1936), 13. Title of the organ varied; hereafter cited as Section *Bulletin*.

[15] *New York Times*, Feb. 9, 1934; memorandum by Major V. H. Cornell, March 16, 1934, Grant Wood to Rowan, Jan. 20, 1934, RG121/105.

[16] "Minutes of Meeting" of Advisory Committee, Jan. 10, 1934, Bruce to [Regional Chairmen], March 7, 20, 1934, RG121/116.

[17] *New York Times*, April 29, 1934; clippings from *Washington Post*, April 21, 1934, *Washington Herald*, April 24, 1934, RG121/110; *National Exhibition of Art by the Public Works of Art Project*, catalogue (Corcoran Gallery, Washington, D.C., 1934).

[18] Clipping from Norfolk (Virginia) *Virginian Pilot*, April 23, 1934, RG121/105; clipping from *Detroit Free Press*, April 21, 1934, RG121/110; memorandum, Bruce to Watson and Rowan, April 5, 1934, RG121/105.

[19] PWAP Press Release, nd, RG121/105; clippings from *Washington Post*, April 25, 1934, *Washington Star*, April 25, 1934, RG121/110.

[20] Clipping from *Washington Daily News*, April 26, 1934, RG121/105; *Journal of Electrical Workers and Operators*, XXXIII (June 1934), 235; *New York Times*, May 27, 1934; memorandums, Ann Craton to Bruce, April 5, May 3, 1934, RG121/106; C. Powell Minnegerode to Bruce, May 22, 1934, RG121/109.

[21] Ellsworth Woodward to Bruce, March 16, 1934, Watson to John Gaw Meem, May 25, 1934, RG121/105; clippings from *New Haven Sun Register*, Jan. 28, 1934, *St. Louis Globe-Democrat*, March 18, 1934, RG121/110; clipping from *Los Angeles Examiner*, March 12, 1934, RG121/111.

[22] Merle Armitage to Rowan, Oct. 22, 1934, April 10, 1935, RG121/123; Ellsworth Woodward to Bruce, March 16, 1934, RG121/105; *New York Times*, March 11, 1934.

[23] *New York Times*, April 23, 1934; Ann Craton, "Public Works of Art Project Report Covering Its Activities and Liquidation," typescript [1935], RG121/105; Forbes Watson, "Art and the Government in 1934," *Parnassus*, VII (Jan. 1935), 14; Bruce to Dows, Sept. 7, 1935, RG121/122.

14 Ben Shahn (Section of Fine Arts), detail of *Worker with Electric Drill*, study for fresco panel in the Bronx Central Post Office, New York City

3

The Bureaucracy of Art

Edward Bruce hoped to advance American art and improve national taste by putting before the public what he judged to be America's best—art acquired solely on the basis of its quality. To pay for the effort he contrived to siphon small portions of the funds Congress voted government agencies. His financial mainstay was the federal building fund, enlarged in the early depression years as a pump-priming device. Restrictions on the use of the building fund money enabled Bruce to place art only in new federal buildings. To dispense art more widely he sought operating capital from other agencies. Wherever he found it the problem immediately arose of how to maintain the quality he insisted upon in face of the often compromising regulations, restrictions, and personality of the benefactor.

After the transfer of the art unit from the Treasury Department to the new Federal Works Agency in 1939, an uprooting which cost him the important protection of Secretary of the Treasury and Mrs. Henry Morgenthau, Jr., Bruce's fortunes began to decline. When Germany attacked Poland and World War II leaped into the American conscience, defense programs preoccupied supporters of the art unit and absorbed the money in the public building fund. Bruce failed to find other suitable patrons, and the administratively created unit withered away. Perhaps Bruce's agency would have lasted if, at the peak of its success, he had worked harder to imbed it in congressional statute and obliged Congress to provide funds directly to it. Had Congress refused, and its mood was uncertain, Bruce's work and effectiveness probably would have ended then.

From the beginning Bruce had preferred to deal with officials of the executive branch who held power to aid the cause of American art through the device of the administrative order. Early in PWAP, Mrs. Elinor Morgenthau, wife of the Treasury Secretary, had become a strong enthusiast of public art. She awakened the interest of her husband, and together the Morgenthaus bolstered the President and Mrs. Roosevelt in their natural inclination to look kindly upon Treasury art efforts. Several days before PWAP released its last artists, Bruce placed before Secretary Morgenthau a new scheme to subsidize art. The plan eliminated the question of employing artists on the basis of need and avoided asking Congress for money at a time when a project to employ individuals who did not specifically require relief would surely find opposition. Bruce proposed to create a Division of Fine Arts in the Treasury and to finance it with existing Treasury and Public Works Administration funds. The Treasury Department held $144,618,000 to build 233 federal buildings: post offices, federal court and office buildings, marine hospitals, and executive department buildings in Washington's federal triangle. Bruce asked that Roosevelt, by executive order, set aside 1 percent of the cost of each building for embellishments. In addition, he asked for a $100,000 allotment from the PWA to start the division, pay the staff for a year, and execute work begun or requested during the PWAP. Specifically, PWA's tangible return would include pictorial records of CCC camps, PWA work, national parks, designs for products made in the Subsistence Homesteads and Tennessee Valley Authority, more murals by Indians, and paintings and murals of the American scene for American embassies. By the time the Division spent the PWA's $100,000, the program for embellishing federal buildings would be fully developed, Bruce believed, and would "prove its value sufficiently to make it a permanent part of the Treasury organization."[1]

Morgenthau approved the plan, at least that part of requiring a PWA allotment, and applied for the money on May 11, 1934. But Public Works administrator Harold Ickes took the position that the building program should be in the PWA, not in the Treasury. In accord with Ickes's wishes the Board of the PWA passed the allotment on condition that PWA operate the program. Morgenthau opposed giving up Treasury responsibilities,

and matters remained at an impasse until Roosevelt settled the controversy in favor of the Treasury in a cabinet meeting on May 18.[2]

Ickes reluctantly included $100,000 for the Treasury project when he sent Roosevelt his next list of proposed PWA expenses, but the President wrote across the figure: "Only enough to keep organization going until July 1, pending later plans." Ickes told Bruce the President wanted to include music, the theater, and other cultural activities in the new project, and could not consider it in detail until after Congress adjourned for the summer and he returned from a trip to Hawaii. His proposal shattered, Bruce immediately arranged a "session" with President and Mrs. Roosevelt. While no one envisioned exactly how to develop music or the theater, the First Family assured Bruce that the new division would concern itself with quality rather than the individual need of participants. The President, Bruce reported, "told me that even if some of the money comes from the relief organizations, that will be all the relief there is to it." Roosevelt invited Bruce and Morgenthau to come to Hyde Park later in the summer when they would work out a definite plan.[3]

Bruce spent most of the summer painting the landscape around Peru, Vermont, and trying to work up a program to present to the White House. He opposed establishing a Ministry of Fine Arts on the European model. Such ministries, he felt, did more harm than good by becoming bureaucratic and so "old fogey" that the kinds of things they supported had usually died a good many years before they took them up. Bruce believed he could influence art and sculpture through federal building decoration, although he admitted that "when it comes to music and . . . the theatre I am pretty much at a loss as to what would be the best thing to do." The responses Bruce's assistant, Edward Rowan, received when he asked some 50 creative writers—thinking they too might be included—what government might do to help the needy among them and the general cause of their field of expression compounded the indecision. Mark Van Doren suggested that the government start literary magazines, John Dos Passos that government subsidize a publishing house, Upton Sinclair that art be socialized as in his EPIC plan, Thornton Wilder that government do nothing. In the midst of the confusion Bruce discovered that Morgenthau's pet hobby was landscape gardening and schemed to include a director of landscape gardening in the new division. The end of the summer found the funds of the art unit exhausted, Bruce wondering if they could not generally direct the relief artists without the responsibility of employing them, and Rowan arranging the Treasury's artist file according to "good, medium, and bums."[4]

Bruce did not get his Division of Fine Arts. He lacked a clear plan of finance, scope, and administration. A deepening rift between Secretaries Morgenthau and Ickes ruined Bruce's chance of PWA financial support. And a program of the magnitude envisioned by Roosevelt would be subject to congressional scrutiny and probably require a congressional appropriation. When asked about one of a number of the privately advanced plans for the support of art that circulated in the summer of 1934 as an alternative to his own, Bruce told the press that "the federal government is too much concerned right now with unemployment, industrial recovery, and other vital matters to give immediate considerations to an art scheme which might, however erroneously, be deemed an unnecessary experiment by the general public."[5] In short, practical politicians knew better than to create a controversial agency during the 1934 congressional campaign.

Morgenthau and Bruce on September 11 agreed on a less ambitious project. The core of the former PWAP Washington staff would dispense the funds for decorating the new buildings being erected under the large building program. Custom decreed that some artistic embellishment be part of new government buildings, and therefore no legislation was necessary. The change was that the art unit, not the architect, would take charge of the decorations. At the same time Morgenthau made it known that he preferred government buildings to look less like mausoleums and that architects stress economy and utility. Ickes, anxious that his public works money go as far as possible, had already eliminated ornamental stone carvings on PWA buildings. In the interest of both cost and beauty, Roosevelt announced, there would be no more large expenses for elaborate scroll work, gold leaf, or cornices. Some of the money thus saved would be

used for interior art. The new unit appeared on the organization chart of the Treasury Department's Procurement Division, which since June 1933 had determined the policies and methods of procurement, warehousing, and distribution of property, facilities, structures, improvements, machinery, equipment, stores, and supplies. To manage all that, two subdivisions split the work: the Branch of Supply and the Public Buildings Branch. The latter repaired, operated, and maintained existing federal buildings, acquired land, let contracts for new buildings, and, through its office of Supervising Architect, prepared the drawings, specifications, and estimated costs for most of the new buildings. Here, appended to the Supervising Architect's office, with a view toward cooperation between artist and architect, the new Section of Painting and Sculpture took its place in the bureaucratic hierarchy.[6]

The Section's first task, said Morgenthau's order which created the art unit, was to secure for new federal buildings art of "the best quality available." In that pursuit the Section would try to develop American art, reward outstanding talent, and "so far as consistent with a high standard of art" employ local talent. Interested citizens whose artistic judgment had the respect of the Section would aid in selecting and criticizing artists. Artists would be chosen "on the sole test of their qualifications as artists." More specifically, "whenever practicable," anonymous competitions would determine which artists received commissions. Morgenthau's administrative order also stipulated that "certain artists, because of their recognized talent," would be entitled to receive work without competition.[7]

Morgenthau's order did not reserve 1 percent of each building's cost for art as Bruce had hoped. Nor did it guarantee that each new building would contain paintings and sculpture. As the machinery developed, the Section of Painting and Sculpture scrutinized the architects' plans for the buildings, made suggestions for embellishment, and argued for changes in the plans that lacked desirable mural or sculpture space. In cases where the Section and the architects agreed and the director of the Procurement Division approved, the Section received a financial "reservation"—amounting in theory to about 1 percent of the sum allocated—for art work. If the actual construction of the building exceeded estimated costs and required use of the "reservation," the building contained no art.

Architects understandably were reluctant to create special spaces for murals or sculpture when there was no certainty that the latter would materialize. In the first two years, over one-third (83) of the new buildings costing over $1,000,000 had no reservation for art. Reservations on other buildings averaged considerably less than 1 percent. Bruce continually sought either a guaranteed 1 percent for art or a $1,000,000 lump allotment from building funds.[8] Receiving neither, the Section argued its case for each new building.

Bruce contended with Treasury regulations, procedure plans, approval requirements, and change-resisting bureaucrats. In addition, the Commission of Fine Arts seemed determined to thwart any but the most formal and traditional art in Washington. Believing in "the personal touch as far as I can do it," Bruce battled for his program with an endless round of conferences, luncheons, planning sessions, dinner parties, and long work days. By the end of June 1935 the Section had completed 29 competitions and planned others.[9]

The intense activity probably contributed to a heart attack Bruce suffered in early June. During his long convalescence Mrs. Elinor Morgenthau worked with the Section staff and kept her husband informed, as she said, so that he could "prod 'those in power' as he saw fit." Bruce's heart attack left the left side of his body partially paralyzed and in 1937 his physician advised him to resign. Although he submitted a letter of resignation, he immediately reconsidered and determined to devote whatever energy he had to what he called "my big dream of my life."[10]

For an individual without a major political office, Bruce attained unusual influence with first-rank New Dealers and the Roosevelts. His Washington home became a fashionable meeting ground for politicians, bureaucrats, and artists, and he enjoyed easy access to the White House. One might conjecture that Bruce and the President shared a common spirit of handicapped men leading exceptionally active lives. In any case Bruce idolized Roosevelt and sent him baskets of fruits and figs for Christmas, and scores of memorandums, letters, and illustrations of the art

work—much of it trivia and obvious flattery. Roosevelt's typical response was to instruct an assistant: "Prepare a nice line for him —Dear Ned."[11]

The achievement of the Section, and presumably its ability to operate on leftovers from building funds, so impressed Roosevelt that he told Mrs. Morgenthau as early as 1936 that plans ought to be made "looking toward making the Art Section a permanent part of the government." Two years later, and after four years of trial and tenuous existence, Morgenthau issued a new Treasury Department order which changed the name of the Section of Painting and Sculpture to Section of Fine Arts, made it a permanent section of the Treasury Department, and authorized it to "continue and further extend" its activities.[12] At the time, October 1938, Washington was already full of talk about reorganization of the executive branch. When it occurred in July 1939 the entire building program (and the art unit) were transferred from the Treasury Department to the new Federal Works Agency. Of course, the action invalidated Morgenthau's order making the Section a permanent part of the Treasury. The period of security was short.

Almost as short, and less happy, was the system devised for putting art in already constructed federal buildings and new buildings without financial reservations for art. After Congress passed a huge emergency relief appropriation in May 1935, Bruce applied to the dispensing agency, the Works Progress Administration (WPA), for money to hire 500 unemployed artists to decorate some of the Treasury's 1,900 nearly artless buildings. Although the WPA planned a much larger art project of its own, Bruce made a strong case for a grant to the Treasury Department. The 1,900 buildings were under the jurisdiction of the Treasury; why fragment authority by permitting another agency to decorate them? The Section already had jurisdiction over art in new federal buildings; why give jurisdiction in the old to another agency? And each of the Section's competitions had yielded three or four designs suitable for federal buildings. With a grant from WPA, Bruce explained, "we could put the artists to work who submitted satisfactory designs . . . decorating old buildings knowing just exactly what we were going to get at the time of their employment." The application for relief money explained that the Treasury would employ the artists half time at low wages (60 hours for $66 a month). The terms were designed to attract only artists unemployed and in needy circumstances, but Bruce insisted employment not be limited to those on relief rolls. WPA granted money, but on conditions that governed all other WPA projects.[13]

Olin Dows, a bright young artist and administrator whom Bruce made chief of the new project, suggested rejecting the WPA money when he discovered that Harry Hopkins "added the clause" that 90 percent of the labor had to come from relief rolls. There would be no difference between the Treasury project and the WPA's new Federal Art Project (FAP) in dealing with artists. Dows believed the projected 5,000-man FAP was too big, would produce "a lot of bad stuff," and would "hurt the Government's patronage of art seriously." He did not want Treasury work confused with FAP work in the public mind. More fundamental, 90 percent of the artists he wanted to employ were not on relief. However, Procurement Division director Christian J. Peoples believed the WPA money, once attained, could be spent with considerable freedom. And Bruce believed that he, the Morgenthaus, and other friends of Treasury art could force Hopkins to waive the relief requirement. Dows relented. The WPA grant on July 21, 1935 of $530,784 created the Treasury Relief Art Project (TRAP). The Section's irregularly published *Bulletin* explained that the fund would be "spent within a year . . . for the purpose of giving work to about 450 artists under the Emergency Relief Appropriation Act of 1935."[14]

The conditions of the WPA grant did not allow freedom in spending. Bruce tried to convince WPA administrators that the Treasury program would relieve artists' material deprivations in the course of obtaining top quality art for federal buildings. But, he insisted, "there are not enough artists on relief to do our job and maintain the quality for which we stand." He could find no one in Hopkins's organization "willing to sit down and talk over the conditions of the Project as an ordinary human being would, and allow . . . a setup which would make it possible to make a reasonable success of it." According to one account, relations between Bruce and Hopkins became strained after an official dinner at which Bruce, "rather drunk and sentimental, piled flattery

so thickly on Hopkins and what he was doing for art that the latter squirmed. . . . He [Hopkins] got up and made a few icy remarks saying that he was not sure of the social importance of art in the life of starving workers; and that his object was to feed them." Bruce came away blustering: "The whole damn thing is like Alice in Wonderland."[15]

Bruce turned to Morgenthau for help while Dows hired a few relief artists who met his standards. Hopkins further frustrated the project when he ordered, on November 1, that only those individuals certified for relief before that date were eligible for employment. There could be no finding the artist and then "getting him on relief." The WPA ruling, on December 6, to reduce mandatory employment of reliefers on all cultural projects from 90 percent to 75 percent disappointed Mrs. Morgenthau. "With this small exemption," she wrote, "I am not at all sure that we can do a decent job. I am almost inclined, if it is not too late, to throw up the whole relief work and concentrate on our other Treasury projects." By that time Dows felt a definite responsibility to the artists already hired.[16] It was too late.

TRAP continued, if not according to the original plan. On the premise that poor art was worse than no art, Dows and Bruce decided to proceed slowly, hiring only such good artists as they found, and to use the grant over a longer period. The administrators backed away from their intent to emphasize murals and sculpture since they considered most relief artists incompetent to design them. The 25 percent of the TRAP artists not on relief —who numbered 60-odd through 1936—designed and supervised teams of relief artists to carry out mural designs. Supervising artists frequently complained that they could find no decent assistants on relief locally, and they could not bring in assistants from out of the vicinity since WPA would not pay for travel by reliefers or away-from-home maintenance. While TRAP artists eventually completed 89 mural and 65 sculpture projects, the bulk of their achievement consisted of over 10,000 easel paintings and prints.[17]

Desiring to maintain a reputation as "the Ritz" of the relief projects, as *Time* magazine dubbed it, TRAP entered a divisive competition with the FAP. Since so many of the best artists lived in New York City, TRAP employed a special assistant, Mrs. Alice

15 Edgar Miller (TRAP),
sculptures at the Jane Addams
Housing Project, Chicago

Sharkey, to administer the project there. Mrs. Sharkey's knowledge of art and her contacts with artists seemingly ranked second among her qualifications to a temperament that enabled her to deal with Mrs. Audrey McMahon, the city's FAP head.

Treasury art officials considered Mrs. McMahon an "ambitious prima donna . . . high strung, impetuous," and a "trifle belligerent." When both projects were forming Mrs. McMahon supplied TRAP with information and lists of artists on relief, agreed to give Mrs. Sharkey preference in hiring, and accepted a "reserve list" of artists which TRAP would employ. A few weeks later TRAP administrators complained that the FAP hired away TRAP artists by offering them supervisory jobs on the FAP, poached on a reserve list, and applied its entire national quota of nonrelief artists to New York City in order to hire the best artists there. The very name "Federal Art Project" struck Dows as "grotesque . . . a piece of inaccurate stupidity." Not all the irritations originated with FAP. Before Hopkins granted the 25 percent exemption from relief employment, Dows had quietly hired twice his nonrelief quota. "If Hopkins knew about it and wanted to," Bruce drafted a letter to Dows, "he could cop your game. . . . Put the artists on the pay roll and 'Hell with him.'" Outside New York, state WPA officials found TRAP confusing. On occasion they tried to supervise TRAP artists, subject them to peculiar state regulations, or stop the work. They received blunt letters explaining the autonomy of "federal" projects.[18]

FAP officers complained that the "august" Section of Painting and Sculpture awarded FAP reliefers commissions for federal murals with the result that many artists quit, leaving FAP work unfinished. Mrs. McMahon and Mrs. Sharkey shared office space, a distressing arrangement when WPA quota cuts forced Mrs. McMahon to dismiss workers and Mrs. Sharkey sat nearby with jobs to offer "quality" artists. Although relations remained civil outwardly, Holger Cahill, national director of the FAP, contended that TRAP should have been a part of the WPA art program from the beginning. And word circulated through WPA headquarters that "If Mrs. Morgenthau had not been so damn ambitious they would never have gotten their project."[19]

While the elitist attitude of TRAP irritated FAP, it infuriated large numbers of organized artists in metropolitan areas. The American Artists Congress, founded in New York City in early 1936, was first to attack and demand that art projects be continued, extended to employ all artists who needed employment, and made permanent. Stuart Davis, secretary of the group, pointedly recalled TRAP's announcement in the July-August 1935 *Bulletin* of the half-million dollar grant "to be spent within a year . . . for the purpose of giving work to about 450 artists under the Emergency Relief Appropriation Act of 1935." Since the same WPA regulations governed employment in both TRAP and FAP, and since Congress intended the Emergency Relief Act of 1935 to relieve unemployment, "by what authority," demanded the Artists

Congress secretary, "does the administration of TRAP arbitrarily refuse employment to artists of professional ability?" At the time, April 1936, Dows admitted employing only 289 artists, but he justified it by quoting the oft-printed qualifier in the *Bulletin* that the Treasury required first-rate work of "professional competence and technical proficiency." Dows argued that the Federal Emergency Relief Administration, WPA's predecessor, had employed the best relief artists in the major art centers and bequeathed them to the FAP, which acquired, in addition, large numbers of artists all over the country whose work would have been suitable for federal buildings. Dows refrained from saying, although he clearly implied, that there was nothing left for TRAP, and challenged Davis to provide the name of even one artist in the hinterlands on relief and of Treasury caliber. As for spending the money within a year, Dows insisted: "There was absolutely no commitment or understanding that it should be spent by that time." Davis did not understand. To him TRAP's explanation meant that 289 artists exhausted the supply capable of producing first-rate work with technical proficiency and professional competence. It also implied, since the FAP easily filled its large quota, that TRAP considered FAP artists lacking in ability. As the Artists Congress viewed them, both groups produced work equal to the general quality of any large group of artists at any time or place. TRAP, in its constant reference to "quality," Davis fumed, failed to understand that "without decent conditions of work for many artists there won't be any 'quality.'" Masterpieces and genius resulted from environment; high quality from a broad base of production. The government art projects ought to use whatever resources they had to bolster demoralized artists and prevent reduction of American art "to a sorry state." That Dows had hired only 289 of his quota of 450 seemed to Davis "a miserable comment" on the administration of the Treasury Relief Art Project. And he communicated the official Artists Congress view of the TRAP administration as "arbitrary, lacking in realistic understanding of the factors involved, and incompetent in that it . . . failed to carry out the purpose for which the Treasury Relief Art Project was established."[20]

The Artists Coordination Committee, formed during the spring of 1936 by delegates of the Artists Congress and other New York art organizations of varying militancy, battled TRAP through its duration over the quality standard and low employment. When Dows challenged the Committee to produce work samples of quality artists who met relief requirements, the Committee declined on grounds that submitting samples would perpetuate the arbitrary standard. At first Dows tried the bureaucratic weapons of declining to meet the Committee personally, ignoring its most vituperative letters, and sending a subordinate into battle without authority to speak for the project. Finally Dows clashed with the Coordination Committee at a meeting and agreed to arrange with Mrs. McMahon for interproject transfer of FAP artists acceptable to TRAP. The committee understood the number "could run very high." It ran to 40, and raised the total of TRAP employment to 356, its highest level.[21]

The organized artists, unsatisfied with the minor concession, agitated for more drastic change. Distrusting Dows, Bruce, Rowan, and Watson, the Committee advocated that every art organization in the United States of over 50 members elect regional boards which would elect a Federal Board of the Government Art Projects to serve on planning commissions and project juries. The Coordination Committee protested TRAP's recommendation of 41 artists to "fascist" Civilian Conservation Corps camps, deplored as "discriminating" and "conducive to hack production" Dows's admission that in "a number of cases" he had requested artists "not to do abstract painting," and demanded that TRAP officials labor to substitute a simple statement of need as requisite for employment in place of the humiliating relief certification.[22]

Dows gave no more ground. The proposed Federal Board of Government Art Projects would be in position to obligate the people's money, yet have no responsibility to the government. And who would represent organizations of under 50 members and the unaffiliated artist? Privately Dows considered CCC camp assignments a good way of eliminating amateurs and testing the "town-livers." TRAP found abstract paintings difficult to place and, although it accepted a few, it asked artists who worked in both methods to do the more popular objective work on the project and abstracts on their own time. "It is reasonable . . . to expect

cooperation . . . in matters of this kind," Dows declared. He refused to discuss the relief qualification, contending that only Harry Hopkins could change it.[23]

The Treasury decided not to apply for another grant from relief funds. Clearly Congress and the President intended the 1935 relief act to provide employment, not selective commissions. Necessary concessions to New York's militant artists resulted in swelling the rolls of easel painters—since few acceptable muralists could be found—beyond the original intent. Whatever number of later distinguished easel artists painted for TRAP in New York, Dows found "most of them . . . not very good," painters of "mediocre things" whose "production ought to be higher." Then in December 1936 WPA further sabotaged TRAP's quality standard by reducing permissible nonrelief employment from 25 percent to 10 percent. These problems persuaded the Treasury to divorce the program completely from relief.[24]

At the end of 1936 TRAP began a slow phase-out. Announcement of the end somewhat quieted the artists with "halfbaked political theories," to use Dows's phrase, and allowed discharging "the least useful artists" while retaining favored muralists until they finished their assignments. Operations during the closing months corresponded—except in numbers—to what Dows and Bruce had envisioned for the project. Indeed, Dows felt strongly enough for the remaining artists and their work that he went to see Roosevelt personally for aid in blocking WPA's attempt to reclaim the unspent part of the grants. From a peak employment of 356 in mid-1936, the number of TRAP artists dropped to 135 by June 30, 1937, to 20 by June 1938, and by October of that year only 2 picture framers remained. TRAP administrators arranged for FAP to absorb many of the relief artists, although some FAP directors hedged at employing TRAP artists—whose "quality" they questioned—at a time when WPA quota cuts required dismissing others.[25]

The Section had hoped to use the WPA grant to expand its operations and thereby strengthen its claim to permanence. But relief stipulations of the WPA proved incompatible with the quality standards of the Treasury. The venture also pitted the Treasury against radical artists who never conceded its right to

16 Reginald Marsh (TRAP), ceiling of the New York Customs House

judge or forgave its greater preoccupation with American art than with American artists. The Treasury withdrew, a little bitter, to seek other means of bestowing quality art upon the citizenry.

Bruce now turned to a plan to create a Smithsonian Gallery of Art. Ex-Secretary of the Treasury Andrew Mellon had recently donated $50,000,000 in old world masterpieces and cash to the government, and plans were in process to house the collection in a National Gallery of Art on the Mall in Washington. Bruce proposed to complement this "mausoleum for dead masters" with a gallery, ostensibly operated by the Smithsonian Institution, dedicated to living American artists. He intended the Smithsonian gallery to encourage contemporary art through buying and selling art, employing artists, making reproductions, giving scholarships, publishing popular and scholarly works, and conducting exhibitions. Moreover, the Smithsonian Gallery of Art should become a great circulating library of pictures for museums, schools, and community groups.[26]

Bruce anticipated more than improved taste and appreciation for painting and sculpture as results of the new gallery. He planned—although he was careful to whom he admitted it—to extend the influence of the Treasury's Section. Secretary Morgenthau's casual comment that the proposed gallery was "outside his bailiwick" sent Bruce protesting to Mrs. Morgenthau that they should consider the plan an integral part of Treasury art activities. "If we succeed in interesting somebody to build the museum and to have it closely associated with the Section," he argued to the Secretary's wife, "it could be enormously successful in developing our program." Bruce confided to Frederic A. Delano, the President's uncle and his chief collaborator in the project, that the Smithsonian gallery seemed "the key to the whole government art project." He told others confidentially, "I conceived the plan . . . and want to have a good deal to say in it myself. . . . It will, I hope, be the culmination of my whole program and what I have been able to accomplish."[27]

Bruce's contention that the Mellon gallery would become America's Louvre and the Smithsonian gallery America's Luxembourg impressed congressmen less than others whose consent he

17 Model of Eliel and Eero Saarinen's winning design in the competition sponsored by the Section for a Smithsonian Gallery of Art

needed for the project. The regents of the Smithsonian Institution responded enthusiastically, seeing in the proposal a place to house and exhibit the thousands of American paintings bequeathed to the government over the years. Although Roosevelt declined to pressure Congress for enabling legislation, he approved the scheme "in toto," noting that it incorporated his oft-repeated idea of improving national aesthetic standards through traveling exhibitions. In March 1937 Senator David I. Walsh of Massachusetts introduced a bill drafted in the Treasury Department with Bruce's assurance that the new gallery also could serve the Senator's dream of a national portrait gallery. Because of the $4,000,000 it committed to the undertaking, Congress defeated the bill. But in May 1938, after much lobbying by Bruce and Delano on Capitol Hill, another Walsh bill passed which granted the Smithsonian a choice plot across the Mall from the Mellon gallery, appropriated $40,000 for an architectural competition to produce a building design, permitted construction through private means, and obliged Congress to maintain the gallery once it had been established.[28]

While Washington bureaucrats fluttered in fear of the impending reorganization of the executive branch in spring 1939, the Section of Fine Arts busied itself with a two-stage architectural competition for the Smithsonian gallery. From the 1,408 simple designs submitted in the first stage, the jury chose 10 for the second, guaranteed the top 10 architects $1,000 each for detailed drawings, and held out $3,500 for second and $7,500 for first prize. Bruce had clearly described what he wanted: "My idea is something genuinely simple and beautiful—no classical columns of any kind. . . . What I would like to see is a one story building with a beautiful garden and suitable courts where people would enjoy coming to." He deplored the weightiness of other Washington buildings and called for light partitions and restrained design. He did not want the new gallery to resemble "that pink marble whorehouse," as he laughingly called the National Gallery of Art.[29] In choosing Joseph Hudnut, dean of the Harvard School of Architecture, and Thomas Mabry, architectural specialist of New York's Museum of Modern Art, to head the jury and handle the technical matters, he guaranteed a design to his liking.

When Eliel and Eero Saarinen's modernistic glass, steel, and concrete plan won the competition, the infighting among temperamental cliques and schools of artists paled in comparison with the feud among architects. Older, conservative architects

44

charged that the Saarinen design—indeed, all the designs in the final stage of competition—showed "complete lack of conformity with . . . the established types of architecture prevailing in Washington." Members of the Commission of Fine Arts gratuitously announced that when the design was submitted to them they would reject it and any other which exhibited a "similar flavor of modernism." Louis Simon, Supervising Architect of the Treasury and nominally Bruce's boss, lamented that radicals sought to destroy his life's work of trying to create something worthy in Washington. Hudnut retorted that the old guard misunderstood the meaning of classical, that they had been hanging colonnades and porticoes on the sides of buildings for 50 years and had succeeded only in making those buildings complicated, false, and restless. And besides, Hudnut fumed, there was no conformity in the styles of already existing structures. Two thousand years separated the Egyptian monument to Washington from the Doric temple of Lincoln, and 700 years more lay between the Lincoln Memorial and the Ciceronian-style monument then being built for Jefferson, and a span of another 1,600 years separated the Jefferson Memorial and the Georgian White House. In all, the irritated competition director computed, buildings of 19 architectural styles faced the Mall.[30]

At the height of this wrangling, with a vacant $20,000,000 plot of real estate and a building design but no money to build it or united front from which to solicit, the reorganization plan of the executive branch uprooted the Public Buildings Administration and Section of Fine Arts and transplanted them in the new Federal Works Agency (FWA). Bruce had reason for apprehension. Reorganization also brought the WPA, including its subsidiary the Federal Art Project, into the FWA. Chances for survival of two art units in the same agency seemed small. And now the Section lacked protectors. Mrs. Morgenthau, declaring herself "really heartbroken" at the turn of events, confessed that her husband could thereafter do little toward getting things done. Secretary Morgenthau did praise the work of the Section to its new overlord, Federal Works administrator John M. Carmody, and Carmody assured Bruce the work would continue and even expand. However, Carmody had neither the political power nor the interest in art of the Morgenthaus. He made Bruce personally responsible for the art going into federal buildings, declined to guarantee the Section's perennial demand for 1 percent of each building's cost, and within a matter of weeks provoked Bruce to complain that except for the Morgenthaus and Roosevelts, no one in the entire government had "the slightest interest" in cultural development.[31]

Events in the autumn and early winter of 1939 seemed to portend an end to the Section's program. When war came to Europe, Bruce wrote bitterly: "All the little bureaucrats with whom it is my misfortune to have to deal, have raised up against me and decided that now that the world is at war we ought to cut out this art muck." Talk of diverting funds from building programs to military preparedness threatened the Section's only source of money, and Bruce's effort to provide other work for the Section by decorating ships constructed under the supervision of the Maritime Commission did not work out. The Maritime Commission, because Roosevelt prodded Commission Chairman Admiral Emory S. Land, expressed interest in Section competitions to provide art for the seven ships of the American President Lines then under construction, but its procrastination suggested other intentions. More depressing, Bruce failed in his plan to gain statutory independence for the Section and incorporate it with the Smithsonian Gallery of Art. Roosevelt had appointed Bruce chairman of a committee to work on the idea of traveling exhibitions. Hoping to satisfy the President, salvage the Smithsonian Gallery of Art and extricate the Section from the FWA, Bruce proposed that the Section become an independent bureau established in the facilities of the Smithsonian Gallery. Carmody opposed independence of the Section on the grounds that separating the tasks of building and decoration one day would invite some economy minded Congress to cut funds for decoration. Roosevelt, who probably never understood Bruce's maneuvering, finally said he would accept a Bureau of Fine Arts created by statute "in Procurement if such a bill passes and if it does not cost additional money." Bruce's plan was to escape Procurement and the program would cost considerably more money, particularly if the government had to pay for the building to house the Smithsonian

Gallery of Art. His plan disappeared up the chain of command; official silence followed.[32]

Drew Pearson and Robert S. Allen splashed the story across their newspaper column on November 25 that Bruce's resignation lay on Peoples's desk because, since the Procurement Division's transfer from the Treasury Department to the Federal Works Agency, Bruce's life had been "miserable." Behind it, claimed the columnists, was a story of red tape, jealousies, and the obstructive attitude of Procurement officials. Bruce publicly denied the entire story.[33] His disclaimers notwithstanding—and the surviving records include no resignation letter—Pearson and Allen had touched at the center of the Section's troubles.

Roosevelt, who did not see Bruce's denial, believed the column. "When a fellow turns up in Washington and proves he can make bricks out of straw," the President chided, "that the bricks are durable and artistic and that nobody else can make them, the President puts a Marine Guard around him and does not let him leave. Do be a good fellow [and announce] that you have been thus chained to the Government of the United States and cannot get away even if you want to."[34] Whatever his inclinations, Bruce could hardly resign. He could only resume haggling with the Public Buildings Administration for embellishment money, continue his search for money to build the Smithsonian gallery with the hope of absorbing the Section into it, and renew his efforts with the Maritime Commission and other agencies to find new work for the Section.

Roosevelt's interest in the following months eased some of the problems. He instructed Carmody to "be good to 'Art in Federal Buildings,'" and sent a presidential assistant, James Rowe, to the Procurement Division with a message to "cooperate and not sabotage." Roosevelt also instructed Rowe to call on Admiral Land at the Maritime Commission to tell him not to let the Marine architects and decorators hand out commissions to their friends as in the past. A presidential order made the Section an integral part of the Public Building Administration and, for the first time, guaranteed 1 percent of each building's cost for embellishment. And when Charles Moore's term expired on the Commission of Fine Arts, Roosevelt appointed Bruce. Bruce left to spend the winter in Key West, he told the President, "with a dancing heart."[35]

Five million dollars to build and endow the Smithsonian Gallery of Art could insure the Section's future. At first raising private funds seemed no problem. Bruce claimed he was "quite confidential" with Andrew Mellon and that Mellon practically assured financing a gallery for modern art to complement his morgue for old masters. But Mellon died and his heirs dropped the plan. Still Bruce felt there should be enough interest among the wealthy people of America to put it through. For a time he sought to finance his potential home through the Guggenheim, Carnegie, and Rockefeller foundations. When no foundation money was forthcoming Bruce's tactics vacillated wildly—beginning with a denunciation of the Rockefellers ("they haven't any taste and they put their dead hand on anything that they put their precious money into"). He then suggested the federal government might better spend its money on the gallery than on "a lot of wholesale WPA theatre projects and music projects." Following that came his suggestion that Congress contribute just half the needed money. By that time, though, world unrest consumed the energies of Congress and made the large private foundations conservative. Bruce began to talk of temporarily neglecting the endowment to concentrate on raising $2,000,000 in small lots for the building. Veteran fund raisers deflated him with the information that in large fund-raising campaigns nearly 98 percent of the money came from 2 percent of the givers and that those givers had, at that time, no money to give. Before Pearl Harbor shattered all hope for the gallery, Bruce had worked out a plan—approved by Mrs. Roosevelt, so he said—to name the new gallery the "Roosevelt Museum of American Art" and call upon the public, through page advertisements in such national magazines as the *Saturday Evening Post*, to "put up a dollar apiece as a memorial to the President for the artistic and cultural development of the country which he . . . sponsored."[36]

Failure to raise money, failure to unite the architectual community to help raise money, and diversion of interest by impending war doomed the Smithsonian Gallery of Art. With it went a niche in which the Section of Fine Arts might have survived

World War II. As it happened the plot on the Mall stood vacant until 1958 when Congress, reflecting the interests of another age, designated its use for a National Air and Space Museum.

The Section's attempt to draw off Maritime Commission funds on a regular schedule ended in failure. Despite Roosevelt's pointed instructions, the Commission continued to obstruct the Section's operation. At one point the Commission initiated a competition on its own for selected artists in the midst of the Section's open competition, to the bewilderment of interested artists. When Bruce induced Roosevelt to chastise Land, the path, once more, smoothed. Shortly H. E. Frick, vice-president of American President Lines, appeared at a meeting of the selection jury to view the winning art. Frick, who impressed Bruce as the kind of vice-president who "might be considered somewhat inarticulate" if "damn" and "goddamn" were eliminated from his vocabulary, announced that if he had his way "there wouldn't be a [god-damn] piece of art in any of the ships." More, he would paint out a good deal of it after a ship's maiden voyage. At length Bruce thought he had pacified Frick and proceeded to commission 27 designs, from the 1,748 submitted, for the *Presidents Jackson, Monroe, Hayes, Garfield,* and *Van Buren.* Before the Maritime Commission delivered the ships, American President Lines head William G. McAdoo repeated Frick's threat to paint over much of the art.[37] So traumatic was the whole experience that the Section gave no further serious attention to the Marine Commission.

For a few months following Bruce's reported resignation, the Section encountered no difficulties in putting decorative art in new buildings. Before 1940 ended, however, Congress and the President drastically cut the building program. Although appropriations already made would busy a small group of artists for perhaps two years, the source of the Section's money withered. Hope centered on extracting money from improvement and maintenance funds. To make such a scheme legal, the Bureau of the Budget ruled, the word "decoration" would have to be in-

18 Willem de Kooning (Section of Fine Arts), detail of mural in the library of SS *President Jackson*

47

serted in the next appropriations bill. For the first time Congress would have to authorize, specifically, the Section's work. A good part of the world was in flames by the time the bill for building repair, alterations, improvement, *decoration*, and preservation went to Congress. The Appropriation Committee's attitude, expressed by Congressman Kenneth McKellar, was that "the painting of all murals ought to be stopped absolutely," that the government "ought not to be thinking about it" during a war. One battleship increased morale more than all the art in America, and if the enemy bombed the United States, the Fine Arts would be a waste of money.[38] The committee denied the Section money for decoration, and thus doomed it.

With building funds practically exhausted, the Smithsonian Gallery impossible, and attempts to acquire new patrons frustrated, the Section struggled to involve itself in the war effort in order to stay alive. Its major efforts concerned establishing an artists corps and a propaganda poster agency.

Even before December 1941 several plans for an artists corps circulated about Washington. Most of them called for attaching artists to military units, government agencies, war plants, and civil defense organizations. Advocates of the corps insisted that the brainless, one-eyed camera, lacking the artist's ability plastically to accent, exaggerate, or restrain, failed to fill the wartime need for dramatic presentation. Some of the plans, including the Section's early version, emphasized placing artists in Army camouflage units. Such talk of using a man's art as well as his feet, of engaging men of advanced years to obscure outlines of important locations was lost on the Army. The camouflage function disappeared from artists corps plans when the Army announced that camouflage activity was "turning scientific," requiring scientific training, and, as a military function, demanded "a soldier first and a specialist afterward."[39]

The probability that the Section's plan would be accepted over all others seemed certain after a cabinet meeting on January 16, 1942. Roosevelt spoke of a letter sent him by Mrs. Morgenthau on the subject of pictures as historical war records. The President desired all departments to give thought and cooperation to the matter and when someone suggested Bruce as the proper person to oversee the project, the President appointed him to incorporate the idea into a plan. Coordination of the government's needs in graphic art and recording of wartime activity, the Section asserted immediately, could best be achieved through a Section of Fine Arts-administered artists corps. Working with Mrs. Morgenthau, the Section came up with a plan, to cost $255,000, for employing 40 artists at war correspondent rank to work in the military theaters and 50 more to record training, production, and changes at home brought by the war.[40]

Roosevelt rejected the Section's plan, for reasons that remain unclear. He had assigned a task to Bruce, asked the executive departments to cooperate, and then refused Bruce's solution. In rejecting the proposal Roosevelt said that he did not question its merits but thought it was not needed since artists already served in the armed forces, and the Army had a plan for an artists corps. Moreover, commercial artists and publishers covered the home front in their normal pursuit of wartime subjects. Perhaps Roosevelt should be taken literally. Or, perhaps Bruce's plan did not encompass what Roosevelt had in mind when he asked for a wartime project. It also seems possible, despite the absence of clear proof, that Roosevelt had lost patience with Bruce. Since the President's letter to Bruce in 1939 "chained" him to the government, Bruce had taken too many problems to Roosevelt, been too serious about too many affairs that must have seemed petty to the President, and when the Section's fortunes declined, adopted a plaintive, almost whining, tone. Or perhaps, as Rowan theorized, Roosevelt turned down the project "because Congress would set up such a howl if it ever heard of it."[41] In any case the Section lost one more opportunity to survive.

For a time the Section tried to work itself into producing war posters. It argued that posters produced by mediocre illustrators and magazine-covermen lacked quality, that government should engage the real artists of America "on a basis less trite and obvious." Privately, Bruce complained that the poster-making agencies viewed the mentality of the public as "something close to the seventh grade." If government was to give the people art in support of the war effort, he insisted, "it should be the best and not directed to morons." If the propaganda agencies of the govern-

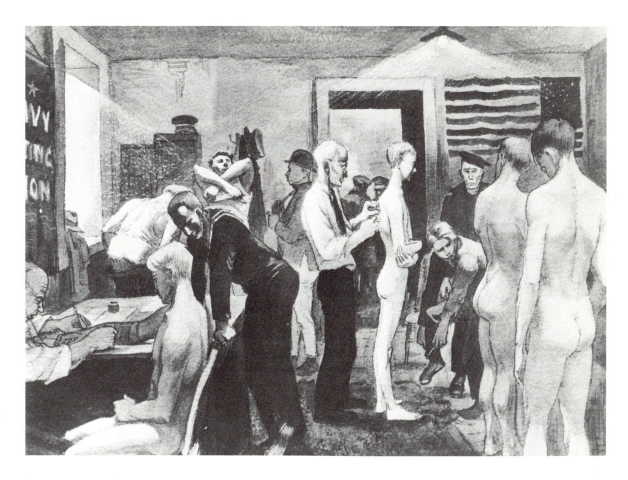

19 Mitchell Jamieson, *Naval Recruiting Station No. 1*, a winner in the competition run by the Section of Fine Arts in 1942 for the Office of Emergency Management

ment would supply the money, the Section would conduct competitions for posters and art in other mediums which, Forbes Watson promised, would "bring out clearly what America means to the People . . . what our ideals are, what we are defending, and what a great country this is." Bruce suggested a coordinated poster campaign around the theme, "My country, the hope of the world." The Section aired its poster ideas at a meeting with representatives of the Army, Navy, Selective Service, Civil Service, Department of Agriculture, Maritime Commission, Social Security Commission, Government Printing Office, and Federal Works Agency. The Section's experience with competitions, its

contacts with artists, its belief that it could select a corps of artists for poster work through competitions failed to impress the assemblage. They argued about the slowness of competitions and "what type of artists would come in."[42] With one or two minor exceptions the agencies shunned the Section and prepared their own posters.

The Section was focusing its effort by early 1942 on Archibald MacLeish's Office of Facts and Figures (OFF), a new agency charged with explaining and advancing the war program. Bruce's supporters informed MacLeish that OFF's graphic propaganda failed to rouse anger, fear and "other raw emotions that arise not between the ears but from the glands." The Commission of Fine Arts, now sympathetic to Bruce, deplored OFF's failure to use the potent force of creative art. "The cold, mechanical, airbrush competence of our present output of posters," the Commission informed MacLeish, "suggests that this has been seen as an advertising job, to be handled with the same technique and by the same men who sell toothpaste and gadgets to the public. We are sick of this kind of product." The OFF, afraid that its graphics division would become "the U.S. Art Department" if it capitulated to Bruce, responded by appointing more artists to its advisory committee. At the same time OFF insisted that the Section's competition system was too cumbersome under war conditions. And the war agency finally admitted that it considered poster-making a "highly technical undertaking more closely allied to the commercial world of advertising than to the fine arts."[43] The OFF opened an office on Madison Avenue, published a guide for poster-makers advising against "symbolic" content, acquired an associate of George Gallup's opinion survey organization as adviser, and that ended that.

During the first months of United States participation in the war, the Section conducted a competition for the Red Cross to obtain pictures and posters interpreting Red Cross activities and a competition for the Office of Emergency Management (OEM) for art depicting war industries at work. The Red Cross competition caused no difficulties, although the organization spent $700 less than the $3,000 allotted and purchased but 71 of the 2,038 items entered. The Office of Emergency Management bought 109 paintings of the 2,528 submitted on industrial subjects. The Section augmented the OEM competition by placing eight artists on salary and sending them to defense plants. Plant guards threw one artist out and police arrested him for working in the street. Another failed to gain entrance because plant officials lacked time "to take care of him," and others spent most of their pay period in waiting rooms.[44] The results, when artists finally set to work, were well received and later widely exhibited, but the experience demonstrated that the Section could not easily engage artists to capture the spirit of the war effort on the scene.

Edward Bruce, in a real sense, gave his life attempting to sustain his dream. Against the advice of physicians he stayed on with the Section to agitate for his version of an art conscious nation. In 1942, when obviously the Section would atrophy altogether if it did not become involved in some way, Bruce's desperate politicking served only to harm his already crippled body. He suffered another heart attack. Too weak to fight the Section's now impossible battles, he refused to resign. Everyone in the FWA understood that replacing Bruce would kill him. Neither Bruce nor the Section recovered. In 1943 both quietly died.

[1] John Morton Blum, *From the Morgenthau Diaries: Years of Crisis, 1928-1938* (Boston, 1959), 92; Edward Bruce, "Suggested Plan for Continuance of the Government Fine Arts Activities Inaugurated Under the Public Works of Art Project," typescript, April 20, 1934, Bruce to Biddle, May 14, 1934, RG121/118.

[2] Bruce to Julius F. Stone, May 19, 1934, RG121/105. The feud between Morgenthau and Ickes intensified in the fall of 1934 when Morgenthau refused to give Ickes complete control over the construction of the new Department of Interior building. See Blum, *From the Morgenthau Diaries*, 87-91; Harold L. Ickes, *The Secret Diary of Harold L. Ickes* (3 vols., New York, 1953-54), I, 221-24.

[3] Henry T. Hunt to Henry Morgenthau, Jr., July 6, 1934, RG121/114; Bruce to Morgenthau, June 5, 1934, RG121/105; Bruce to LeRoy Barton, July 20, 1934, Bruce to Edward Rowan, July 21, 1934, RG121/124; Bruce to Biddle, June 26, 1934, Biddle Papers.

[4] See folder of correspondence with writers in RG121/105; Bruce to Rowan and Cecil Jones, June 18, 1934, RG121/106; Bruce to Henry V. Hubbard, July 30, 1934, Bruce to George H. Williamson, July 9, 1934, RG121/124.

[5] *Washington Post*, Oct. 4, 1934.

[6] William H. McReynolds to Bruce, Sept. 12, 1934, RG121/114; Edward Bruce and Forbes Watson, *Art in Federal Buildings: An Illustrated Record of the Treasury Department's New Program in Painting and Sculpture* (Washington, 1936), 283-84; Blum, *From the Morgenthau Diaries*, 92; *Washington Post*, April 26, 1934.

[7] Treasury Department Order PWB No. 2-c Organization, Oct. 16, 1934, RG121/118.

[8] "Memorandum Concerning the Treasury Department Art Program for the Coming Year," na [1936], RG121/124.

[9] Bruce to Biddle, March 4, 1936, Biddle Papers.

[10] Elinor Morgenthau to Bruce, Aug. 2, 1945, Bruce to Peoples, Nov. 8, 1937, RG121/124.

[11] Dows, "The New Deal's Treasury Art Programs," 54; see also memorandum by Roosevelt, July 17, 1937, AAA Reel NDA/HP1.

[12] Elinor Morgenthau to Bruce, Aug. 18, 1936, RG121/124; Treasury Department Order, Procurement Division, Oct. 13, 1938, RG121/129.

[13] "A Federal Project for Employment of Artists in the Decoration of

Public Buildings under the Emergency Relief Act of 1935," typescript, na, nd, Bruce to Morgenthau, May 22, 1935, RG121/120.

[14] Dows to Donald J. Bear, Nov. 8, 1935, RG121/119; Dows to Bruce, July 15, 1935, RG121/122; Bruce to Peoples, Nov. 2, 1935, RG121/124; Section *Bulletin* No. 4 (July-Aug. 1935), 8, No. 5 (Sept. 1935), 8.

[15] Bruce to Dows, Nov. 29, 1935, RG121/122; Bruce to Elinor Morgenthau, Nov. 3, 1935, RG121/122; Bruce to Peoples, Nov. 2, 1935, RG121/124; George Biddle Diary, Sept. 9-13, 1935.

[16] Dows to Bruce, Dec. 5, 1935, RG121/124; Elinor Morgenthau to Bruce, Dec. 10, 1935, Dows to Bruce, Dec. 13, 1935, RG121/122.

[17] "Final Report of Treasury Relief Art Project," typescript, RG121, final report file; Bruce to Cecil Jones, Dec. 11, 1935, RG121/118.

[18] Cecil Jones to Bruce, Nov. 29, 1935, RG121/119; Dows to Alice Sharkey, Nov. 13, 1935, Cecil Jones to Bruce, Sept. 14, 1935, draft letter, Bruce to Dows, Aug. 21, 1935, Cecil Jones to George H. Gannon, Oct. 19, 1935, RG121/118; Dows to Bruce, Nov. 20, 1935, RG121/122.

[19] Maria Ealand to Bruce, Aug. 12, 1935, RG121/122; Holger Cahill to Agnes Cronin, RG69/211.5.

[20] Stuart Davis to Dows, April 29, 1936, RG121/122; Dows to Davis, April 8, 1939, RG121/119; Davis to Dows, April 29, May 26, 1936, RG121/118.

[21] Memorandum by Dows, Dec. 21, 1936, Davis to Dows, June 18, 1936, RG121/119; Dows to Alice Sharkey, May 28, 1936, Sharkey to Dows, June 5, 1936, RG121/120.

[22] Artists Coordination Committee to Dows, Aug. 6, Oct. 12, Nov. 2, 1936, RG121/119.

[23] Dows to Sharkey, June 23, 1936, RG121/120; Dows to Frederic Knight, Sept. 1, 1936, Dows to Artists Coordination Committee, Nov. 6, 1936, RG121/119.

[24] Memorandum, Cecil Jones and Watson to W. E. McReynolds, Feb. 26, 1937, RG121/119; Dows to Sharkey, April 24, 1936, RG121/120.

[25] Dows to Bruce, April 3, 1936, RG121/119; "Final Report of the Treasury Relief Art Project."

[26] "Program for a National Competition for the Smithsonian Gallery of Art," na, nd, RG121/124.

[27] Bruce to Harold Mack, July 15, 1939, Bruce to Elinor Morgenthau, March 2, 1939, Bruce to Delano, June 17, 1939, Charles Butler to Bruce, Feb. 24, 1939, RG121/124.

[28] H. J. Res. 599, 75 Cong., 3 Sess., S. J. Res. 99, 75 Cong., 1 Sess.; Bruce to Elinor Morgenthau, March 8, 1934, Delano to Bruce, March 4, 1937, RG121/124.

[29] Frederic A. Delano and Charles G. Abbot, "Report of the Smithsonian Gallery of Art Commission," typescript [Jan. 11, 1940], Bruce to Hari Lindeberg, May 17, 1938, RG121/124; Peggy Thomson, "Peggy Bruce: Of Art and Salty Memories," *Washington Post Potomac*, Sept. 15, 1968, 50.

[30] Francis P. Sullivan, "Architecture," *The American Year Book* (New York, 1940); Bruce to Archer W. Huntington, Dec. 5, 1939, Gilmore D. Clarke to Delano, July 22, 1939, Joseph Hudnut to Bruce, Dec. 7, 1939, Joseph Hudnut, "Program of the Smithsonian Gallery of Art," nd, RG121/124.

[31] Elinor Morgenthau to Bruce, July 9, 1939, Bruce to Arthur Hays Sulsberger, Nov. 17, 1939, Memorandum, Bruce to Inslee Hopper, July 18, 1939, RG121/124.

[32] Memorandums, Roosevelt to James Rowe, Dec. 14, 1939, Bruce to John W. Hanes, Oct. 30, 1939, AAA Reel NDA/HP1; John M. Carmody to Roosevelt, Feb. 12, 1940, Bruce to Roosevelt, Feb. 20, 1940, RG121/118; Bruce to Hudnut, Dec. 5, 1939, RG121/124.

[33] Clipping from *Washington Times-Herald*, Nov. 25, 1939, Section of Fine Arts Press Release, Nov. 25, 1939, RG121/124.

[34] Memorandum, Roosevelt to Bruce, Dec. 28, 1939, Bruce Papers.

[35] Memorandums, Roosevelt to Rowe, Dec. 22, 1939, Roosevelt to Carmody, Dec. 19, 1939, Rowe to Roosevelt, May 22, 1940, AAA Reel NDA/HP1; Federal Works Agency Administrative Order #12, April 12, 1940, RG121/118; Bruce to Roosevelt, Jan. 26, 1940, Bruce Papers.

[36] Bruce to Frederick P. Keppel, nd, RG121/122; Bruce to Thomas D. Mabry Jr., July 31, 1938, Bruce to Hudnut, Feb. 6, 1939, Bruce to Harold Mack, July 15, 1939, Bruce to Elinor Morgenthau, July 28, 1939, Bruce Barton to Delano, May 14, 1940, Bruce to Roland J. McKinney, March 7, 1941, RG121/124. Since 1958 the Smithsonian has assumed many of the functions Bruce planned for it. The National Collection of Fine Arts—exclusively for American work—is now in a separate building; and the acquisition of the Hirshorn Collection in the 1960s signaled a much larger interest in contemporary art.

[37] Memorandums, Roosevelt to Admiral Emory Land, Nov. 14, 1939, May 1, 1940, AAA Reel NDA/HP1; Section *Bulletin* No. 22 (Sept. 1940), 17-18; "Report of the Section of Fine Arts, 1939-1940," typescript, RG121/128; draft memorandum, Bruce to Mr. Bates, nd, Douglass Parshall to Bruce, Aug. 6, 1940, RG121/124.

[38] Memorandum, Harold D. Smith to Miss [Marguerite] LeHand, Nov. 2, 1940, AAA Reel NDA/HP1; Bruce to Paul Manship, March 19, 1942; transcript of hearings, RG121/122; Harold D. Smith to Carmody, Nov. 23, 1940, Smith to Malvina C. Thompson, March 12, 1941, Eleanor Roosevelt to Smith, March 21, 1941, Office Files of the Bureau of the Budget (Washington, D.C.).

[39] Memorandum: "Plan to make use of artists in the national emergency," by Manuel Bromberg, Nov. 1941, Dows to Daniel Catton Rush, Jan. 14, 1942, Homer St. Gaudens, "Camouflage Notes," mimeographed, Oct. 14, 1941, RG121/141.

[40] Philip B. Fleming to Harold D. Smith [May 1942], "Mr. Bell's Report" (excerpt from memorandum on cabinet meeting, Jan. 16, 1942), RG121/141.

[41] Rowan to Dows, July 18, 1942, RG121/124; Roosevelt to Gilmore D. Clarke, July 21, 1942, RG121/141.

[42] Memorandums, Watson to Bruce, Feb. 21, 1941, Hopper to Bruce, March 27, 1941, RG121/124; Bruce to Delano, April 10, 1942, Bruce Papers.

[43] Max Stern to Archibald MacLeish, March 23, 1942, RG121/122; "Minutes of Meeting" of Commission of Fine Arts, May 2, 1942, RG121/131; Allen Grover to Stern, nd, RG121/118; Thomas Mabry to MacLeish, March 7, 1942, RG208/320 (Records of Office of War Information, National Archives); *How to Make Posters That Will Win the War* (Washington, 1942).

[44] *American Artists Record of War and Defense*, catalogue (Smithsonian Institution, Washington, 1942); Office of Emergency Management Press Release PM2394, Feb. 3, 1942, memorandum, W. B. Phillips to Robert W. Horton, nd, memorandum, Dows to Lt. Col. L. M. Wright, Jr., Jan. 20, 1942, RG121/141; Pauline Ehrlich to Donald B. Goodall, April 30, 1942, RG121/122.

20 The Post Office, St. Louis, Missouri. Edward Millman and Mitchell Siporin (Section of Fine Arts) won a $29,000 competition for murals in the building

4

The Art of Bureaucracy

Edward Bruce's Section of Fine Arts labored from 1934 to 1943 at the threefold task of commissioning art which satisfied the government and public, the artists who produced it, and its own quality standard. If the unit occasionally failed in its first two objects, rarely did it in the third. The Section staff knew the kind of art it wanted, made it clear to artists, and handled the commissions in a manner that gave some control if the work went wrong. In its attempt to establish an image at once dynamic and dignified, dynamism often came to mean winning favorable publicity, and dignity came to mean avoiding bad publicity. The influence of the Section on art, then, was one of caution. Still, considering the problems of obtaining funds for decorating federal buildings and the deliberate process of acquiring the decorations, the Section placed before the nation an impressive amount of mural, sculptural, and other art.

The heart of the Section's plan for dispensing art in public buildings was the competition. Before World War II smothered it, 15,426 artists submitted 40,426 sketches in 190 competitions.[1] Each competition concerned decoration of a specific building chosen by the Section for its mural and sculpture spaces and the size of its financial reservation for art. Typically the Section requested "some expert" in the vicinity of the building to chair a competition committee consisting of the architect of the building and one to three people, often suggested by the Section. The amount of the prize varied since it depended on the difference between the appropriation and the actual cost, but the Section tried to obtain reservations to provide muralists about $20 per square foot and sculptors a comparably modest amount. Artists learned of the competitions from the Committee members, local newspapers, and the Section *Bulletin*. The competition committees, or juries, sent interested artists theme suggestions and blueprints of the building. Most competitions were "invited" (open to artists selected by the Section) or were limited to artists born or residing in a locale, state, or region. Less than 15 of the 190 were national competitions.

Competition rules required artists to submit designs, generally a 3-inch to 1-foot scale, with no visible identification. The juries marked the unsigned work and accompanying blank envelope containing the artist's name with corresponding numbers. About three months after announcing a competition, the jury looked over the offerings, made its recommendation (by number), and shipped all the designs to Washington. There the Section staff placed the designs around a large room, studied and discussed them for a week or ten days, and opened the envelopes only after picking the winner. In a few cases the Washington staff disregarded the local jury recommendation or failed to find any design worthy of execution.

The winning artist signed a contract, furnished a performance bond, provided his own materials, and paid for whatever help he required. The Treasury paid one installment of the award when the artist signed his contract, a second when the Procurement Division pronounced the work half completed, and the third and largest when the artist installed the mural and received Procurement Division approval.[2]

Local juries headed by local culture barons, plus the anonymous submission of artists' sketches, gave the system an aura of fairness. Bruce hoped to make the award decisions—ultimately made by his own staff—palatable to losers and factions among artists. To achieve his goal of improved taste in America he knew that he must convince people that his was a worthwhile movement and that the Section's system produced art of the highest quality. Bruce also insisted that competitions shielded the Section against political pressure. "You can't imagine what a protection it is," he wrote, "to be able to thank a Senator for his kindness

and calling our attention to such and such an artist and assuring the Senator that we will give him an opportunity to compete in our next competition." Moreover, the Section argued that comparatively unknown artists, by winning and carrying out "less complex undertakings" in local post offices, could "prove their right to be invited . . . to design murals and execute sculpture for the great buildings" in metropolitan centers. A final reason for competitions was that Roosevelt liked them. He felt they gave "youth and experience . . . equal opportunities."[3]

The emphasis on competitions confused the Senator with the artist friend, a great part of the interested public, and many of the artists who participated. In truth, most of the art commissioned by Bruce's office did not win a competition. While the Section held 190 competitions it eventually awarded 1,371 commissions. Most of the commissions for which there were no competitions went to artists who the Section felt submitted outstanding designs in previous competitions. Of the first 572 artists to receive jobs, for example, 184 won competitions, 382 received work on the merit of their designs, and 28 were appointed outright. Thus, it was not so important to win a competition as to enter one and make an impression on the Section staff. The Section's *Bulletin* assured artists that their chances for commission by the Section were "very different" from their chances when they entered a competition for a single mural or sculpture. Bruce wanted the good artists to understand that the Treasury would commission "all the outstanding designs which were submitted." At the same time he could fend off persistent amateurs and artists of alien creed by bucking responsibility for commissions back to the local juries. Incompetent and out-of-favor artists who solicited work received polite letters regretting that no jury had recommended their work and the advice to enter other competitions where their work would come before another jury and perhaps receive a recommendation.[4] Despite Bruce's harping that the Section wanted only to secure for the government the best art in America and also his insistence that Section members who judged the designs possessed catholic taste and judgment based on wide experience, the awards made without competitions could not but reflect the Section's aesthetic bias. And the work awarded through competitions could not but reflect the conscious and unconscious bias of the juries, the chairmanship of which the Section controlled.

Artist reaction to the competition system varied. Most refrained from open protest, but more than one Section administrator returned from a field trip aware that artists doubted the ability of local juries to produce an intelligent and fair verdict. Erica Beckh Rubenstein, the first serious student of Treasury art, extracted admissions from a number of artists that they recognized the artistic bias of the Section, compromised their principles for money, and learned to "paint Section," that is, suspend their own creative inclinations to paint potboilers they knew pleased Section officials.[5]

The Artists Union shrieked hostilities against controlled juries and officialdom's aesthetics in the pages of its magazine, *Art Front*. Local juries of school principals, directors of libraries, and prominent local citizens, the typical article harangued, "ran hog wild" rejecting the sketches of hundreds of artists when clearly they lacked qualifications to judge. The union demanded that juries consist of artists and that every organization of 50 artists or more be represented in an artists' group which would serve on juries and on federal planning commissions. But "planning commissions," which the union evidently thought made the assignments for jobs where there was no competition, did not exist. The Section never considered creating one, never understood why artists should think selection and planning belonged to them instead of the government, or why the union questioned its integrity. Other artists' organizations demanded that the juries consist of previous winners and runners-up, that 80 percent of the awards be made through such juries, that artists be spared performance bonds and red tape, and that the minimum competition award be $1,000.[6]

Aside from bias by the award makers, the most frequently heard objections to competitions held that participation meant hardship for losers. Creditable sculpture and mural designs required technical, theoretical, and emotional concentration over an extended period, so the argument ran, and artists, generally in unenviable financial straits, could devote the necessary time to competition sketches only at considerable personal sacrifice and expense. Since the artists designed the work for a specific building, it had no usefulness elsewhere; competition wasted the energy of all but one artist. And private clients, influenced by government practice, began to expect artists to furnish competitive designs without compensation. The militant artists of New York demanded the Section limit competitions to invited artists who would receive salaries while they designed. Many other artists simply declined to enter competitions when the labor of designing two or three sketches brought no remuneration.[7]

The higher an artist considered himself in his profession, the more he was apt to oppose the idea of competitions. Some objected to contributing time, material, and expense to an enterprise in which most of the competitors lost, and others resented the status reduction inherent in open competition. As one member exclaimed at a National Sculptors Society meeting: "Our honourable president and his colleagues could hardly be expected to agree to compete with high school girls and any old nincompoop!"[8]

One serious objection held that the competition system did not secure the best murals because the best sketches won competitions. And the ability to make a winning sketch had nothing to do with the ability to paint a great mural. Another objection to the principle of competitions was that compromise was inherent in it. As one prominent sculptor put it, the choice of a painting or sculpture by a jury "necessarily reflects personal preference, based on personal judgment, multiplied by agreement, reduced by disagreement, with compromise the inevitable sum total."[9]

Considering the scarcity of work, the artist Robert Cronbach told the American Artists' Congress, the competition system put a greater premium on securing the job than on doing it. Artistically, financially, and in the sense of social prestige, he said, the artist felt at the peak of achievement when he received the award. Painting the mural constituted a slight letdown.[10]

Enough artists shunned competitions by 1937 to prompt Bruce to complain that he had difficulty finding good artists. The marked letdown in artists' interest, he admitted, left "some pretty rotten stuff" for juries. "The honest fact of the situation," he la-

21 Maurice Sterne, Henry Varnum Poor, Edgar Miller, and Olin Dows were the jury who in 1939 chose a mural design for a post office in each of the 48 states. This was the largest mural competition conducted by the Section of Fine Arts; 1,477 designs were submitted

mented in a dark moment, "is that we get no real support from the artists." Privately, Bruce called the question of competitions and juries "a thorn in my side." And his aide Dows admitted the jury system rarely obtained the best art; the restricting influence of group advice rendered "safe" art.[11] But to eliminate competitions would invite political pressures and bring more charges of artistic prejudice; to modify the system according to artists' de-

mands would lessen Bruce's control over Treasury art and conceivably result in work offensive to the public or the Treasury or Congress.

Although Bruce failed to engender the crusader spirit he felt artists owed their government, his idea of competition was democratic and, whatever the flaws, spread the work among more artists than had the pre-New Deal system. The mural competitions raised the level of mural understanding and technical skill among the nation's artists. Finally, competitions enabled many young artists to prove themselves and the system did unearth new talent.

When Bruce formed the Section he decided that he should, "for the sake of the movement, take a middle course." He vowed to oppose classical "ladies in cheesecloth" and abstractionist "tripe," and deal with social protest by stopping the "Mexican invasion on the border." What he admired and wanted for the Treasury Department was the representational competence, the ability to render detail literally, of the academic artist applied to wholesome American themes. The Section chief never tired of telling artists that people wanted something that reminded them of the country round about, or of complaining when he viewed the distortions then in vogue that "nobody seems to know how to draw any more." The kind of art he sought gave him, so he said, "the same feeling I get when I smell a sound, fresh ear of corn." Inviting his guests to study the Section art around the Section's warehouse where he held frequent luncheons, Bruce promised that "you will . . . when you leave, feel that your soul has been refreshed and that this world seems a little cleaner than when you came." He wanted art to be "pleasant." Government art, he told artists, should make people's lives happier and not be solemn or intellectual. "There is too much intellect about it and not enough feeling," he said of art he disliked. "The artist's business is to help people to see and enjoy seeing and not think. We are all thinking too much and laughing too little." When he showed Roosevelt and the Cabinet a group of mural sketches he particularly liked, Bruce testified: "They make me feel comfortable about America." So it was that perhaps 50 percent of Treasury art depicted local activity, and the Section busied itself with letters admonishing artists to proportion figures realistically, to change the size of a tree or the pitch of a roof. When Ward Lockwood painted a photograph-like Daniel Boone and companions emerging majestically from the Kentucky woods, Bruce thought it might be "the best thing" an artist had done for the Treasury.[12]

The 8,500 artists who received the Section's free *Bulletin* well knew Section thinking on mural art. Positions emerged in articles

22 Ward Lockwood (Section of Fine Arts), detail of mural in the Lexington, Kentucky, Post Office, showing Daniel Boone and his companions

by Watson and Bruce, articles reprinted from journals, and reprinted letters solicited from respected artists. The *Bulletin* made clear that public murals and sculpture must be in language understood by the public. It advised that complicated or highly intellectual ideas were "a great drawback," and that too many murals were overcrowded, lacked simplicity of design, and attempted to tell too much. Great murals focused on simple content and possessed visual freshness and reality which spoke more clearly than any other thing. The tendency to use art as a weapon of social criticism struck *Bulletin* editors as purely negative in character when the need was for murals to deal constructively with the chaos and conflict. The reminder that Florentine artists during the Renaissance were "so imbued with the glory of Florence that they would do nothing which did not enhance that glory" boded ill for socially critical and abstract art alike. "The Treasury Department Art Program is not a school," Bruce editorialized, "yet fortunately, it cannot help functioning to an extent as a school."[13]

The manner in which Bruce operated the Section resulted from political as well as aesthetic convictions. Converted from Republicanism in the beginning of the Roosevelt era, his philosophy incorporated self-sacrifice, philanthropy, and noblesse oblige. He directed the PWAP without personal compensation and declined more than actual expenses during the early months of the Section of Painting and Sculpture. "I want to have the pleasure of feeling I am contributing my own time to the cause," he explained. Later when he became one of the New Deal's $6,500-a-year men, he spent sizable amounts of his own money for Section activities not covered by government sources. He viewed the New Deal not as reform and temporary sustenance which government owed the people, but as the wilful mortgaging of the future by the nation's affluent to relieve human misery. This view enabled him to speak of New Deal supporters as "cheerful givers."[14]

The corollary to cheerful giving, Bruce believed, was grateful receiving. If the government bestowed art on a local post office the community should accept it in the taste-improving spirit of the giver. If the government offered artists a new opportunity to work, Bruce expected all of the artists in the country to cooperate and show their enthusiasm. The philanthropist's code held that it was proper for the giver to set any conditions on the gift, unthinkable to offer the receiver a part in setting conditions, and bad form for the receiver to complain about conditions or insult the giver. Thus, artists who offended the Section's aesthetic or political sensibilities risked exclusion from patronage. Yasuo Kuniyoshi, whose artistic ability the Section respected, never received the job he wanted because he scandalized the Section with a mural sketch which dealt, in Rowan's words, "with a buxom woman being raped in Central Park with the two fingers of God Almighty pointing to where X marks the spot." And the Section decided to award no further contracts to the artist and union leader Stuyvestant Van Veen because he "said inimical things about the Section." When the artists in the Congress of Industrial Organizations demanded an accounting of Treasury art expendi-

tures and legal citations authorizing Section practices, Bruce ignored them. Federal Works administrator Carmody had to explain to irate CIO officials that since Bruce had "given everything but his life to the program . . . questionnaires that suggest a desire to run his business may annoy him."[15]

Bruce's handling of decorations for the Department of Justice and the Post Office Department buildings in Washington, the largest and most important Section project, aptly illustrated his philosophy and Section policy. He rejected George Biddle's idea that a self-appointed group dedicated to the ideals of the New Deal should decorate the Justice building. It could be handled more efficiently and safely, Bruce believed, if the Section chose the artists, supervised them, and obliged each individually to the government through contract. Hoping to initiate the Section's program with a spectacular achievement, the Section decided to consider decorations for the Justice Department building and the new Post Office Department building as one huge project and bring in the best-known artists in America to do the work.

Dividing decorations for the two buildings into 22 painting "units" and 10 sculptural "units," the Section insured selection of the most popular artists by foregoing a competition and asking each member of an appointed committee to submit 32 artists' names. The 11 artists and 2 sculptors who won commissions by being mentioned twice more than the rest included most of Biddle's original group. But Thomas Hart Benton, suspicious of government patronage from the first, and Grant Wood declined the offer in favor of previous or better-paying commitments. When the Section pressed Benton to do the work at a later date, he frankly admitted he had declined primarily because he feared meddling. "You and others [would] share responsibility with me," he wrote Rowan, "and to an extent that you feel you have to watch me and pet me along to keep me from running you onto the brink of possible difficulty."

While the artists prepared sketches and models on "the history of justice" and "the history of the post" for the spaces assigned them, the Section held an invited competition among the artists less mentioned by the Committee to secure designs for the remaining units. The invited competition yielded 91 mural designs

23 George Biddle at work on his murals in the Justice Department building, Washington, D.C.

24 George Biddle (Section of Fine Arts), *Life Ordered with Justice*, mural in the Justice Department building, Washington, D.C. The artist's brother, Francis Biddle, was the model for the man seated behind the table, and Edward Rowan, assistant director of the Section of Fine Arts, for the one hanging his coat

on themes of justice, 314 on post office subjects, and 62 sculptural models. A jury looked over the sketches depicting justice—offerings which emphasized chain gangs, evictions, third degrees, electrocutions, battling juvenile delinquents, and gangsters—and rejected the lot. From the post office themes the jury selected 8. Later, the Section appointed artists to decorate the remaining units.[16]

Of the many approvals required before the artists could begin painting—Section staff, Supervising Architect, Director of Procurement, Commission of Fine Arts, architects of the building, and frequently officials in the building concerned—that of the Commission of Fine Arts was the most difficult to secure in the early days. The work being prepared for the two new buildings, the Commission charged, illustrated quickly outmoded themes, ignored the beautiful, and promoted social theories "at variance with established ideas of the fundamental rights and duties of citizenship."[17]

Accused in 1933 by the Commission of creating embarrassing work the government "would wish to avoid," George Biddle found himself once again the center of controversy. Biddle's proposed mural panels in the Justice Department depicted woebegone workers, pinched-face tenement dwellers, and a contrasting happy family to illustrate his theme: "The sweatshop of yesterday can be the life ordered with justice of tomorrow." Unenthusiastic toward the work, the Section nonetheless sent it to the Commission of Fine Arts which, to use Biddle's phrase, "after due rumination and cud chewing, brought up a considerable balch of mephetic disapproval." The Commission found Biddle's composition disturbingly busy, the figures crudely drawn and grotesque, the colors gaudy, and the style—influenced by French and Mexican work—"intrinsically un-American and ill-adapted to express American ideas and ideals." A politely unfriendly correspondence ensued during which time other artists completed sketches for the Justice-Post Office project. On November 25, 1935 the Commission met for 25 minutes to view 48 items, found numerous "infelicities of line and detail," "dry and meaningless" relationships in the compositions, and disapproved or required changes in the work of six more artists.[18] The reaction of artists and the Section bordered on hysteria.

Biddle indicted the Commission for censoring style, for daring to dictate what was un-American, for insisting that painters suck on "the dried up tit" of a "weak, thin-blooded, sugar-coated imitation of the French Beaux Arts Prix de Rome," a style which manifested itself in a schoolboy conglomeration of "helmets and urns and fasces and white triumphal bulls and chariot wheels and little cuty girls with budding breasts and French empire dresses." Boardman Robinson, whose murals the Commission required changed, wondered why he took the job and lamented, "I am far away and broke and my exasperation knows no bounds." Bruce, who personified his troubles, had tried to believe that Commission chairman Moore meant well, "but just don't [sic] know a hell of a lot." Now Bruce wrote, "I am . . . getting to hate his guts."[19]

Bruce asked the Procurement Division to authorize Biddle's rejected sketches on the grounds that the Commission was unsympathetic to contemporary art, thoroughly reactionary, and professionally unqualified to pass judgment on mural painting. With Mrs. Morgenthau's assurance that the time had come when the Section must definitely buck the Fine Arts Commission and go ahead with what it thought was right, Procurement director Christian J. Peoples ordered Biddle to proceed with his mural. No one in memory had dared flaunt the Commission's advice and the Section feared the consequences. None of the Section's worst fears materialized, for the Commission kept its invective to itself and, although it continued to demand the most annoying changes, never objected so strenuously that it resorted to public debate. Although Bruce continued to think of Moore as a man of no mind or feelings, the Section could operate without pandering to the Commission. A few art editors wrote of Washington's "whispered art war," but the dispute never reached the general public or became political. It was victory enough, Bruce reckoned, particularly being so close to election.[20]

While the Section rejected the Commission of Fine Arts' right to dictate changes in artists' work, it defended its own instruction to artists on the grounds that "in the final analysis, the members of the Section will be responsible for the work that goes up." None of the distinguished artists commissioned for the Justice-Post Office decoration escaped the heavy, if well-meaning, hand of Section supervision. Conspicuous examples of advice included instructions to Biddle to paint the happy family liberated through justice in his mural much happier than in his sketches, to Henry Varnum Poor to depict the Bureau of Prisons more a place of social readjustment than punishment, to Leon Kroll to replace the doves with clouds in his "Victory of Justice," to Rockwell Kent to give his depiction of mail delivery in the tropics more tropical flavor, to Reginald Marsh to draw the monumental instead of the easel-like, to Doris Lee to paint heads, bodies, and horses in more realistic proportion. John Steuart Curry finally submitted an uninspired design showing a robed judge backed by military figures saving a victim from a lynch mob because his first several designs failed to convey the idea of justice to the Section's staff. The artists received constant "suggestions" and "requests" bearing on colors, drawing, composition, mood, and theme.[21] All understood that Section approval preceded payment.

Maurice Sterne, the artist who received the largest number of votes from the special Justice-Post Office advisory committee, suffered perhaps the worst injustice at the hands of the Section. Sterne's "unit" was a series of 20 panels for the library of the Department of Justice illustrating, from antiquity to the present, "Man's Struggle for Justice." After spending four years on the panels, Sterne believed they were among the most important of his career. Most of the critics who saw them on brief exhibition before their delivery to the Section thought them distinguished.[22]

One of the Sterne's panels, "Cruelty," drew protest from Monsignor Michael J. Ready, spokesman for the National Catholic Welfare Conference in Washington. "Cruelty" showed a collapsing figure carrying pieces of molten iron in a trial by ordeal, with Pope Innocent III and a number of monks supposedly halting the act. The inscription beneath the panel explained that the fourth Lateran council in 1215 prohibited trial by ordeal. Ready objected that the clerics appeared to be countenancing the affair rather than protecting the victim. For the Monsignor the panel was a caricature of ecclesiastics and a baseless identification of the Church with the practice of ordeals. In the future, he said, "millions of good citizens with little skill in art appreciation" would visit the library, see "welcome evidence of a decadent Church in the ancient medieval age" and ask: "Why didn't popes

a thousand years earlier stamp out such cruelty?" When the Attorney General's office "suggested . . . consideration to be given" to altering the panel to preclude the possibility of misunderstanding and controversy, and that the Section not install it, cautious officials considered the suggestion an order. "It is absolutely *impossible* to alter this panel," Sterne exploded, "because the main importance of my job is the composition—each panel, though complete in itself, is integrally only a part—a detail of the whole—changes would throw the whole thing out of gear and if I made any change in one, I would have to repaint all the twenty murals." A visit by Monsignor Ready to the Section worsened matters. He objected, according to Bruce, to the offensively Jewish character of the figures in the panel, wanted the title and caption changed, and insisted the expression of the clerics in the panel reflect the Church as a champion of suffering humanity, "not a sadistic wretch."[23]

Bruce turned for help to an influential Catholic acquaintance, Father John La Farge, son of the painter John La Farge. Bruce recounted for the priest his life history from minister's son to Treasury art chief. Working out a fair program for artists caused one stroke, and doctors, he confided, considered him on the verge of another. Such sacrifice and suffering, however, was small price for the resulting salvation from dire want of a whole generation of artists. "As a disciple of the dear Jesus whose servant you are," concluded Bruce's maudlin plea, "I pray to you my dear Father that you advise me." Now, Maurice Sterne—Jewish immigrant, recipient of numerous awards, man to whom success meant everything, considered by Bruce the best draftsman in the country—by every rule of law and justice was entitled to payment and installation of his work, but an honored cleric blocked it.[24]

La Farge interviewed Sterne, looked at his work and advised him, so Sterne told his wife, to change the faces of the churchmen in the mural "to prove their Christian intention." The prelate wrote Bruce that if Sterne refused to change the murals, he (Sterne) simply would have to revise his philosophy of life into a larger philosophy which could take within its scope certain outstanding failures.[25]

Bruce reacted bitterly. He pronounced La Farge's reply a piece of "Jesuitical sophistry," complained that "the Church . . .

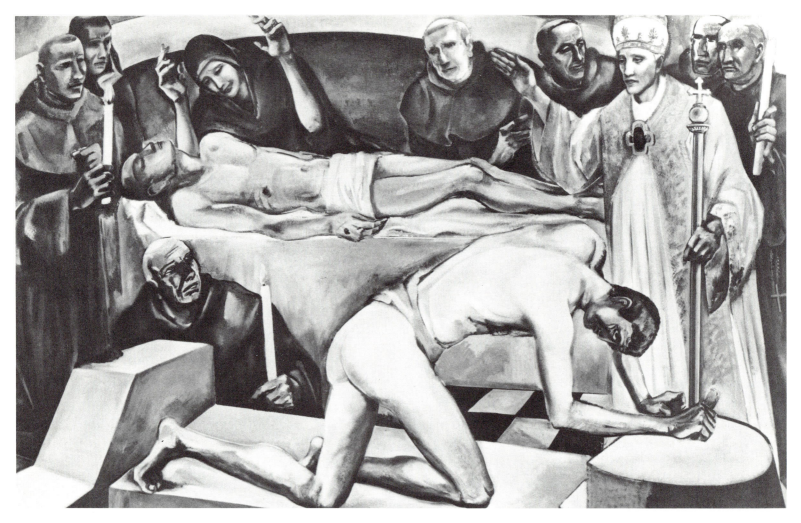

25 Maurice Sterne (Section of Fine Arts), *Cruelty*, one of 20 panels in the library of the Justice Department building, Washington, D.C.

The way in which Sterne portrayed Pope Innocent III and other clerics at a trial by ordeal aroused Catholic objections

ordered" the Section not to hang the panel because it was painted by a Jew, and sarcastically referred to Federal Works administrator Carmody and Public Buildings administrator W. E. Reynolds—both Catholics—as Father Carmody and Father Reynolds. The failure of other intermediaries convinced Bruce that "the Holy Inquisition continued unabatedly in its benign career."[26]

Almost a year passed before Solicitor General Francis Biddle, in his words, "poured a little oil on the top father, whom Ned Bruce had ruffled a bit." At an arranged luncheon Ready learned from his Catholic friend, presidential assistant Tom Corcoran, and Biddle that a situation had arisen in the Justice Department building over some murals, the result of "the stupid and provincial outlook of some myopic busybody." Moreover, these little incidents could swell into a journalist's delight and "Maurice Sterne had so many friends." Ready professed ignorance and, although he insisted he was only a social worker, found himself with Biddle inspecting Sterne's murals after lunch. When Biddle asked for objections, the Monsignor had none. A few days later, on January 23, 1941, Sterne received authorization to install his murals.[27]

The teapot affair never reached the public, nor did awareness of Sterne's murals; and therein lay the injustice to Sterne. "I put in four years on this job," he exclaimed, "and four years is quite a slice off the outer edge of my age!" While he painted and while the bureaucrats stalled, Sterne went broke paying $1,500 annual premiums on his performance bond. The work, then, caused Sterne hardship, ranked among his best, and consumed precious years. Once installed, he believed it entitled to proper recognition. Bruce, however, lacked confidence and felt "the venom and intolerance of the Church is very deep-seated, and if anything is done which they consider as crowing over them or bragging about a victory they can, by calling up their loyal cohorts in Congress, put the Section of Fine Arts and the whole program out of business overnight." For that reason, Bruce told his friend and mentor, "we must put the murals up without fanfare."[28] The "millions of good citizens" Monsignor Ready predicted would troop

through the Justice Department library to view the murals never came. No one told them they were there.

The caution of the Section affected Maurice Sterne more than the other distinguished artists who worked on the Justice-Post Office project. Some received considerable public attention, although not quite the dignified sort hoped for by the Section. Use of family, friends, and government officials as models provided George Biddle some compensatory publicity. Biddle even painted himself at a sewing machine in a sweatshop and placed Secretary of Labor Frances Perkins nearby. When the wife of former New York mayor "Jimmy" Walker insisted one face was that of Mrs. Wallis Simpson, friend of King Edward VIII, a flock of reporters and photographers delighted in real and fancied "identifications," including singer Rudy Vallee, Representative Maury Maverick of Texas, and Irma, the third girl from the left end at the local Gayety Burlesque. The newsworthiness of Biddle's friends and the comic relief called attention to the art. Some thought his social realism was "Moscow propaganda" or advertisement that the Justice building was "a possession of the Jewnited States." Others thought Biddle a genius. Mrs. Roosevelt stopped by to check progress and called the work in her newspaper column "very nice" and "a very interesting record for the future."[29] The dialogue was not learned, but for a change it was about art.

The artist Rockwell Kent contrived for even more public attention than did Biddle, to the everlasting embarrassment of the Section. Illustrating expansion of the postal service, Kent painted Alaskan Eskimos attending the departure of mail in one panel and a group of barefoot, Negroid Puerto Rican women receiving a letter in a second. After Kent installed the panels the newspaperwoman Ruby Black received an anonymous suggestion to examine the scribbled letter in the Puerto Rican panel. Miss Black finally found an Arctic explorer who identified an Eskimo dialect and translated the letter: "To the people of Puerto Rico, our friends! Go ahead. Let us change chiefs. That alone can make us equal and free."[30]

Rockwell Kent possessed three qualities the Section of Fine

Arts did not: belief in artists as visioned social idealists, an intuitive ability in handling publicity, and an impish sense of humor. For the "noisome cesspools" of Puerto Rico, he said, and for all colonial problems, there was but one solution: freedom. Perhaps Kent recalled Michelangelo's portrait of an obstructive cardinal (on which the maestro painted the ears of an ass) in the hell section of the Sistine Chapel's Judgment Day mural or the publicity Diego Rivera received when he painted Vladimir Lenin's head in a Rockefeller Center mural. In any case, Kent admitted that he had included the letter in his mural and tipped Miss Black in order to further a cause and to amuse himself with the embarrassed writing of "pettifogging underlings" in the Procurement Division. Within an hour of the message translation, Kent recalled, a nation ignorant of Puerto Rico, its desperate plight, and the "usurpations practiced against it by ourselves, was alive to it all."[31]

Shouted Rafael Martinez Nadai, leader of Puerto Rico's Coalitionist party, "NO! Caramba, it cannot be," when he saw Puerto Ricans portrayed "as a bunch of African bushmen." Anthone Dimond, Alaska's delegate to Congress, chimed in that Kent had made Eskimos look "like a bunch of rebels," and Postmaster General James A. Farley demanded a different message—in English. Obviously having fun, Kent told reporters, "I think it's a swell thing when people want independence and I think it's the most American thing one can do to wish them luck." Admitting his own sneakiness, he told the ladies of the Women's International Press Club to "sneak a point of view" into their stories and justified it on grounds that everyone should take sides on issues. He offered to revise the mural without charge showing the president of the Puerto Rican senate tearing up the message. At a White House dinner party Kent found himself seated next to Mrs. Morgenthau who turned to him and said, "Mr. Kent, you have a priceless sense of humor!" and shook with laughter.[32]

Some Americans, the Post Office Department, and Secretary Morgenthau's underlings were not laughing. While the *Washington Post* editorialized of the mural that a laughing and tolerant public would want it to stand, other editors, from Bridgeport, Connecticut to Butte, Montana, described the murals in terms like "subversion" and "conspiracy." Peoples promised Farley a change and denied Kent the $1,950 owed him because the message constituted a deviation from the design sketches approved by the Section.[33]

After refusing Kent's offer to substitute a phrase from Lincoln's first inaugural address which mentioned the right of oppressed minorities to revolution, the Section tentatively agreed to: "May you persevere and win that freedom and equality in which lies the promise of happiness." Before final agreement could be made, the decision had to be approved by Bruce's superiors. The only acceptable message to Procurement and higher Treasury chiefs, it turned out, was: "To commemorate the far-flung front of the United States Postal Service." Kent would not consider it and, to the delight of the press, contended that until paid he owned the painting and threatened to sue the Treasury if anyone touched it. Finally the Treasury paid, according to Bruce's public statement, in order to "clean up that panel and once and for all shut that guy up." Ever after the postman of the mural handed the Puerto Rican women a blank sheet of paper.[34]

The Section failed to achieve the spectacular successes in art, public response, and government-artist relations it anticipated when it initiated the Justice-Post Office project. Kent said that his experience impaired his faith in government. Henry Varnum Poor described an empty feeling about government work. Biddle, writing in the *American Scholar*, theorized that however competent the Section staff, the circumstances of their existence affected their performance and the artistic result. The grocer's outlook and mentality embedded in the performance bonds, vouchers, and red tape of the Procurement Division caused it to handle artists with the same delicacy as political building contractors. Procurement's "continual nightsweat lest it be shortchanged" and its fear of congressional investigations caused it, often stupidly, to censor the artists. The result, Biddle believed, was that the Section never got an artist's worst work, but rarely did it get his best. Biddle judged most of the work "technically able and unimaginative."[35] Of course the Section staff disagreed with Biddle's judgment and rationale. True, the original dream glowed more brightly than the depression decade reality, but the

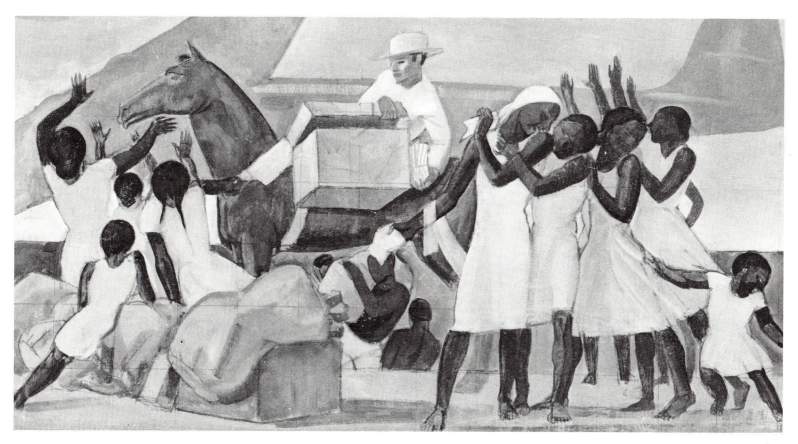

26 Rockwell Kent (Section of Fine Arts), study for mural in the Post Office Department building, Washington, D.C.: a letter—left blank in the study—arrives in Puerto Rico from Alaska

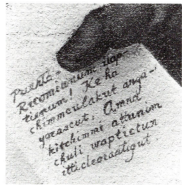

27 Detail of the controversial letter in Rockwell Kent's completed mural. The message, an appeal for independence, was deleted by government order

65

28 Lloyd Ney (Section of Fine Arts), mural in the New London, Ohio, Post Office

Section could proudly point to a large and respectable body of murals, sculpture, and other art.

Of the 1,118 Section-decorated buildings in 1,083 cities tallied in the Section's last formal report the majority were post offices. Awards for post office murals varied from $200 to $300 to $26,000 (awarded to Anton Refregier for the Ricon Annex of the San Francisco Post Office). While the Section accepted local history and life as suitable subjects for post office murals, it frequently squeezed artists into schemes to glorify the postal service. That there are few inspirational ideas in delivering the mail perhaps accounts for some pedestrian work. Only one post office muralist, Lloyd R. Ney, managed to install an abstract work. Rowan, knowing Ney's aesthetic convictions, invited him to submit de-

signs for the New London, Ohio, Post Office. After making designs Ney got endorsement letters from leading New Londoners and turned up, broke, in Key West to badger Bruce for Section approval. Ney's work and his arguments about spirit in art left Bruce unmoved, but he felt guilty at having asked Ney for a design when the Section actually disapproved of his art. Bruce rationalized: "It isn't a bad idea to have one experimental picture in the project, as this abstract art stuff is certainly getting a lot of attention these days." Besides, the town was small and the project not very important.[36]

The concern of the Section for post office art culminated in 1939 with a nationwide competition for designs to decorate a post office in each state. The scheme attracted 1,477 designs from 972 artists, the largest number to participate in any Section mural competition. For some time Bruce hoped to arrange for each post office to sell picture postcards of the local mural. This small enterprise might have increased interest in post office art and even returned the government's investment. Had it not been for postal regulations, the inconvenience of manufacturing several sizes of cards for various shaped murals, and resistance to innovation, something might have come of it.[37]

The Section commissioned slightly more than 300 sculptures. The contemporary emphasis on murals, the higher cost of sculpture, and the Section's failure to build a reputation for its sculpture as it had for its murals kept the number low. Bruce tried to gain control of the major sculptural project of the decade, the $3,000,000 Thomas Jefferson Memorial in Washington; but the commission of politicians and old guard philanthropists which Congress appointed to oversee it distrusted the whole idea of competitions. Bruce went so far as to suggest to Morgenthau that he provide enough pure silver from the Treasury, with strings attached guaranteeing a competition, to cast the statue. Instead, Jefferson's Roman Pantheon-like memorial was built with Bruce bemoaning "the complete breakdown of our whole program." And when in the final stages the commission asked the Section's advice, Bruce refused, pronouncing the entire proceeding "undemocratic and consequently opposed to the spirit of a memorial to Jefferson." Of all Section sculpture—interior and exterior, aluminum Benjamin Franklins and limestone eagles—Michael Lantz's "Man Controlling Work," two stocky men controlling a pair of rearing draft horses, received the most public attention. Lantz, a $94 a month WPA employee, won the $45,000 commission in a national competition to beautify the new Federal Trade Commission building at the apex of the federal triangle in Washington. At the time enthusiasm for the dramatic figures prompted an optimistic newspaper to predict that they would become as familiar as the lions of Trafalgar Square.[38]

Most sculpture, like most murals, achieved respectability, but occasionally, as in the case of murals, a piece embarrassed the Section. The sculptor Heinze Warneke's matched eagles atop the new Social Security building, one observer wrote, looked like

29 Heinz Warneke (Section of Fine Arts), full-scale clay model of one of two eagles for the top of the Social Security building, Washington, D.C.

they had "washed down pistacio ice cream with Irish whiskey." After a respectable interval Social Security officials ordered them removed. In accord with the time-honored, sealed bid method of disposing of surplus property, the taxpayers sold their $5,000 "limestone dodos" to an Alexandria, Virginia automobile distributor for $25.[39]

The list of Section achievements included more than murals

30 Jack Tworkov (Section of Fine Arts), *River Kids*, watercolor purchased by the government in 1940 in the competition for decorating the federal leper hospital, Carville, Louisiana

and sculpture for federal buildings. The work of TRAP, the Section's subsidiary financed with relief funds, included 10,000 easel paintings (mostly destined for federal hospital wards), mural hangings, curtains, posters, copies of portraits, and decorative zinc plates for bird cages at the National Zoological Park, models for honorary medals for the military, and a small experiment in rehabilitation and aesthetics in the federal reformatory in Chillicothe, Ohio.[40] The Section's traveling exhibitions, totaling upwards of 1,000 photographs, easels, and mural designs, reached civic clubs, Rural Electrification lobbies, Army Service Clubs, public libraries, and museums through the generosity of the Carnegie Corporation. Indeed, Carnegie's $6,000 annual gift, supplemented by Bruce's donations, paid for all activities not allowable from building funds or contracts with other agencies.

Carnegie money did most in 1940 when the Section added $3,000 of it to the $6,000 in government funds available for decorating the remodeled federal leper hospital in Carville, Louisiana. In the Section's only easel competition, Bruce held out the money to watercolorists, promising $30 for each work the jury selected. The competition yielded 10,000 watercolors. When all the government money was spent, Carnegie money sent hundreds of the watercolors on tour, during which viewers could purchase them for $30 each. Carnegie's grant enabled the Section to parlay the Carville allocation into $18,212 for the watercolorists.[41]

Impressive though the record was, it might have been greater but for the depression-sharpened characteristic of bureaucrats to guard their administrative satrapies' against joint enterprises which might, somehow, erode their prerogatives. The results hardly seemed commensurate with the energy Bruce put into interagency art. The Section chief did arrange the design selection for the long-circulated "Jefferson nickel" and a briefly printed 1-cent stamp. But neither Felix Schlag of Chicago, who won the $1,000 prize in the competition the Section conducted for the Mint, nor Elaine Rawlinson of New York, who won $500 for designing the commemorative stamp of George Washington, received an opportunity to try again because the sponsoring agencies declined to permit the Section to control operations traditionally in their province.[42] Then, too, there was the painful memory of the Maritime Commission.

If skeptics remained unconvinced of the near impossibility of interagency art cooperation, there remained the humiliating incident of the 1939 New York World's Fair. After Bruce required Roosevelt's intervention to persuade Fair Commissioner Edward J. Flynn that the United States Pavilion should be decorated through Section competitions, the Section chief felt obliged to pacify Flynn by appointing a jury consisting of four artists, two of whom held Fair jobs given by Flynn, and five laymen, including Flynn and his second in command. When the jury failed to agree on a winning mural design for one space, the juryman-artist Eugene Savage, under contract by Flynn to decorate the Fair's Communication Building, introduced a design not under

31 Elaine Rawlinson (Section of Fine Arts), winning design for a 1-cent stamp   32 Felix Schlag (Section of Fine Arts), winning design for a 5-cent coin

discussion, convinced the jury's lay members of its superiority, and with their votes overrode the objection of Bruce and the other artist members. The creator of the second-rate design thus selected was James O. Mahoney, co-signer with Savage of the contract to decorate the Communications Building. Bruce parried artists' demands that the Section invalidate the award, and referred the matter to the Fair commissioners, among whom sat Savage. The commissioners announced that the award would stand, and Bruce announced that the matter was closed. It was not. George Biddle, finding himself spokesman for leading artists' groups, published letters in the *New Masses* documenting Bruce's failure to champion justice as artists saw it. Bruce, who earlier expected the World's Fair to provide "a culminating statement" of the Treasury's art program, blathered abuse upon the

World's Fair Commission, "the little long-haired boys" who had organized, and Biddle whose disappointment at not being Section chief, he reckoned, "gnaws at his vitals."[43]

The Section appeared more impotent in guaranteeing fair play for artists when, a few days before the fair opened, it failed to stop Commissioner Flynn from destroying a $4,000 prize-winning statue of Abraham Lincoln. The sculptor Louis Slobodkin's 15 foot statue of a young, sinewy Lincoln splitting a rail broke up under sledge hammer blows after some of Flynn's guests scoffed at it during a preview. This time Bruce joined the artists in calling Flynn "cruel," "stupid," and "cowardly." Although Flynn eventually permitted Slobodkin's half-size working model to be exhibited in the pavilion, the statue was not replaced. Justice of a sort came to the sculptor through Harold Ickes who liked the statue and decided to place a new cast of it in a pleasant courtyard of the Interior Department building.[44] The experience clearly drew the never-answered question for the Section: How could it gain the confidence and cooperation of the agencies from whom it solicited work, produce art in good taste for them, and avoid becoming their lackey?

The Section intended its trying negotiations with agencies and its considerable influence over artists to produce quality art which the critics and public would praise. The reaction of critics and the public, of course, was beyond Section control. Art critics supported or attacked the Section according to their feelings toward the style they described as contemporary realism, since that style characterized so much Section art. Critics of academic bias felt strongly that mural art ought to be closely related to the architectural style of the building and room containing it. Only when subject, design, and colors harmonized with the rest of the building would the mural be a part of the wall, not a mere painting on it. Accept that view, other critics argued, and the government classical architecture of Washington, imitated and bastardized in public buildings across the country, would force American artists to paint in the manner of Raphael, to produce art wholly unrelated to the mood of the times. Few government muralists tried to reconcile the contemporary American scene with what the Section considered the architectural sins of the fathers.[45]

33 Fletcher Martin (Section of Fine Arts), *Mine Rescue*, rejected study for mural in the Kellogg, Idaho, Post Office

34 Fletcher Martin's executed mural in the Kellogg Post Office, showing the arrival of a prospector named Kellogg

The same critics who demanded that art conform to architecture branded Section art "lightweight stuff," based on casual and trifling conceptions unworthy of wall space. They saw in the "banal sentimentality" of post office "illustrations" failure to conceive mural painting as a noble, scholarly art. The symbolism of antiquity, not the fads of the 1930s, made for timelessness. And they believed that important buildings demanded important art. When Treasury art went to the White House these critics protested that nothing less than acknowledged masterpieces should hang in the White House, "no painting less important, for in-

stance, than Whistler's 'Mother.'" Presumably art in buildings in Washington and small towns across America need be relative to the importance of the agency occupying the structure. Despite these adverse judgments, most critics praised the Section for bringing art out of the studio, the museum, and the pink tea salon and bringing it into the post office. They approved competitions as a democratic device for breaking what one called "the stranglehold of the romantic-escape school . . . on officialdom." By discouraging artists' attempts to capture eternal verities in noble allegories, they believed, the government stimulated murals more alive, easier to live with, more understandable. Still other critics supported the Section's contention that its easels for hospitals, ship art, and monumental decorations represented a faithful cross section of contemporary standards, resulting—depending on one's view—in something for everyone or aesthetic Babel.[46]

General public reaction, so far as it existed, varied widely. Many vociferous laymen considered art frivolous during the economic emergency, absorbing energy which should be channeled into productive tasks—on the plow handles or in the ditches. Professional New Deal haters, decrying the boondoggle in the arts, lumped Section artists with the WPA cultural employees and dismissed them as "sorry daubers, spavined dancers, ham actors, and radical scriveners" luxuriating on the dole. Bruce admitted that nine out of ten people, if they had heard of the Section, thought it was simply a branch of the relief organization. That so few people understood the distinction between the Section's emphasis on art and the WPA's emphasis on relief in large part resulted from the Section's aversion to publicity, especially if it involved controversy. Practices such as asking commissioned artists not to grant interviews unless authorized, Olin Dows reflected 30 years later, were quite wrong. Better that the Section be talked about, even unfavorably, than be ignored, as it was by most people.[47]

Infrequently the people who lived with the art rallied to protest. The sensitivity of the Section to criticism usually brought change. Residents of Port Washington, New York objected to the artist Paul Cadmus's designs for the local post office showing the resort town's summer people engaged in youthful sports, and especially to a girl clad in shorts in a yachting panel. Cadmus, on

35 Tom Lea (Section of Fine Arts), *Back Home, April 1865*, mural in the Pleasant Hill, Missouri, Post Office; the postmaster wrote to Bruce in appreciation

Section orders, reworked his design and put pajamas on the "hot stuff" in the yachting panel. Westward on the prairie, the Cheyenne Indians pitched a tepee on the lawn of the Watongo, Oklahoma, Post Office until the artist Edith Mahier changed the Indian ponies in her mural which Chief Red Bird said resembled oversized swans and Indian children who looked like cornmeal bloated pigs. The artist Joseph Vorst repainted the post office mural in Paris, Arkansas, when local civic groups objected that the lone farmer pushing an antiquated plow in the first mural failed to reflect the progressive nature of the community. In the mining community of Kellogg, Idaho, Local 18 of the Mine Workers and Smelt Workers praised Fletcher Martin's dramatic design, "Mine Rescue," as distinctly appropriate for the post office while local industrialists rejected it as not in harmony with existing conditions. The industrialists carried and Martin eventually installed a noncontroversial scene of purely local interest. In Maryland the director of Glendale Children's Tuberculosis Sanitarium ordered receiving room walls whitewashed after the artist

Bernice Cross had decorated them with scenes from Mother Goose. The director considered the work "unsuitable to the dignity of a public institution."[48]

In Washington, Secretary of the Interior Harold Ickes easily ranked as the most vociferous among laymen demanding influence over the art they saw daily. Ickes, who knew what he liked but not why, insisted on personally approving each decorative design for his department's new building. When the Section presented him the work of the 17 artists and sculptors the Secretary accepted 7 and rejected 10. Branded "a complete Tzar" by the Section, Ickes even supervised the execution of designs he accepted. And when the Secretary, whom everyone knew could and would cancel the project if defied, asked for a spoonbill or an egret in a swamp scene, or structural support in a construction scene, or "more American faces" on workmen in the panels, the Section beseeched the artists to oblige.[49]

When artists turned up in local post offices after Pearl Harbor a discouraging number of communities shouted down the Sec-

71

tion's argument that art enobled, raised morale, and helped men to maintain some perspective during war. From Mobile, Alabama; Yakima, Washington; Orofina, Idaho; and Riverton, New Jersey, came protests that the war threatened to bankrupt the country and that spending money on nonessential murals undermined the morale of the citizens whom the government had asked to sacrifice and economize. It mattered not to postmasters, Granges, and Chambers of Commerce that the decorations resulted from 1939 or 1940 appropriations. The government should set examples in economy and divert money from nonessentials to defense projects. Without effect Bruce circulated a resolution passed by the now friendly Commission of Fine Arts endorsing the Section's work as a means of keeping culture alive during the war. "No resolution passed by any set of persons on earth," wrote Judge John McDuffie in typical response, "could ever convince me that the continuance of the work of your Bureau is an essential activity of the government during a very serious war." Pressures on the Post Office Department led to its recommendation, in November 1942, that the Section abandon post office decoration for the duration. And that ended post office art.[50]

While much of the public remained oblivious to the Section of Fine Arts and a small minority resisted it after Pearl Harbor, another part accepted its work in gratitude and pride. In an era when the local post office was a place of some leisure and conversation among townsmen, pleasant, easy-to-understand murals and sculpture did affect the art consciousness of many patrons. Residents of small towns like Big Spring, Texas, brought their out-of-town guests into the post office to view the art, and in rural America, ladies' clubs traveled from post office to post office on art tours. The post office mural or sculpture was the first work of original art in many communities. Bruce always kept copies at hand of a letter from the appreciative postmaster of Pleasant Hill, Missouri. Postmaster Basil V. Jones had written: "In behalf of many smaller cities, wholly without objects of art, as ours was, may I beseech you and the Treasury to give them some art, more of it, whenever you find it possible to do so. How can a finished citizen be made in an artless town?"[51]

How indeed? For those Americans who accepted on faith the idea that exposure to the fine arts of painting and sculpture

brought spiritual and emotional betterment, whatever aesthetic and bureaucratic controversies consumed Section energies, and however short of its goal fell the Section's achievements, putting some art in a thousand towns warranted all its efforts.

[1] "Final Report of Section of Fine Arts," typescript, RG121/ special file.

[2] The Section ignored the jury recommendation in the mural competition for the Wenatchee, Washington, Post Office, to cite one example, and commissioned no art as a result of the competition for murals for the Springfield, Ohio, Post Office. The best summary of the mechanics and technicalities of competitions is Bruce and Watson, *Art in Federal Buildings*.

[3] Bruce to William Zorach, Feb. 21, 1936, Bruce to Hildreth Meiere, Jan. 12, 1937, RG121/124; Section *Bulletin*, No. 1 (March 1, 1935), 4, No. 11 (Sept. 1936-Feb. 1937), 7.

[4] See, for example, Rowan to Joseph Pistey, Jr., Feb. 19, 1941, and Inslee Hopper to Salvatore Reina, May 24, 1940, RG121/126; Section *Bulletin*, No. 2 (April 1, 1935), 7; Bruce to Rowan, April 8, 1936, RG121/124; Bruce to Biddle, April 9, 1940, Bruce Papers. Officials of the Section reported slightly varying statistics. Forbes Watson, in *The Edward Bruce Memorial Collection*, catalogue (Corcoran Gallery, Washington, 1943), mentions 1,371 works in 1,205 communities.

[5] Erica Beckh Rubenstein, "The Tax Payers' Murals" (unpublished Ph.D. dissertation, Harvard University, 1944); memorandum, Cecil Jones to [Section staff], March 31, 1937, RG121/129.

[6] See "Reports" folder, RG121/129.

[7] Anita Weschler to Hopper, April 5, 1938, RG121/138; Bianca Todd to Bruce, April 7, 1939, RG121/122.

[8] Heinz Warneke to Bruce, Nov. 23, 1938, RG121/124.

[9] Biddle, *American Artist's Story*, 278-82; notes for speech, nd, William Zorach Papers (Archives of American Art, Washington, D.C.), AAA Reel NY 59-1.

[10] Typed speech by Robert Cronbach, RG121/122.

[11] *New York Times*, July 28, 1940; Bruce to Lucile Blanche, March 21, 1937, Bruce to Maurice Sterne, March 10, 1938, RG121/124.

[12] Bruce to Merle Armitage, Dec. 12, 1934, RG121/123; speech by Bruce to artists, nd, speech by Bruce at luncheon for Carmody, Sept. 9, 1939, speech before cabinet, Jan. 20, 1939, Bruce Papers; clipping from *Baltimore Evening Sun*, Nov. 3, 1939, Bruce to Rowan, June 20, 1938, RG121/124; "Minutes of Meeting" of Commission of Fine Arts, May 17, 1940, RG121/122; Rubenstein, "The Tax Payers' Murals," 152-54, 211-12. Public acceptance was clearly a part of the definition of the "middle course" art Bruce desired. George Biddle, piqued at Bruce's compromises and "face-saving policy" in selecting artists for the Justice Department building, protested: "After all, we want an arrangement which will produce the nine finest mural units." "No," Bruce returned, "we want the nine mural units which will make possible the best and largest number of art projects in America in the next five years." George Biddle Diary, Oct. 10, 1934.

[13] Section *Bulletin*, No. 1 (March 1, 1935), 5, No. 7 (Dec. 1935), 6, No. 10 (June-Aug. 1936), 10-11 No. 11 (Sept. 1936-Feb. 1937), 3, 4, No. 21 (March 1940), 4.

[14] Bruce to Roosevelt, April 20, 1936, AAA Reel NDA/HP1; Bruce to Peoples, Dec. 15, 1934, RG121/124. Bruce was not wealthy. He was able to work without compensation and spend his own money on the Treasury art program because of the $50,000 fee he had received as a lobbyist for the West Coast Chambers of Commerce. See Bruce to Harlan F. Stone, Nov. 10, 1942, Bruce Papers.

[15] Memorandum, Rowan to Members of the Section, Dec. 12, 1940, RG121/126; memorandum, Rowan to Bruce, Watson, and Ealand, Dec. 21, 1939, RG121/129; Carmody to Richard Lewis, June 7, 1940, Bruce to Rowan, April 8, 1936, RG121/124.

[16] Section *Bulletin*, No. 2 (April 1935), 3-4; memorandum, Dows to Peoples [Dec. 1935], RG121/118; Belisario R. Contreras, "The New Deal Treasury Department Art Programs and the American Artist, 1933-1943" (unpublished Ph.D. dissertation, American University, 1967). The eleven artists selected first were: Thomas Hart Benton, John S. Curry, Rockwell Kent, Leon Kroll, Reginald Marsh, Henry V. Poor, Boardman Robinson, Eugene Savage, Maurice Sterne, and Grant Wood; the two sculptors, Paul Manship and William Zorach.

[17] Moore to Peoples, Jan. 3, 1936, RG121/118.

[18] Biddle, *American Artist's Story*, 287; Moore to Rowan, Nov. 26, 1935, RG121/118.

[19] Biddle, *American Artist's Story*, 290; Boardman Robinson to Biddle, Dec. 8, 1935, Bruce to Biddle, Nov. 10, 1935, Biddle Papers; Bruce to Dows, Jan. 21, 1936, RG121/122.

[20] *New York Times Magazine*, Aug. 2, 1936; Peoples to Biddle, Dec. 9, 1935, Biddle Papers; Elinor Morgenthau to Bruce, Dec. 10, 1935, Bruce to Dows, Jan. 21, 1935, RG121/122.

[21] Memorandum of Mr. Dow's trip to New York, May 1, 1936, RG121/129. For fuller exposition of Treasury relations with individual artists see Contreras, "The New Deal Treasury Department Art Programs and the American Artist: 1933-1943," and Francis V. O'Connor, "New Deal Murals in New York," *Artforum*, vii (Nov. 1968), 41-49.

[22] Bruce to William V. Griffin, June 10, 1940, RG121/124.

[23] Michael J. Ready to Carmody, April 19, 1940, Jan. 21, 1941, Edward G. Kemp to W. E. Reynolds, Feb. 29, 1940, Sterne to Bruce, March 21, 1940, RG121/124.

[24] Bruce to Rev. John La Farge, July 15, 1940, RG121/124.

[25] Vera Sterne to Bruce, nd, La Farge to Bruce, July 18, 1940, RG121/124.

[26] Bruce to John Dewey, Oct. 8, 1940, Bruce to Dows, May 31, 1940, Bruce to Sterne, Jan. 15, 1941, RG121/124.

[27] Francis Biddle to George Biddle, Jan. 30, 1941, Biddle Papers; Francis Biddle, *In Brief Authority* (Garden City, 1962), 137-39.

[28] Bruce to Sterne, Dec. 19, 1940, RG121/124.

[29] Clippings from *Washington Daily News*, Jan. 30, July 21, 1936, *New York Sun*, Feb. 21, 1936, *New York Daily Mirror*, Dec. 30, 1936, *Washington Post*, May 14, 1936, Biddle Papers; *Time*, xxviii (Nov. 30, 1936), 19; Biddle, *American Artist's Story*, 304-05.

[30] See Rockwell Kent's two accounts of the incident: *This Is My Own* (New York, 1940), 303-12; *It's Me O Lord* (New York, 1955), 501-05.

[31] Kent, *It's Me O Lord*, 501, 502.

[32] Clippings from *Washington Star*, Sept. 12, 1937, *Baltimore Sun*, Nov. 3, 1937, *Washington Daily News*, Sept. 21, 1937, RG121/124, *Time*, xxx (Sept. 20, 1937), 21; Kent, *It's Me O Lord*, 504; *New York Times*, Nov. 6, 1937.

[33] Clipping from *Baltimore Sun*, Nov. 6, 1937, RG121/124.

[34] *New York Times*, Nov. 4, 1937; memorandum, Watson to Peoples, Nov. 1, 1937, clipping from *Washington Daily News*, Jan. 25, 1938, RG121/124.

[35] Kent, *It's Me O Lord*, 311; George Biddle, "Art Under Five Years of Federal Patronage," *American Scholar*, IX (July 1940), 327-38.

[36] Bruce to Watson, Jan. 26, Feb. 14, 1940, Lloyd R. Ney to Bruce, nd, RG121/124; "Final Report of Section of Fine Arts."

[37] "Report of Section of Fine Arts, 1939-1940," typescript, RG121/128; Bruce to Dows, Nov. 14, 1935, RG121/118.

[38] Bruce to Morgenthau, Nov. 30, 1937, Bruce to Zorach, April 5, 1938, Bruce to Fiske Kimball, Jan. 15, 1940, Section Press Release, Jan. 26, 1938, RG121/124; clippings from *Washington Star*, Feb. 4, 1938, *Washington Herald*, Jan. 29, 1938, RG121/124.

[39] Clipping from *Washington Daily News*, Sept. 15, 1941, RG121/124.

[40] See "Final Report of the Treasury Relief Art Project."

[41] The Carnegie donation was $10,000 in 1940. See Bruce to Roosevelt, Nov. 6, 1939, AAA Reel NDA/HP1; Bruce to Frederick Keppel, Jan. 5, 1942, RG121/118.

[42] Section *Bulletin*, No. 13 (March-June 1937), 9, No. 14 (July 1937-Jan. 1938), 3, 10, No. 17 (Sept. 1938), 16.

[43] Clipping from *New Masses*, Nov. 22, 1938, Biddle Papers; Report of Jury Meeting for Judgment of the Mural Competition for the Federal Building at the New York World's Fair, Arthur Emptage to Bruce, Nov. 10, 1938, Hopper to Bruce, Sept. 26, 1938, Bruce to Sterne, March 6, 1939, RG121/124; Bruce to Roosevelt, Dec. 19, 1937, RG121/138.

[44] Report on the Destruction of Statue by Louis Slobodkin, na, nd, RG121/124; *New York Times*, May 4, 1939; clippings from *Washington Times-Herald*, May 21, 1939, *Washington Daily News*, May 12, 1939, *Washington Post*, Nov. 2, 1939, RG121/124.

[45] Address by Cass Gilbert, Jan. 4, 1934, in RG121/124; *New York Times*, July 15, 1934.

[46] *New York Times*, June 12, 1934; *New York Times Magazine*, Aug. 2, 1936; clippings from *San Francisco Argonaut*, July 18, 1941, *New York Post*, March 2, 1940, RG121/137; *Forum*, xcvi (Dec. 1936), 293.

[47] Clipping from *Baltimore Evening Sun*, March 24, 1938, RG121/124; Dows, "The New Deal's Treasury Art Programs," 74; Bruce to Joseph Alsop, Oct. 27, 1939, RG121/124.

[48] Frank T. Cornell to LeRoy Barton, Jan. 31, 1936, Dows to Bruce, Feb. 6, 1936, Bruce to Dows, Feb. 15, 1936, RG121/122; Bruce to William F. King, Nov. 22, 1937, RG121/124; clippings from *Louisville Courier Journal*, June 15, 1936, *Washington Post*, Nov. 23, 1937, Sept. 15, 1940, *Little Rock Gazette*, Oct. 29, 1935, *Boise Statesman*, Nov. 4, 1935, RG121/137.

[49] Report of July 14 and July 16 meetings between Secretary of Interior and Rowan, Aug. 4, 1937, Bruce to Millard Sheets, nd, RG121/118.

[50] Orofino, Idaho Chamber of Commerce, to Compton I. White, Feb. 12, 1942, Mrs. Mervil E. Hass to Walter Myers, March 4, 1942, F. J. Buckley to W. E. Reynolds, Nov. 19, 1941, John McDuffie to Bruce, Jan. 23, 1942, RG121/118; Resolution . . . of Broadway Grange No. 647, Yakima, Washington, nd, RG121/122.

[51] Basil V. Jones to Treasury Department, June 6, 1939, RG121/124. (The Texas artist Tom Lea had painted the mural in the Pleasant Hill Post Office.)

36 Philip Guston (FAP), *Work
—The American Way*, mural
for the WPA building at the
World's Fair, 1939

5

WPA — Patron

America's first large-scale subsidy to artists involved much more than the projects directed by Edward Bruce. The Federal Art Project (FAP), a small division of the Works Progress Administration (WPA), received nearly 14 times more money, aided perhaps 10 times more individuals who considered themselves artists, and brought infinitely more art to the attention of its patron, the American taxpayer. As has been shown, Edward Bruce organized his projects to obtain for federal buildings the best art available. In the process he believed he could improve the economic and social position of American artists and raise the level of taste of the American public. The Federal Art Project developed separately as a part of the relief program. The principal objectives of the New Deal relief agencies, and thus the objectives of the FAP, were the provision of sustenance to destitute workers and the preservation of their languishing skills.

In keeping with the ideas of social service that relief administrator Harry Hopkins had brought into the Roosevelt administration, the FAP was designed to enable destitute artists to retain their dignity and, at the same time, to offer useful products and services to the community. Holger Cahill, the director of the FAP throughout its existence, held more catholic views of art than did Bruce. And while Cahill yearned as passionately as Bruce for a more art-conscious American public, the FAP director believed that encouraging volume of production, rather than parading a few of the "best" artistic creations, was a more appropriate means of achieving the goal. The important differences between the

75

projects of Edward Bruce and Holger Cahill did not end with the purposes of their creation and the philosophies of the directors. The Section of Fine Arts suffered because of its obscurity and because no legislation guaranteed its future. The FAP was perhaps too well known in some unsympathetic quarters, and the annual legislation which gave it life eventually became a part of a conservative attempt to curb the powers of the President. Compared with the course of the Section of Fine Arts, that of the Federal Art Project was turbulent, free wheeling, and for most artists, exciting.

The FAP resulted from the inability of the Roosevelt administration to end the depression. Reform of the monetary system, schemes to raise prices by limiting competition and production, and millions of dollars to prime the economic pump had failed to bring recovery. In the second winter of the New Deal, 4,300,000 families and 7,000,000 single people received government aid, and another half-million farmers, ineligible for direct assistance so long as they owned land, just as desperately needed help. Harry Hopkins had been denied continuation of the Civil Works Administration, in effect an employment as much as a relief agency, by New Dealers and conservatives who opposed its cost, "socialist philosophy," and potential for political manipulation of the unemployed. Congress had forced the relief administrator to change the alphabet-agency letters on his door and try to cope with the unemployment problem through the reactivated Federal Emergency Relief Administration. Hopkins never had liked the FERA. In his view, the law which created it gave too much control to state welfare agencies—staffed by individuals unenlightened by the ideals of efficiency and service which moved him. FERA dispensed relief primarily in the form of doles, and the few opportunities to work in return for pay were on low-standard, make-work projects which discredited the principle of work relief. Now, in December 1934, Hopkins asked the President to consider a better program.[1]

The plan which Hopkins presented to the President called for ending the dole, expanding the rural rehabilitation projects, and giving other reliefers jobs on useful projects. By working for a small salary, the unemployed, whose condition usually was no fault of their own, could escape the humiliation of accepting handouts. Every worker would receive "a total sum adequate for the maintenance of health and decency," albeit at a rate determined by the nature of the work done. Hopkins proposed a wide range of construction and service activities to preserve languishing skills. In addition to home building, rural electrification, reforestation, highway, school, and hospital construction, his proposal called for "a variety of service and professional projects."[2]

Hopkins intended from the beginning that artists were to take part in the new program. Edward Bruce's proposals to Roosevelt in late 1934 to make a pictorial record of the public works program came to Hopkins's desk, and the fiery relief chief promised to work out some kind of cultural program the moment Congress passed a relief bill sufficiently flexible for the purpose.

The Emergency Relief Appropriation Act passed by Congress in April 1935 was a triumph for Hopkins. It gave money and broad power to provide unemployment relief. At first, administrators hoped most of the work projects could be placed in existing federal agencies—the Public Works Administration, the Bureau of Public Roads, and, for artists, the Treasury Department. Perhaps at Roosevelt's urging, Hopkins approached Bruce about heading a large project for artists.[3] However, the relief administrator failed to follow up his early contact when, in late spring 1935, the President's advisers concluded that the unemployed would receive more money more quickly if he used his executive power to create a new agency to handle most of the work projects. In August, therefore, Roosevelt signed an order creating the Works Progress Administration. Some 50 existing agencies, claiming previous commitment by Hopkins or singular ability to undertake special work, received small WPA grants; among them was the Treasury Department, which used its money to create the Treasury Relief Art Project. The vast part of the money now available for the unemployed, including those in the arts, would come from the WPA.

During the muggy Washington summer Hopkins detailed his relief agency employees to work with newly hired planners to outline hundreds of work projects. In an old opera house on the fringe of the capital's government complex, scores of planning groups staked out work areas—on the stage, in the orchestra pit, in the balcony, and in the aisles. Four small groups of six or eight members each, thus ensconced, sweated out guides for employment of artists, actors, musicians, and writers.

Among the planners of relief work for artists none was more influential than Mrs. Audrey McMahon. An able and intensely energetic woman, Mrs. McMahon was president of the College Art Association, editor of *Parnassus*, and the wife of an eminent art historian. More important, for the past three years she had been a central figure in administering aid to the huge community of artists in New York.

Mrs. McMahon had been involved with work projects for artists since late 1932, by which time it was clear that gallery exhibitions of the work of destitute artists, barter art festivals, and drastic price reductions could not save New York City's artists. Mrs. McMahon and fellow College Art Association activist Mrs. Frances Pollak had appealed to a special municipal committee for money to provide work for destitute artists, and between December 1933 and August 1934 they helped some 100 individuals with $20,000 of the committee's money. The women operated out of the offices of the College Art Association, donating their own time. Mrs. McMahon supervised muralists who decorated churches, schools, and neighborhood houses, and Mrs. Pollak tutored art teachers who offered arts and crafts courses in 12 neighborhood centers. When the municipal committee had exhausted its resources, the New York state relief administration supplied limited funds to continue the work, and put the two enterprising women on the payroll. Then, in November 1933 when the Civil Works Administration was formed, Mrs. McMahon and Mrs. Pollak received federal funds to expand their work. With considerably less acrimony than accompanied Mrs. Juliana Force's PWAP project, art teachers went to work in boys' clubs and settlement houses, murals and easel paintings went into city high schools, and a new poster division served the city's government and noncommercial institutions. When CWA collapsed, New York state's Temporary Emergency Relief Administration again became the patron of artists under Mrs. McMahon. The number of art teachers, muralists, easel painters, and poster-makers on the New York payroll between the end of CWA and Mrs. McMahon's trips to Washington to meet with the planning committee fluctuated between 300 and 400.

Audrey McMahon brought the WPA planning committee not only her experience in administering work relief to artists, but also detailed knowledge of the extent of trouble among artists. She told the committee that some 1,800 additional artists in New York City wanted help. She noted the need to provide work for textile and fashion designers, stage designers, artists' models, illustrators, commercial artists, photographers, art research workers, poster painters, and other artistic specialists. Not surprisingly, the scheme which emerged from the planning committee bore the mark of Audrey McMahon.[4]

Of course, the planners had to adopt their scheme to the administrative as well as philosophical requirements of the WPA. WPA, it developed, would consist of two types of projects: nonfederal and federal. Nonfederal projects required a "sponsor" in each state, some agency which would pay a part of the cost in return for work which supplemented its own activity. Federal projects required no local "sponsor," undertook work which ordinarily would go undone, and received a larger part of their instructions from WPA officials in Washington. The projects for artists, writers, actors, and musicians were designated "federal" projects, a status which pleased the planners. State WPA officials would be responsible for the nonprofessional aspects of the cultural programs—payrolls, offices, relief certification, etc. Professional staffs in Washington would direct the creative work and vouch for its quality. The four cultural projects fell within the Professional and Service Projects Division of WPA, and shortly acquired the collective identity of Federal Project Number One, or Federal One.[5]

To work out details and lay plans for action when the money should arrive, Hopkins began to look for directors for the units. He drew Henry Alsberg out of the FERA to guide the writers project, and Hallie Flanagan from Vassar College for the theater project. He asked Nikolai Sokoloff, former director of the Cleveland Orchestra, to head a project for musicians. He asked Mrs. McMahon to take charge of the project for artists. But Mrs. Mc-

Mahon, deferring to the objections of her husband, declined. Shortly, the name of Holger Cahill came before the WPA chief. A friend introduced Cahill to Mrs. McMahon, and Mrs. McMahon offered his name to Hopkins. About the same time, Miss Ann Craton, an assistant in the FERA and sister-in-law of the artist Peter Blume, carried Blume's recommendation of Cahill to Hopkins's top assistant, Jacob Baker. As a result, Hopkins summoned Cahill to Washington for an interview.[6]

Cahill did not soon forget his unpleasant first encounter with federal bureaucrats. He had gone to Washington believing, for some reason, that his hosts wanted criticism of the PWAP, and he delivered it with force—going so far as to say that the government's efforts in art were "unimportant." An agitated insider took him aside and told him: "Don't denigrate things!" Cahill did manage to deliver himself of some views on what needed to be done. His main point was that the artistically impoverished South and rural America should receive special attention. On the train back to New York, Cahill encountered a startled WPA official who informed him that he had "stood up" Harry Hopkins, who expected to discuss the art project with him that evening. When Cahill learned that Hopkins indeed wanted him to take the job, he went drinking with his artist friend Stuart Davis. Then he called other friends, including Francis Henry Taylor, the director of the Worcester Museum. Taylor told him that the head of the FAP would have "a dead cat" thrown at him every few minutes, but that he could not decline because such an invitation was like being drafted. Davis, Taylor, and others also told him that Jonas Lie, ex-President of the conservative National Academy of Design, would probably be chosen if the post remained vacant.[7] Somewhat reluctantly Holger Cahill accepted the offer to become director of the Federal Art Project.

Forty-two year old Holger Cahill was neither artist nor, in the formal sense, art critic; he was a museum curator, organizer of art exhibitions, aspiring writer, and art lover. His personality and attitudes, if less obviously than in the case of Edward Bruce, soon would have their effect on federal subsidy to artists.

The road from his birthplace in Minnesota to Washington

37 Holger Cahill in the early 1930s, before he became director of the Federal Art Project

had been circuitous and full of adventure for Holger Cahill. His family was of Icelandic background and had gone west before the turn of the century to take land, but had remained tenants. His father, Cahill judged, "was a failure in almost everything he did out there," and his mother, "a European peasant woman," raised her son in an atmosphere of marital discord. When Cahill was ten the parents divorced and he was farmed out to a number of families who "needed a boy around the place." These guardians pressured him to be confirmed in the Lutheran church and to commit himself to a life of following the plow. But young Cahill thirsted for knowledge and adventure. In his thirteenth year he ran away to Canada where he earned a living as a farm hand. At age 16 the future art project director made his way to Vancouver and took a job as a coal passer on the *Empress of China*. In Shanghai he jumped ship only to find a terrifying cholera epidemic, and hastily worked his way back to North America. After a series of menial jobs, including one punching cattle, he settled for a year and a half in the main office of the Northern Pacific Railroad. There he had the time and inclination to begin night school. There, also, he settled on a career in journalism, and, he recalled, began to "read Tolstoi by the acre." The railroad job did not last, and Cahill drifted to Milwaukee where he found employment on a lake steamer carrying ore from the Mesabi. Shortly he quit in Cleveland, and learned in that city that he was a failure as an insurance salesman. Then, with his money sewed in his underwear, he hopped a series of freight trains to New York City. The night lights of the metropolis, the adventurer thought, "was the most fascinating sight in the world."[8] Holger Cahill was not yet 20.

A job as night short-order cook gave him time and money for courses at the New School for Social Research and at Columbia. His interests were writing and socialism. He took a course from Thorstein Veblen and frequented a bar popularly known as "The Hell Hole," where the literary entourage of Eugene O'Neill and a number of artists gathered. Soon Cahill was a frequent and familiar figure in Greenwich Village. He was "gay and debonair," and "terribly blond," the girls recalled. And, except for some "rather odd" neckties, "he wasn't a bit Bohemian looking."[9]

Cahill liked New York and the Village. He resented the charge that Villagers were in flight from the reality of their homes. A flight, he said, was also a search, and Villagers had come in search of a spiritual environment which did not exist in their home places. The city and the events of the time changed Cahill. He came to be less interested in politics and more interested in writing. The socialism of the Village, he discovered, "was not very deep"; and then there was the disillusionment which followed the Russian Revolution. Cahill refined his position to that of "the old American left wing tradition . . . like the Populists of the '90s."[10]

After World War I Cahill worked as a reporter for small New York papers and concluded that he was not a good newspaperman. He tried writing biographies at 1/2¢ a word for the American Biographical Encyclopedia, but soon changed to freelance writing. In 1919 he began to study art seriously. The impetus came from the publisher of *Shadowland Magazine* who offered him 5¢ a word for an illustrated article each month.[11]

About the same time Cahill experimented with a theory of aesthetics of his own design which he called Inje-Inje. According to his own account, the ideas were stimulated by an obscure book he chanced to read about a South American Indian tribe so primitive that the language consisted of the two words, "Inje-Inje." All other communication was through gestures. "I said, 'Holy mackerel, this would be a wonderful basis for aesthetics. We've heard so much of nuance and all kinds of things, how about a little simplicity for a while!'" He interested the artists William Gropper, Mark Tobey, and John Sloan, the writer Malcolm Cowley, and the poet Orrick Johns in exploring the artistic possibilities. The idea of Inje-Inje was to eliminate "nuance and prettification . . . and the lies." In theater the face and hands of actors should be masked because they knew too much about lies. The script should have the repetitiveness of a popular ballad. The cult recognized as musical instruments only the human voice, the African signal drum, and a Filipino flute played as a percussion instrument. For art, William Gropper's collage created from newspapers seemed appropriate. Inje-Inje, Cahill admitted, had some common characterists with Dadaism, which was becoming popular at the time. Dada, however, was destructive, illustrating that man and art had reached "the end of the line." Cahill and his friends in the Inje-Inje movement indeed believed that there was "something outrageous, something violent, something vulgar, something in bad taste in American life" and that it must be reflected in art. But unlike the Dadaists, the adherents of Inje-Inje sought to transcend the vulgar "into the beautiful," to retain the optimism that seemed such a part of the American tradition. Cahill also thought the Inje-Inje movement owed more to the growing interest in primitive art than to the Dada movement.[12] In any case, Inje-Inje left its mark only on the few who had joined Cahill in the experiment. By 1920 it was forgotten.

An outlandish publicity stunt catapulted Cahill into a position of opportunity and prestige. As agent for the Society of Independent Artists he concocted a story of a painting by a dead woman which had mysteriously appeared at the Society's exhibition, and mysteriously returned each time it was removed. At-

79

tendance tripled, and job offers poured in to the author of the hoax, among them a chance to study folk art in Sweden for a summer and an offer to work with John Cotton Dana in the Newark Museum. Cahill accepted both, and remained at the Newark Museum from 1922 until Dana died in 1929. Under Dana, he formed the Museum's collection of contemporary American art, and later, having become an expert on American folk art, organized for the Newark Museum the widely heralded exhibitions "American Primitives" (1930) and "American Folk Sculpture" (1931). While working at the Newark Museum he also wrote three biographies: *Pop Hart* (1928), *Max Weber* (1930), and *A Yankee Adventurer: The Story of Ward and the Taiping Rebellion* (1930). From Newark, Cahill moved to the Museum of Modern Art in New York as director of exhibitions, a position he held in 1932-1933 in the absence of the director, Alfred H. Barr, Jr. During that short tenure he wrote three long catalogue texts for exhibitions he organized; most important were *American Folk Art* (1932), based upon the Abby Aldrich Rockefeller Folk Art Collection which was later installed at Colonial Williamsburg, Virginia, and which Cahill had helped to form, and *American Sources of Modern Art* [Maya, Aztec, Inca] (1933), the first of the museum's outstanding exhibitions of the art of "primitive" cultures. He was to write, through the years, a number of other catalogue texts for the Museum of Modern Art.[13]

When Cahill became director of the FAP, he recognized that art spoke "to a very limited number of people." Still, he refused to concede that art appreciation was *their* exclusive birthright; they were merely the few who had time and opportunity to enjoy art. That there was widespread ignorance and apathy was "no fault of the mass of people who had no voice in the matter and whose interest in art was not even invited."[14]

Cahill hoped to give WPA artists a sense of participation in American life and, at the same time, give Americans the feeling that they were getting something by subsidizing artists. His guiding principle, he said, was to make a connection between art and daily life. Such a grand objective, he reasoned, would enable him to preserve the skills of older artists and to encourage the younger ones. Art would become a part of daily life as a result of a gen-

eral movement involving large numbers of artists. The dozen or two Parisian artists of the early twentieth century to be remembered by history probably would not have been stimulated to such heights of creative endeavor had not some 40,000 fellow artists been daubing energetically in the City of Light. Thus, he reasoned, an occasional great work would come from the mass of FAP artists; not from favoring a few "good" artists. Painters and sculptors who did not excel could still contribute to integrating art with daily life.[15]

In this attempt to aid artists and improve the quality of national life, the priorities of WPA's purposes rang clear. "Never forget that the objective of this whole project," Hopkins told his staff, "is . . . taking 3,500,000 off relief and putting them to work, and the secondary objective is to put them to work on the best possible projects we can, but we don't want to forget that first objective, and don't let me hear any of you apologizing for it because it is nothing to be ashamed of." Cahill never apologized for relief work, nor was he ever ashamed of the "best possible" project WPA could devise for artists on relief. Yet, Holger Cahill's deepest allegiances were to things artistic, not things bureaucratic or social problems.[16]

Cahill took a room in a Washington hotel in August 1935 to await the President's promised allocation of money and to organize a staff—rather a difficult task without money. He sought out Thomas C. Parker of the art institute at Richmond, Virginia, whom he had met while working on the Williamsburg restoration, and offered him the assistant directorship. Cahill considered Parker level-headed and respected him as a printmaker. He was also from the South, an important asset in Cahill's mind, and betrayed his origins in his speech. Parker soon proved himself a meticulous administrator. The new FAP chief also called in Mrs. Mildred Holzhauer, a former assistant in New York who had introduced him to Mrs. McMahon. Mrs. Holzhauer's first task was to help choose people to direct the project in each state. As the roster of directors began to fill out, Cahill asked nine of the leaders to double as "field supervisors," as intermediate link in the chain of command.[17]

An attempt to produce efficient operations and harmonious relationships within the WPA scheme, with its gerrymandered jurisdictions and obscure boundaries, would have exasperated even the most experienced civil servant. Cahill came to see that if each state WPA was to handle matters of administration and employment and his office was to exert technical direction, he had to make the most of directives, field trips, and especially his control (in theory) over the directors of the state art projects. The directors of the FAP in each state, because of the spongy hierarchy and their own physical proximity to state WPA chiefs, potentially had more influence than the national director of the FAP.

The heads of each state art project were to be appointed by Cahill, the regulations read, "in agreement with" the state WPA administrators. Reaching agreement sometimes proved difficult since, as Cahill pointed out, "most of these administrators are engineers or construction people, not much interested in the art program, and who consider artists and art lovers a rather queer lot." In a few states WPA administrators or politicians blocked the appointment of art project directors. Cahill always believed that Vice-President John N. Garner, "a terrific old drunk," had ordered the WPA chief in Texas to "be careful of those art projects." In other states, like Missouri, where politics dominated the relief program, Cahill installed directors only after considerable "pulling and hauling."[18]

The idea of the planners was to appoint directors who were celebrities or who, at least, were well known in state art circles. When no one in Washington or New York could suggest appropriate leaders in the South and West, Cahill's assistants, armed with a one-paragraph letter of introduction, set out to talk to local artists, musuem directors, and art teachers. Locally known personalities would be in a position, one of Cahill's colleagues explained, to "thunder back at the critics and say, 'This *is* or *is not* Art. You, the horse doctor, a mere administrator, are no judge.'" Celebrities, time would demonstrate, often lacked the most rudimentary administrative skills and had to be relieved. A few others, almost in stereotype of the artistic prima donna, would use the power at hand in support of whim, vindictiveness, and blind prejudice. Naturally, such leaders antagonized the

workers—a problem to which WPA became increasingly sensitive. Mrs. Increase Robinson of the Illinois project (a Polish woman who married Increase Robinson and took his name when he died, Cahill explained derisively) was destined to go on "leave" from which she never returned. An investigation showed that Mrs. Robinson played favorites, established herself as "Queen Bee," antagonized prospective recipients of the art, ran the project like a production machine, and proved unable to handle labor relations. In Pennsylvania a sizable minority of project workers were to become vociferous in their contention that state director Mary Curran was guilty of "favoritism and discrimination, dictatorship, anti-unionism, inability, social waste and official lethargy." When they enlisted the sponsorship of John Dewey and distributed a pamphlet, *Philadelphia's Shame*, charging that the retention of the director promoted "social disorder and flagrant fascism," Cahill would discover enough truth in the charges to relieve Miss Curran.[19]

In selecting and dealing with directors Cahill was fully aware that one of them would be almost as important as the rest combined. New York City was the cultural capital, and at least 40 percent of the nation's artists lived in New York. Clearly Mrs. Frances Pollak and Mrs. Audrey McMahon were the best qualified candidates. Cahill decided against Mrs. Pollak, a gentle and cultivated woman, because with each crisis she would be "on the phone" or "sitting in my lap." He later came to believe that Mrs. McMahon could be ruthless and in some ways deserved the name others used behind her back, "Iron Woman." In summer of 1935, however, he needed someone who would "run things." Mrs. McMahon was a good choice and the federal director never regretted it.[20]

While he grappled with staffing problems and writing the project rules, Cahill learned something about the Capital City and the way of government. Cocktail party talk that Washington was America's Left Bank notwithstanding, he "always detested" the city. The slums, the overcrowding, the heavy architecture depressed him, as did most of the people. He had lost all his fascination with politics and avoided the hangouts of politicos. For Cahill, Washington was simply "a filing cabinet town."[17]

He discovered in October that WPA had not processed his appointment papers or those of his assistants. He had to loan his aides money and threaten to quit to rectify matters. Then, suddenly, money for project operations was on the way and Harry Hopkins expected WPA officials from across the country to be in Washington within a week for "the kick off." Informed in New York, Cahill "swore about three dollars worth over the telephone." He was learning the principle, he reflected later, that "government dawdles for months and then suddenly informs you that it wants a task accomplished day before yesterday."[22]

The local officials who converged on Washington in October learned that the President had allocated $2,952,663 for artists to last six months. Hopkins, having borrowed the idea from Cahill, told them that in India and China the disappearance of demand had resulted in the loss of invaluable craft and art skills and traditions which might require hundreds of years to recapture. The FAP, he promised, would prevent such loses to America by assuring continued production. The visitors then received hours and reams of instructions on WPA's administration system and returned to their homes to begin work projects.

Getting started in the traditional art centers posed no problem. In Massachusetts, Connecticut, New York, Illinois, and California, FERA was already paying local artists up to $1.03 an hour for 100 hours a month. The FAP merely took over financing and technical direction. In other states, especially those where PWAP had been small and there had been no FERA program, FAP organizers experienced varying degrees of success. They created state advisory committees, mostly composed of former PWAP advisers, which they hoped would lend prestige and comment and guide artists to the state FAP. Despite the relative inactivity of the committees, some 5,300 artists—1,000 of them former PWAP artists—joined the FAP during the first year.[23]

Cahill put all his strength into his assignment. For more than a year his work day, more often than not, extended from 8:00 in the morning to 3:00 the next morning. He wanted to help artists, of course, but much of his drive came from a strong sense of personal loyalty and obligation to Harry Hopkins. The new director's responsibilities required knowledge of administration, art,

and public relations. The latter involved addressing numerous groups and meetings. He had always considered public speaking "a low form of art" and admitted that it "terrified" him. But he sought teachers and he learned.[24]

With so many projects to oversee Cahill showed little patience for petty technicalities and intraoffice power struggles. It made him "very angry" when "people would come busting in . . . asking about requisitions." About the time the state FAP programs began to operate smoothly, Jacob Baker, Hopkins's assistant in charge of Professional and Service Projects, recommended that complete control of all the cultural projects be turned over to the state WPAs. It was true that many state WPA chiefs found the divided authority troublesome and considered technical direction from Washington an unwarranted intervention. It seems more likely, however, that Baker was prompted by the move of Ellen S. Woodward, Hopkins's assistant in charge of women's projects, to gain control over all the white-collar workers on WPA. The matter was complicated by pressures brought by Pat Harrison, powerful Senator from Mississippi, on behalf of Mrs. Woodward, and by Baker's attitude that a woman ought to "yes" a man and not assume men's responsibilities. Cahill did not object to eventual transfer to the states, and he was personally ready "to get out," but he felt, as did the directors of the theater, writers, and music projects, that they needed "a great deal more time to build up professional quality" under federal guidance. When a joint appeal to Baker by the four directors brought no action, Hallie Flanagan and Cahill made an appointment to see Mrs. Roosevelt. (Cahill considered Henry Alsberg of the writers project weak, and Nikolai Sokoloff of the music project a "fuddy duddy.") The First Lady found her visitors "quiet, polite people" who offered logical arguments and explained why they would have to resign if Baker acted. She confronted Hopkins and disputed his defense (no doubt conditioned by talks with Baker) that Federal One directors were "abrupt and . . . very imperious." She asked whether the present "difficulty might be with Mr. Baker." Hopkins shortly concluded that it was, eased out Baker, and placed the cultural projects in a new Women's and Professional Division under Ellen Woodward. Federal control was re-

38 Harry Hopkins speaking at a luncheon, with Eleanor Roosevelt and Ellen S. Woodward of the WPA's Women's and Professional Division on his left. On his right is Florence Kerr, Mrs. Woodward's successor

tained, but at what effort. "I frankly confess that I drank more than I had in years," Cahill said afterward.[25]

While the principle of federal control over the technical aspects of the cultural projects had been temporarily resolved, the tensions between technical directors and state WPA administrators had not. Each state administrator and state FAP director determined—sometimes after interminable feuding—the point at which project administration stopped and technical direction began. There were problems when the FAP directors felt that administrative actions affected the technical performance of reliefers. Scheduling workers, requisitioning materials, acquiring project sites, and negotiating rentals were among the most common jurisdictional disputes. The ways of the arts projects required exceptions to WPA procedures which seemed unnecessarily troublesome to many state administrators. Where the art project lacked strong local support and where state FAP directors proved incapable of dealing with people or paperwork, state WPA chiefs felt justified in assuming greater control. A study ordered by the Women's and Professional division in 1937 concluded that the arts projects were "a distinct drag on the State Administrations" and recommended that they be directed entirely from Washington, thus absolving the states "from every vestige of responsibility."[26] The recommendation was lost, and almost reversed in 1939 when Congress reduced the national officers to little more than "advisers."

A good many of Cahill's difficulties in running the FAP resulted from the fact that its existence was so precarious. If Hopkins, or perhaps Mrs. Roosevelt, should lose interest, the "administrative gumshoes" who occupied the second ranks of WPA would gladly eliminate the FAP—or so it seemed to Cahill. No one could guarantee that WPA would last for more than one year. It depended upon annual and occasional supplementary congressional appropriations which both the President and Congress hoped to discontinue as soon as possible. Moreover, no routine procedure ever developed for allocating a portion of WPA's money to the FAP. The components of Federal One made formal requests from time to time, but the amounts and the rationale were subjects of discussion between the President and Hopkins, and the President and the Director of the Bureau of the Budget. Mrs. Roosevelt also presumably influenced her husband's decisions via casual or intentional comments when she returned from teas or outings with Mrs. Ellen S. Woodward and Mrs. Florence Kerr, the successive directors of WPA's Women's and Professional Division. None of these conversations is a matter of record, and one author, with the concurrence of the chief of the WPA financial division, concluded that "the documentary evidence in the WPA files is the facade behind which are hidden the processes by which decisions were made."[27]

The tentative future limited the kinds of activities Cahill could initiate to promote his goal of uniting art with daily life. Should prosperity emerge from its heralded position "just around the corner," FAP would expire with no way of completing what it might have begun. Even while prosperity remained a fugitive, Cahill could never be certain of numerical strength for any scheme. WPA headquarters handed down monthly employment quotas which shriveled when the economic indicators went up and bulged when they turned downward.

Had conditions been otherwise, the FAP probably would have had a "promotion bureau." In the past Americans had turned out

for cultural events when promised the appearance of some star or known master of art. WPA lacked stars, and most of the state directors showed lack of imagination in devising new techniques to involve people in the new condition of the arts. Some state directors aimed to impress "the best people" while others adopted the patronizing idea of enlightening the "underprivileged." In Boston, for example, a FAP gallery in affluent Beacon Hill was one of the director's proudest achievements, while in Louisiana nearly all the director's energy went to carrying art education to children in the bayous and hill parishes.[28] Of course the WPA's Division of Information funneled publicity to the media. But the Division of Information served an organization in which the combined cultural projects amounted to less than 1 percent. Moreover, the Division relied primarily upon the glib, traditional, easily recognized "government issue" press release. A dynamic promotion bureau, fired with Cahill's rhetoric and the imagination and freedom to appeal to all levels of society, would have brought greater changes in American attitudes toward art. Effective promotion, Cahill's superiors correctly argued when the subject came up, was a long-range undertaking—and they never seriously considered establishing such an appendage.

Cahill had to deal with other features of WPA which confounded him as much as the uncertain future. He could never efficiently promote art and artists and at the same time adhere to the WPA's pattern of employment, its rules, and the changing desires of those who ran it.

WPA had been conceived in terms of masses—masses of people engaged in mass efforts. It did not accommodate well individual types of activity and people who had never experienced the controls of mass production or the usual disciplines of industry. One of the first complaints the new director brought to Hopkins was against the ruling that placed artists on "force account," that is, a working schedule which was checked by a timekeeper. Finding the relief chief at a cocktail party sitting on the floor and leaning against the host's fireplace, Cahill told him the decision was "perfectly silly." Artists, who had always worked at times and places of their own choosing, should work under an honor

39 Mabel Dwight (FAP), lithograph

system in which supervisors would consider the artist's presentation of a specified amount of art as proof that he had put in the required hours. Cahill's experimenting boss allowed him to try the honor system in a number of states; but in almost every case state administrators eventually demanded a return to the force account. Their typical reaction was: "You're going to have us all in state prison before you're through." Although he was overruled, Cahill still preferred the honor system. He liked to tell of poor Mabel Dwight, an old woman and excellent printmaker, who had to come into Manhattan from Staten Island each day to sign in and then go home to work. She was nearly deaf and worried so that she would not hear her morning alarm clock that she sat up all night. Mabel Dwight was representative of untold others to whom the ways of WPA were foreign and overwhelming.[29]

WPA's inability to adjust to the habits of artists had something to do with the decision of many artists to organize unions to deal with the WPA. "The inevitable sense of being inconsiderately whip-sawed from hope to disappointment in a series of inadequate, experimental, impermanent and sometimes callously handled operations," one unionist recalled, "gradually forced artists to join with one another to procure and protect some means of livelihood." He was supported by the popular artist Rockwell Kent who explained that when artists—essentially proud, independent people—ask for help, "they need it desperately," and when essentially peaceful artists resort to strikes, "they need to desperately."[30]

A decision by Congress in 1936 to change the method of payment for WPA employees convinced other artists of the value of unions. Under the original plan artists on relief had worked 96 hours each month. The amount of the paycheck depended upon each worker's skill classification: unskilled, intermediate, skilled, or professional. The 1936 law required state administrators to pay the "prevailing wage" rate in the area for each type of work. Thus, while all WPA laborers in the same skill category would receive the same monthly wage, some, because of a higher prevailing wage rate for their occupation, would earn it in fewer hours. Among Federal One workers, only the musicians and actors had previously worked for hourly wages, and immediately the long-established musicians unions and Actors Equity became important in establishing WPA wage rates. To make the most of one of the few negotiable aspects of WPA employment, writers and artists flocked to infant unions in their crafts.

The existence of artists unions, one must note, was not simply a result of intimidation by bureaucracy and the need to establish WPA wage rates. In a sense, the chain reaction of crises precipitated by the economic collapse underscored the old but now urgent question of what exactly government owed the citizenry. Most artists gratefully accepted FAP jobs as an alternative to molting on home relief. These persons tended to view the WPA as temporary, and accepted its inconsistencies while yearning for the restoration to health of the market economy. Other artists, those who were caught up in the radical movement of the 1930s, theorized that among each man's rights was that of working at the occupation for which he had talent and interest. The depression, which was no fault of the working classes, was depriving workers of the right to work in their chosen occupations. Government, in their view, had the responsibility and the power to ensure this right. Radicals viewed WPA as a program in the right direction, but they wanted to change the rationale for it and modify its operation. They looked to unions to apply pressure for change.[31]

Harry Hopkins had sensed what could happen in bureaucracy suddenly grown fat. Hoping to prevent projects from bogging down in technicalities, he had ruled in the beginning that no lawyers would write the how-to-do-it instructions.[32] Indeed, Cahill took much of the responsibility for writing the field procedures for the cultural projects. In the end, it mattered little whether lawyers or national directors worked out the details. They had to conform to general WPA practice, and that involved deference to state relief officials, many of whom did not understand, or care to understand, the special problems of creative persons.

WPA's regulations and its principle of shared authority by state and federal government bedeviled Cahill from the day he ordered state directors to enlist artists. The first requirement for work on the FAP was to be on relief. Cahill soon realized that each of the local relief boards which determined eligiblity for relief applied a different standard, meaning there were hundreds. Rural and southern artists, at least as destitute as their northern city cousins, frequently remained without work because of the more rigid relief requirements in the farm belt and the South. The second requirement for work with the relief agency for artists was to be accepted by the state FAP. There were as many standards for selecting FAP workers from among the reliefers as there were art projects.

How would state project directors select from among the reliefers? Would the quality of the applicant's work be judged, and if so, by whom, and upon what criteria? Federal guidelines were imprecise about workers' qualifications, although Cahill's view that the measure of talent depended upon the judge and that the

40 Sculptors' workshop in Chicago. The WPA feared that artists would not work the regulation number of hours without supervision

important goal was to establish a broad base of production was widely circulated. State project directors tried several methods of screening reliefers who claimed to be artists. In some states special committees reviewed each applicant's work; but often, as in California, directors abandoned this procedure when committeemen presented individual lists of artists they wished to employ. In some instances, need affected the decision more than competency. In one southern California case, for example, the director hired a 67-year-old applicant with six dependents because the art project paid $85 a month while the applicant's WPA job tending the community gardens paid $55. Most frequently the state director, or his appointed agent, passed judgment on the qualifications of each applicant. In general, reliefers who could prove they had once been professional—defined as making money from art—found jobs, as did young people not previously employed whose work showed promise or whose schools recommended them.[33] In the press of establishing projects and filling quotas, most states took on a high percentage of mediocre if not incompetent artists.

Cahill could exercise little more control over what happened to most of the FAP art and services than he could over the selection of those who produced it. While none of the cultural projects required an official "sponsor" in each state to pay the nonlabor and part of the labor costs (as did construction projects), WPA chiefs did not want to give away FAP services and products. Moreover, Congress and the President prodded them to recover from the states as much of the cost of all projects as possible. The presidential order creating WPA did not specify the proportion of costs to be paid by "sponsors." As the depression dragged on, the "contributions" of states became less, until by 1937 there was talk in Congress of denying WPA money to states which did not pay 25 percent of all project costs. The President was just as anxious to decrease the load on the federal treasury. He thought "it would be a fine thing if . . . we could bring the average of contributions up to as close to 40 per cent as possible." When he noted that sponsors' contributions ranged between 10 and 23 percent, he chided Hopkins: "More contributions please!"[34]

"Federal" projects or not, the top officials of WPA insisted that all of the cultural projects reclaim something from those who benefited. Admission charges defrayed part of the cost of the music and theater projects, and the sale of books some writers project expenses. The FAP was required to rely upon "co-sponsors," a status bestowed on any public institution or agency which contributed in order to become a recipient of art work. In some states a schedule resembling a price list circulated among potential co-sponsors. In other instances co-sponsors donated work space or materials. In no case did the admissions or book sales or contributions approach the 40 percent desired by the President or the 10 to 23 percent averaged by other projects. Co-sponsor contributions generally covered the cost of frame, canvas, and paint—a small part of the $105.50 federal outlay per artist each month. For the cases in which no co-sponsor could be found, Cahill permitted project directors to spend up to 10 percent of the total cost of projects on materials.[35] The work then went into storage for later allocation, or it was shipped to Washington for the exhibition unit Mrs. Mildred Holzhauer headed. WPA rules, in short, meant that "ability to pay" was more important in distributing the products of the FAP than exposing the largest possible number of people to them.

The expensive difference between putting a man to work on a sewer and putting him to work on a drawingroom comedy or a mural was noted repeatedly inside and outside the government. The cost per person to the federal government for all WPA workers, the vast bulk of which were classed as construction workers, was about $60 a month. The higher wage scales of professional workers and the high scales for urban areas which contained the cultural projects explained the roughly 70 percent higher cost. The difference did exist, however, and prompted Roosevelt to demand cost cuts and many congressmen to demand complete abolition of the projects.

In July 1937 Roosevelt shocked state WPAs by ordering budget director Daniel Bell to withhold federal funds from projects to which state sponsors contributed less than 20 percent, and a few months later in the same economizing spirit the President ordered Federal One to cut its man-year cost to $1,000. To meet the new requirement Cahill would have to fire the highest paid artists, reclassify the 91 percent in professional wage categories (who drew over $1,000 a year) to lower skill and wage categories, or glut the projects with enough $720-a-year unskilled labor to make the average $1,000. Obtaining enough additional co-sponsor contributions to reduce the federal cost was out of the question. Roosevelt's demand seemed to spell doom for the FAP. Thomas Parker glumly discounted the alternatives. Dismissing top artists would decrease the amount of co-sponsor contributions, since fewer people would want the less competent work which would result. Packing the projects with unskilled laborers would decrease quality and support even more. Mass reclassification at lower rates would have "a most disastrous effect" on morale and constitute "flagrant discrimination" against professionals. Cutting man-year costs to $1,000, Parker concluded, would make the FAP a mere relief employment program with "no justification for continuance on cultural grounds."[36] Only in

face of united opposition from the four cultural project directors and considerable public clamor, and only in June 1938, did Roosevelt decide to permit Federal One to operate at the acceptable man-year cost of $1,200.

While Cahill struggled with the problems of relief bureaucracy and learned to think from one presidential decision to the next, artists—over 5,000 of them—had been at work. Before the FAP had existed a year, project workers in New York were conducting tours of galleries, teaching drawing in CCC camps, organizing a design laboratory, sending teachers into settlement houses to teach girls "art and originality in dress and good taste with economy," and offering courses from kindergarten art to creative home planning. Already 30,000 Oklahoma City residents had looked and tried their hands in their FAP-directed art center. Many FAP operated art centers, which enjoyed early success in the South and West, doubled as workshops where poster-makers, model builders, photographers, and stage designers on relief offered their services to WPA, local fire and police forces, and community enterprises of a hundred kinds. By the end of the first year thousands of easel pictures in oil, watercolor, tempera, and pastel alternately delighted and appalled the schools and public agencies which had become "co-sponsors." FAP murals, sculpture, and graphic art entered public consciousness as a widening minority argued their merits: quality or junk, good taste or subversive, economical culture or ruinously exorbitant for depression taxpayers.[37] For artists, the New Deal had brought renewed hope to most, and to many, real excitement.

Holger Cahill fitted into the hierarchy of WPA better than his oft-spoken disdain for the civil servant class might suggest. He built good relations with state administrators and artists, and acquired more influence in the high councils of WPA than the other cultural project directors. He took orders, and he accepted the position of Roosevelt and Hopkins that WPA was only temporary. Insofar as the obstructions built into WPA would permit,

he committed the FAP to integrating art with daily life. He felt, he said, "a good deal like a machine-gunner who'd been told to hold a place," but with permission "to get out" should his unit collapse.[38] He held his place until WPA disintegrated during the Second World War.

The fortunes of the FAP in the war on poverty took many unexpected turns. Congress came to charge in 1939 that the strategy was wrong, that the conduct of the campaign was incompetent, and that many of those for whom the battle was waged were ingrates and subversives. The critics found ample illustration for their charges in the disruptions and political activism on the cultural projects—and almost always in New York City. The cultural projects in New York were indeed special; and while they were not typical, they represented the best and the worst in the government programs. Cahill later admitted that some events on the FAP in New York were "really scandalous," but those events were caused by forces and reactions greater than he could control from the position his commanders had assigned him.

41 Holger Cahill, director of the Federal Art Project, with Edward Rowan, assistant director of the Section of Fine Arts

[1] Hopkins to Roosevelt [Dec. 14, 1934], AAA Reel NDA/HP4.

[2] *Ibid.*

[3] Bruce to Roosevelt, Dec. 19, 1934, Hopkins to Roosevelt, Jan. 4, 1935, AAA Reel NDA/HP1; Bruce to Peoples, March 29, 1936, RG121/124.

[4] Interview with Mrs. Audrey McMahon, March 31, 1970, New York City; McDonald, *Federal Relief Administration and the Arts*, 350-53; Audrey McMahon to Bruce McClure, June 25, 1935, files of Federal Support for the Visual Arts: The New Deal and Now (Library of the National Collection of Fine Arts, Smithsonian Institution, Washington, D.C.).

[5] The Professional and Service Projects Division became the Women's and Professional Projects Division in July 1936 and in November 1939 the Community Service Division.

[6] Interview with Mrs. McMahon, March 31, 1970; "The Reminiscences of Holger Cahill" (Columbia Oral History Collection, Columbia University, New York), 240. Hereafter cited as "Cahill Reminiscences."

[7] "Cahill Reminiscences," 236-37, 332, 335, 339-40.

[8] *Ibid.*, 13-49.

[9] *Ibid.*, 51-58, 596-97. The Cahill transcript includes a short interview with Dorothy C. Miller, whom Cahill met at the Newark Museum and later married.

[10] *Ibid.*, 59-94, 406-08.

[11] *Ibid.*, 77-78, 95, 103-06.

[12] *Ibid.*, 117-22; John I. H. Baur, *Revolution and Tradition in Modern American Art* (Cambridge, Mass., 1951), 28-29.

[13] "Cahill Reminiscences," 78, 190-97; McDonald, *Federal Relief Administration and the Arts*, 377-79; Dorothy C. Miller Cahill to author, April 22, 1972.

[14] "Mr. Cahill's Lecture before the Metropolitan Museum of Art, March 28, 1937," mimeographed, Emanuel Benson Papers (Archives of American Art).

[15] Holger Cahill, "Speech for Southern Women's National Democratic Organization in New York City on Sunday, Dec. 6, 1936," Holger Cahill Papers in files of Federal Support for the Visual Arts; Cahill to Maury Maverick, Aug. 28, 1936, RG69 (Records of the Works Progress Administration), Entry 211.5.

[16] Hopkins quoted in McDonald, *Federal Relief Administration and the Arts*, 32.

[17] *Ibid.*, 380.

[18] Holger Cahill, "Record of Program Operation and Accomplishment: Art Program," typescript, 1943, 27, in RG69/special file; Cahill to Burt Brown Barker, Dec. 23, 1935, RG69/211.5; "Cahill Reminiscences," 348-49.

[19] "Cahill Reminiscences," 347, 417; Increase Robinson to John A. Holabird, March 19, 1935, Parker to Lawrence S. Morris, March 5, 1938, Parker to Woodward, March 3, 1938, RG69/651.315; Henry Hart, *Philadelphia's Shame* (Philadelphia, 1938); clipping from *Philadelphia Inquirer*, Feb. 9, 1938, RG69/Division of Information files. (Hereafter cited as RG69/DI.)

[20] "Cahill Reminiscences," 504.

[21] *Ibid.*, 405-08.

[22] *Ibid.*, 238-39.

[23] Holger Cahill, *New Horizons in American Art*, catalogue (Museum of Modern Art, New York, 1936), 16; Cahill, "Record of Operation and Accomplishment," 38; Federal Art Project, *Federal Art in New England, 1933-1937* (np [1938]), 12. Most of the projects got under way in November or December 1935.

[24] "Cahill Reminiscences," 364, 448.

[25] *Ibid.*, 351-52, 373, 375, 384-86.

[26] Harold Stein, "Survey of the Federal Arts Projects," typescript, 1937, 39, RG69/211.

[27] McDonald, *Federal Relief Administration and the Arts*, 208-11.

[28] Stein, "Survey of the Federal Arts Projects," 2-3, 35; State Final Report: Louisiana, RG69/651.3115.

[29] "Cahill Reminiscences," 355-58.

[30] Francis V. O'Connor, *Federal Support for the Visual Arts: The New Deal and Now* (Greenwich, Conn., 1969), 48; telegram, Rockwell Kent to Cahill, May 21, 1936, RG69/651.315.

[31] American Artists' Congress Against War and Fascism, *First American Artists' Congress* (New York, 1936); John Taylor Arms, *Art as a Function of Government* (New York, 1937).

[32] Memorandum, discussion with Sol Ozer, by Holger Cahill, nd, Cahill Papers.

[33] See State Final Report file, esp. California, Connecticut, New York City, RG59/651.3115; Nelson H. Partridge to Frank van Leeuwen, Feb. 16, 1936, RG69/Federal Art Project segregated files (hereafter, RG69/FAP).

[34] Roosevelt to Hopkins, July 27, 1937, Roosevelt to Daniel Bell, July 31, 1937, AAA Reel NDA/HP4.

[35] Stein, "Survey of the Federal Arts Projects," 21; *Final Report on the WPA Program, 1935-1943* (Washington, 1946), 102.

[36] Cahill to McMahon, Oct. 31, 1935, Cahill Papers; Parker to Morris, May 11, 1938, RG69/211.5; Bell to Roosevelt, Sept. 17, 1937, Roosevelt to Locals No. 96 and 100, United Federal Workers of America, May 20, 1938, AAA Reel NDA/HP4.

[37] See State Final Report file; Cahill, *New Horizons in American Art*, 20-41; Grace Overmyer, *Government and the Arts* (New York, 1939) 208-17; Ralph Purcell, *Government and Art: A Study of the American Experience* (Washington, 1956).

[38] "Cahill Reminiscences," 379-80.

42 Lucienne Bloch (FAP, NYC), *Childhood*, panel of mural *The Cycle of a Woman's Life* in the New York House of Detention for Women

6

The Cultural Capital

Cities naturally attracted artists. Artists could argue that the metropolis offered them cultural advantages, anonymity when they wanted it, the stimulation of like spirits, diversity of experiences, and the best market for what they produced. With the New Deal, FERA in the larger cities offered relief projects for artists, and in most of those cities obtaining the "relief certification" was less troublesome than elsewhere. When the FAP launched its operations, new art units sprang up in more cities and the FERA units were absorbed and expanded. Since the FAP based its employment quotas on an area's employable—available —artists, it surprised no one that 25 cities containing 20 percent of the population harbored 75 percent of FAP workers (63 percent of all Federal One workers). What did astound some indi-

viduals was the extent to which New York City overshadowed other cities as a cultural center. New York, in December 1937, employed 44.5 percent of all FAP artists, and, even so, Mrs. McMahon could not employ all the needy artists who applied.[1]

The concentration in urban centers of the arts projects was inconsistent with both political reality and the philosophies of the projects. A few urban congressmen represented the majority of workers and beneficiaries. Rural districts, many of which received less than a proportionate share of the relief dollar and no arts projects service, favored cuts for relief schemes in general and for the arts projects in particular. More even distribution of artists and art projects might have softened the resistance.

Concentration in a few urban areas also prevented the cultural

93

projects from realizing their announced intention to "drive roots into all American soil and to permeate all American culture."[2] New York City, despite its cosmopolitan posturing, was in fact as provincial as Dodge City or Kokomo. As many people lived in the Dakotas and Texas as in New York City, but during the FAP's first year not one artist examined the life or permeated the culture of the three states.

Cahill and his superiors in the Women's and Professional Division recognized the problem. There was simply little they could do about it. Their plans to transfer relief artists out of high density areas ran afoul of state relief boards in areas where artists were few. Since each board set its own standard for relief eligibility, the artists proposed for transfer sometimes did not appear sufficiently destitute to merit certification. More often an arbitrary residence requirement stymied redistribution of art talent. There was the fact, too, that most states did not want another state's public charges. As for the artists, many expressed reluctance to leave their urban ghettos so long as the possibility existed that the FAP might end suddenly and leave them stranded in the boondocks. With a few exceptions, Cahill had to deal with artists where he found them.

The physical presence in New York City of nearly half of the FAP artists was one reason Cahill could expect Mrs. McMahon's project to receive frequent notice from the public and Congress. New York City was also home for the nation's most famous critics and most influential museums. They could be relied upon for a running commentary on the quality of federal art. The New York based communications media, especially the wire services and radio networks, could be relied upon to spread the news of any irregularities beyond the boundaries of the city.

While hardly anyone doubted that the FAP's best work would come from New York, the national director had cause for concern from the beginning. Artists who had worked on the art projects of FERA were not reexamined as to need or competence before their transfer to the FAP. In the fall of 1935 both city relief board and FAP supervisors relaxed their standards as hundreds upon hundreds of new supplicants streamed through their offices. Two years later an investigator commissioned by Mrs. Woodward estimated that perhaps 25 percent did not in fact qualify for relief and that 10 percent were amateurs and incompetents. If there were trouble, the New York City administrator of the WPA would have to answer for placing individuals on relief who did not qualify, and Holger Cahill and Audrey McMahon would have to explain the amateurs and incompetents.[3]

The calibre of artists on relief worried Cahill. Like Edward Bruce, he believed that artists who had escaped the humiliation of relief produced better work than those who had not. Unlike Bruce, Cahill carefully refrained from voicing that view in public. When Hopkins ruled in December 1935 that the arts projects might temporarily employ a fourth of their quotas from people not on relief (instead of the 10 percent permitted by the original orders), Cahill's public reaction was that the larger exemption would permit the FAP to enlist needy artists who had been unable to get on the projects because of the stringent requirements in some states. But he wrote Mrs. McMahon that he wanted to use the exemption "particularly for artists whose talent is needed to improve the standard of work." At the same time he announced a "second phase" of the project in which he desired directors to criticize the work produced "very severely" to see that those who offered art in the name of the FAP possessed the requisite talent. "Too heavy a load of poor work will sink us very soon," he warned.[4] Poor work abounded—and not only in New York City. According to Cahill the pieces sent to Washington from southern California were not worth transporting across the continent. North and South Carolina at first yielded only one artist the FAP director deemed competent to undertake projects. Every state had artists and administrators who polluted quality.

The federal director, although he had his own ideas about what constituted high quality, could not bring himself to establish arbitrary quality standards as had the Section of Fine Arts. The work of relief artists, in his view, "wasn't always great quality. It wasn't always even good quality. . . . But Congress didn't appropriate money for that. It appropriated money to preserve the skills of the unemployed." Moreover, Cahill did not believe a quality standard, regardless of who made it, could last. History had proved the definitions by contemporary critics wrong more often than right. This did not mean that Cahill despaired of fostering creativity which history would remember. He was willing to take some chances. "I think we must be liberal in these matters," he concluded. To employ "a handful of important artists . . . it would be worthwhile carrying a great many lesser lights."[5]

Cahill wanted the FAP to operate in such a manner that "the genuine creative talent comes to the top" and the "lesser lights" worked in socially constructive ways. All artists should have the chance to demonstrate their talents, he explained, but "when it has been pretty completely demonstrated that they are not qualified for creative work, I think we should endeavor to work out other types of projects for them."[6] The "practical" arts projects (those which required skill but not creative imagination) and the educational services of the FAP, in theory at least, would be used to give specialists an opportunity to exercise their skills, to drain off the least creative into other work, and thereby protect the quality of murals, sculpture, easel painting, and graphic art.

In the end, maintaining the quality of art caused the FAP fewer headaches than the unions and political activities of artists. The American Artists Union, local affiliates of the United Office and Professional Workers, United Federal Workers of America, Brotherhood of Painters, Decorators, and Paperhangers, and the more militant Workers Alliance attracted project artists in every major city. When WPA began paying at prevailing wage rates in 1936, unions in the Midwest and West worked for and achieved wage agreements, according to Cahill, which made for efficient project operations and sound labor relations. The eastern projects, he believed, were hindered by the union efforts. The organized artists established such high prevailing wages—thus many fewer working hours—that the projects suffered. Project administrators told of animosity between artists and nonprofessional project workers who had to work more hours for the same or lesser wages. When the union tried to remedy the problem by taking in all project workers, many union artists who were not in government projects left the unions, with the result that project employees comprised practically the entire union membership.[7]

The unions, especially on the east coast and most strongly in New York City, moved to employ collective bargaining on vari-

43 New York City artist (FAP) for the Index of American Design, interior of a Victorian Pullman parlor car

ous issues: selection of artists, job security, working conditions, sick and leave pay, expansion of the project. For the first year or two at least, they evidenced naiveté and inability to comprehend the system. State administrators could determine prevailing wages in a given area. They could not alter congressional or presidential dictates or regulations passed down from Hopkins's office. Unions never understood this fragmented authority, or if they did, their response—applying pressure by indirect means—failed miserably. Typically, the unions confronted the state art project director, the national FAP officers, or state WPA administrator with their grievances. Frequently these officials dismissed categorically union demands, however legitimate, because they lacked authority to grant them. Some administrators, because of anti-union prejudice or conviction that the program demanded loyalty to regulations, responded belligerently. In more than a few instances, the unions concluded that the forces of reaction permeated WPA's art project.

The FAP first experienced the wrath of organized artists in late 1936. At the time the number on the federal art rolls was near the record high, some 5,300 individuals. Cities had recently received more money for art projects, after Cahill had withdrawn money from some 25 rural states on grounds that he had overestimated their unemployed artists. Even so, some urban artists remained in need. They were frustrated by a WPA ruling of November 1, 1935 that only individuals certified for relief before that date could be employed. Then, on March 6, 1936, WPA froze relief employment. Artists who had managed to stay off relief until after November 1935 now felt their government had discriminated against them. Groups of artists, complaining that "we must show that we need jobs," had to be carried by police from FAP anterooms in New York City.[8] Sit-down strikes seemed to the artists a way to move those officials who had made the rulings. They were wrong. And they were wrong about the effect of their disruptions which accompanied layoffs after the 1936 elections.

The substantial cut in the relief program resulted partly from Roosevelt's reluctance to continue deficit spending and partly from his belief that private employment could now sustain many workers currently on WPA. Neither artists nor FAP administrators shared the President's beliefs. Besides "tremendous hardship" for artists, Mrs. McMahon complained from New York, the "deplorable decision" would so decimate the art project manpower as to impair if not nullify the value of the project as a cultural service. On December 1 those New York artists who believed their rights included gainful employment as artists and who saw no opportunities in the private sector marched to 6 East 39th Street and packed into Mrs. McMahon's offices on the eighth floor. Elmer H. Englehorn, an assistant of the New York City WPA chief, came in to chastise the strikers. He said that he recognized most of the artists and that if they did not leave immediately he would fire them and put their names on a "blacklist." The demonstrators, now desperate, decided to remain in the office until leaders in Washington reversed the decision for layoffs and saved them from Englehorn's threats. Police came. After spokesmen for the artists and the police mounted desk tops, charged each other with responsibility for any violence or property damage which might result, the artists locked arms behind an iron railing, and the police waded in. For more than an hour police wrenched links from the human chain and dragged them from the building. The crack and thud of fists and nightsticks mingled with the shouts and curses and cries from both sides. The melee ended with 219 artists under arrest and 12 artists and policeman under medical care. This incident was the most violent, but in Chicago sit-down artists temporarily and less spectacularly stopped work in the local office. In other cities artists joined other WPA workers in filing petitions against relief retrenchment.[9] In this atmosphere charged with resentment and emotion, the bureaucracy of the FAP began to pare the rolls to conform with the new quotas.

Project supervisors refused to help Mrs. McMahon thin her roster. The New York director, acting on instruction and information available to her, released artists who had outside income, who least served the needs of the project, and who produced the lowest quality work. Still, she knew that some remained on the project with outside resources, that some essential artists from the viewpoint of quality and needs of the project received pink

44 Stuart Davis (FAP, NYC), detail of mural for radio station WNYC; for many years obscured by a curtain, the mural was valued in 1965 at about $100,000. Davis was secretary of the American Artists Congress

separation slips, and that her limited contact with projects hardly qualified her to judge which were nonessential workers. Knowing that the procedure was vulnerable to attack, she briefed Cahill, "I have therefore refused to explain it."[10]

Mrs. McMahon's troubles had only begun. From more than 2,500,000 in October 1936, WPA rolls dropped to less than 1,500,000 a year later. While economic indicators showed improved health for the economy, the American Federation of Labor estimated that 8,000,000 workers still needed jobs. Practitioners of the arts contended that private employment opportunities for them had not improved at all. The WPA cuts, proportionately distributed among the projects regardless of varying private opportunities, occurred amid echoes of Roosevelt's ringing speech at Madison Square Garden on October 31, 1936. "Of course we will provide useful work for the needy unemployed," he had told his audience, that was one of the things for which he had "only begun to fight." Edna St. Vincent Millay, writing eloquently what floated crudely through union halls, barber shops, and gasoline stations, considered it bad taste for Roosevelt to bite so soon after his reelection the hands that fed

him "so many nourishing votes." Under its motto "It is not patriotic to starve," the *WPA Defender* printed Miss Millay's piece
arguing that recent events illustrated but one more version of the
ancient game labeled by the English "Not Cricket," the French
"Pas tres chic," and the Americans "Double-crossing."[11]

The objections of artists against cuts went further than insistence that the President keep his word. The relief program, quite
unintentionally, revealed art as an important factor in contemporary culture. It would be blind, perhaps even perverse, the writer
Lewis Mumford cautioned the President, to weaken seriously the
arts projects. In the opinion of Stuart Davis, secretary of the
American Artists Congress, such an act would be criminal or
worse. When government began supporting culture because private patronage disappeared, it recognized its obligations to culture in the way it recognized obligations to industry, farming,
and banking. Federal patronage resulted in "a new and immense-
ly valuable cultural growth, far greater and more valuable than
the cultural state which it was initiated to defend and uphold."
The logical conclusion, Davis insisted, was to make the federal
arts programs permanent. "In other words," he explained, "the
original intention of an emergency stop gap has been changed by
social dialectic into its opposite." The administration could not
now claim ignorance of, or renege on, an obligation it had already recognized.[12] How, then, could WPA talk of cuts?

The problem was that neither Franklin D. Roosevelt, Harry
Hopkins, Congress, nor the American people saw so clearly as
Davis the imperatives of the obligation they had accepted. Congress brought on a confrontation when it reduced WPA funds in
the spring of 1937 by 25 percent. For Federal One this further retrenchment meant elimination of some 11,000 jobs between the
end of April and the middle of July, about 3,000 of them in volatile New York City. Roosevelt added to the tension when he took
advice from director of the Bureau of the Budget, Daniel W.
Bell, and ordered a further cut in numbers of WPA workers not
on relief—to less than 5 percent.[13]

To help cope with existing and anticipated reaction in New
York City the national directors of the cultural projects managed
to wrest the administrative responsibilites for the projects from
the New York WPA. They did so by creating a special administrative unit for Federal One in the city, with the theater project
under William Farnsworth and the other projects under Harold
Stein, a sensitive New Dealer who believed the unions performed
a real service in the cause of eliminating project irritations and
injustices. City WPA administrator Lieutenant Colonel Brehon
B. Somervell, whom leftist workers branded a fascist when he
ordered their WPA work exhibited with no signature and closed
at least one exhibition as unfit to be shown, seemed anxious to be
rid of the arts projects.

The new project officers proceeded to eliminate workers according to instructions from WPA headquarters. And those dictates, strangely, did not require dismissals of the least needy and
retention of the most destitute. Instead, a worker's future depended on a complex weighing of the value of his project, his
"employability," his "indispensability to the project" and the
length of his service. Stein created a Joint Appeals Board for
Federal One composed of the technical adviser to the Social
Security Board in New York, the personnel director of Blooming-
dale's Department Store, and a New York Civil Liberties Committee lawyer. The board passed on matters of discrimination involving relations with unions, race, and the like, but it lacked
power to order reinstatement on grounds of need.[14]

In May, New York's union artists took drastic action against
the cuts. At 4:00 o'clock on Friday afternoon, May 14, some 200
artists sat down in the arts project building, sent out for soup and
chicken, and settled in for the night. Next morning they marched
to Textile High School and voted with representatives of other
activist organizations for a WPA work stoppage on May 27. On
that day only the radical Workers Alliance and unions sympathetic to it walked out. No more than a sixth, by the largest estimate, of Colonel Somervell's 169,000 relief workers participated,
but of 9,000 relief workers in Federal One, 7,000 took to
the streets.[15]

Holger Cahill tried to stay out of the fracas. In spring 1937 he
was looking forward to seeing the Federal Theatre Project produce a play he had written. He had enjoyed good relations with
the unions and publicly sympathized with many of their objec-

tives. Some union officials, notably Stuart Davis and Harry Gott-lieb, were personal friends. Nonetheless, Cahill's liberalism was too conventional for him to appreciate the tone of the artists unions. "These people were pretty wild, you know," he said after everything was over. "They were strange. They were left-wingers who thought that if they could get a portrait of Marx or Lenin into a meeting, this somehow would bring about the revolution."[16]

As the date of the greatest mass of layoffs neared, Somervell, Cahill, and Mrs. McMahon agreed that since they had no power to grant concessions they should not meet with the unions. One night Stuart Davis and Harry Gottlieb kept Cahill up until daybreak trying to convince him to meet with the artists on the New York project. When they departed in the morning Gottlieb's last words were: "Cahill, I have known you for twenty years, at least. I never knew you could be such a mean son-of-a-bitch." As it turned out Cahill and Mrs. McMahon did meet with union representatives before the layoffs. Mrs. McMahon, according to Cahill, broke down and told him, in tears, that she would have to leave New York if they refused to hear the grievance committees. When they assembled, some of the representatives cried, some shouted and screamed. In one instance a speaker shook his fist in Cahill's face and shouted: "You are responsible for every unemployed artist! . . . You and Harry Hopkins and President Roosevelt!" Cahill remembered thinking at the time: "These people are psychopaths, they are basically unemployable, and you can't do anything with them."[17] He fielded the questions and charges as best he could, and stayed away from New York for the next few weeks.

Mrs. McMahon had no choice but to continue to follow orders, issue the pink dismissal slips, and dock the pay of workers who participated in work stoppages. Her list of 2,000 artists waiting to get on the project convinced her that private employment opportunities did not exist. More requests for art in public places poured into her office than the project could possibly fulfill. Thus the need of artists for employment and desire for their service increased despite the more heartening general employment statistics and the resulting cuts into WPA quotas. Thomas C. Parker, Cahill's assistant admitted: "We are faced with a problem which cannot be solved."[18] In June artists and fellow Federal One workers—no better off—made a desperate attempt to get them to try.

June 22, a Tuesday morning, 2,248 Federal One employees in New York City received their pink slips. In the building at 235 East 42nd Street, housing offices of the writers, artists, musicians, and historical records projects, an immediate sit-down stopped all work. By 9:30, 36-year-old Minnie Wallenstein had reflected long enough on her dismissal from a $19 a week clerical job on the writers project to become hysterical. By 10:00 she had tried to jump out a second-story window. A block down the street 300 dismissed workers, many of them sobbing women, stormed the theater project offices in the Chanin Building. At the Federal Music Theatre on 54th Street 5 male and 12 female dancers forced indefinite postponement of scheduled concerts and rehearsals for "The Tales of Hoffmann" with a sit-down and hunger strike.[19] A shaken administrator in the theater project telephoned strikers' demands for reinstatement to Ellen S. Woodward, who pointed out that only cases of discrimination were subject to appeal, expressed her "sorrow" for any hardships, and blamed it all on Congress. Strike leaders were insulted and telegraphed her that her attitude was unforgivably heartless and bureaucratic. Next day, 60 strikers barricaded themselves in the payroll division offices, holding up pay checks for those still in Federal One and virtually paralyzing arts projects throughout the city.[20]

Thursday, June 24, Audrey McMahon agreed to face individually the artists her pink slips had separated from the project. Into the night some 45 ex-workers pleaded their cases. Beside them stood their dependents, who, often with tears, added their pleas. When the ordeal ended, the former president of the College Art Association telegraphed leaders in Washington for exemptions from the cuts. "You have, no doubt, wondered how it was," she wrote Cahill the next day, "that I could in the face of my instructions, wire you for exemptions. I did so because I felt that the dismissals as they now stand will be profoundly disastrous." The parade of sick and pregnant wives, humbled parents, rickety and malnourished children, cases of tattered dignity and of abject despair deeply moved her. "Until last night," she confessed, "I had no way of actually recognizing the need concealed be-

45 Louis O. Guglielmi (FAP, NYC), *View in Chambers Street*

neath these employees, and I know you will forgive me, therefore, that I also cannot conceive of it. I have not before made requests from you away from administrative instructions. . . . I do now ask whether nothing can be done. . . . I beg you to carry similar cases as far as you are able."[21]

While Mrs. McMahon was being confronted by destitute artists, 25 girls prepared a macabre procession around the Federal Music Theatre. At midnight they marched, at funeral pace, in black robes, faces chalked to resemble death heads, to dramatize the state of their starving colleagues inside.[22]

On Friday afternoon dismissed workers packed around administrator Stein's third-floor office. They would not leave, they announced, or permit Stein to leave, until someone with authority established an appeals board to review every dismissal on Federal One. Safety engineers sent up their opinion that the floor could support the weight of the 600 people on it only if there was no commotion. Stein then wisely declined a police escort out of the building. On orders from his captors, the Federal One administrator made several telephone calls to WPA officials in Washington, repeating the conversation to the ex-project workers who were sitting on his desk and who crowded his private office. Word came from Washington that Deputy Works Progress administrator Aubrey Williams told the small delegation sent by New York strikers: "We are agents of law and I don't know what we can do to help you . . . we cannot grant exemptions." Williams reproached the delegates for their strike and warned them that such tactics might well cause the public to demand an end to WPA. Mrs. Woodward's blunt assertion that the lack of outside employment opportunities could not affect the necessity for layoffs infuriated the strike strategy committee. They declared they were prepared to hold Stein until they got "satisfaction," from President Roosevelt if necessary.[23]

Once Stein's captors convinced themselves that he lacked authority to grant concessions, they ordered him to bring in Mrs. McMahon and such other project directors as had not left town. While this group conferred, the 5 women and 2 men not yet carried from the Federal Music Theatre passed their one hundredth hour without food. Outside the besieged project building, police

100

kept the picket lines from blocking night club entrances on 42nd Street. At 4:00 A.M. on Saturday the strike leaders and administrators emerged from conference. The administrators would inform Hopkins that they considered the method of dismissal unsound and did not wish to carry out dismissals according to the method. Administrators would recommend a neutral review board with power to retain all needy artists who met FAP's quality standard and with power to transfer needy workers who lacked technical competence to other projects. They would recommend extending the effective date of pink slips until the board could function. As soon as the recommendations were typed and signed, cheers went up, strikers left the building, and a physician began feeding orange juice to dancers too weak to move in the Federal Music Theatre.[24]

The cheers had come too soon. On Monday morning Aubrey Williams rejected the recommendations. WPA accounts had only so much money; rescinding the dismissals would necessitate compensatory dismissals in other states or on other projects. In light of that reality, Cahill wrote Mrs. McMahon, "It is not clear to me just what you would like me to do." In rejecting the demand for a New York City review board to consider dismissals on the basis of comparative need, Hopkins's lieutenant in charge of Women's and Professional projects, Mrs. Ellen Woodward, argued that if New York City received such a jury, in fairness the cases of all 2,000,000 WPA workers should be reviewed. That, she bluntly asserted, was neither practical nor financially sound. Mrs. Woodward saw nothing to be gained by further discussion.[25]

A few militants persisted. Philadelphia artists, part of a delegation refused an audience with Hopkins in Washington, were "bruised about the head and shoulders" by capital police when they declined to leave federal offices. In St. Paul a sit-down in project offices won a review board and transfers to other projects for 55 workers. Fifty discharged employees of Federal One occupied the WPA offices in San Francisco for a couple of days in July. The Harlem Artists Guild continued to demand reinstatement of all dismissed Negroes and exemptions from future cuts on grounds that the conditions among Negroes during the depression entitled them to special consideration. Other artists

joined with white-collar and construction workers in street demonstrations. But WPA had learned quickly. Hopkins ordered Stein to find a building for the headquarters of Federal One in New York away from project operations—one more secure against sit-ins. Then, presumably because Stein had agreed to support grievances of Federal One workers, Hopkins transferred him to Washington and made former finance officer Paul Edwards the administrative head of Federal One in the great metropolis. Security guards shortened the duration of sporadic sit-ins by sealing off toilet facilities. National administrators steadfastly refused to compromise their decisions. And as summer passed, the demonstrations grew less frequent and finally ended.[26]

The protest movement had been an exercise in futility. Greatest discomfort came to people with no real power to force change. Congress, the ultimate source of change, experienced no inconvenience or pangs of guilt or compassion. Because Federal One was so concentrated in a few congressional districts, the arts workers' plight and their disruptions failed to register with the national legislature as matters which required immediate investigation and resolution. It is doubtful that congressmen or the President understood the issues behind the strike. The traditions of American bureaucracy militated against it. Even Holger Cahill, who referred to himself as "a strange fish" in the hierarchy, could explain: "You see, you're always supposed to protect the man above you."[27] Strikers had erred in thinking that if they pressed their immediate superiors hard enough, their superiors would agitate at the highest levels in Washington. Mrs. McMahon shielded Cahill; Cahill shielded Mrs. Woodward and Hopkins; and Mrs. Woodward and Hopkins shielded the President and Congress.

The strikes by WPA workers paralleled Roosevelt's highhanded attempt to "pack" the Supreme Court. The Roosevelt coalition, strained by the struggle over the Court, showed no sign that it would honor a presidential request for a supplemental appropriation—which, of course, would be required to reemploy the agitators. The President, for his part, had no intention of asking for one. Not only did he wish to avoid being embarrassed by

Congress, he believed that prosperity was returning and the need for federal relief declining. He further insisted that "militant tactics have no place in the functions of government employees." A strike by public employees amounted to an attempt to paralyze government by those who swore to support it. Roosevelt called it "unthinkable and intolerable."[28] If WPA workers were not bona fide employees they were close enough to leave the President irritated and unimpressed.

Outside New York City relations between artists and the WPA had been considerably less volatile. Most urban units had suffered trials of various kinds during June and July, and then, according to an in-house study, labor relations quickly returned to "a basically decent and sound state of affairs." If one excluded New York City, the investigator reported, labor relations consisted of the daily give-and-take of any boss-worker relationship, "qualified in a surprising number of cases by a curious and admirable form of professional ethics or by an almost embarrassing sense of gratitude on the part of the workers, especially in the rural districts."[29]

Gratitude and ethics made dull news compared with insults and strikes. Perhaps one-third of the artists on the FAP belonged to unions, and probably less than one-third of the union members could be considered militants. The coverage of the sit-downs and street demonstrations in the national news media gave many people the impression that the writers, musicians, actors, and artists of America had become anarchists. Congressmen, like everyone else, learned most of what they knew about contemporary affairs from the newspapers.

Administrators in WPA and FAP did not anticipate that in the summer of 1938 congressional opponents of Roosevelt's social program would rally for a massive assault. The cultural projects were to be one of their first targets. They would charge radicalism and corruption, and by exploiting the peculiarities of the projects in New York City, they would win their point with a majority of legislators. In June 1939 Congress would legislate the Federal Theatre Project out of existence and reduce the programs for writers, musicians, and artists to local projects financed and directed by the states. The formerly powerful directors in

46 Audrey McMahon, head of the Federal Art Project in New York City, with the director Holger Cahill, at an exhibition in 1938

Washington would become mere "advisers." In general, the quality of the work would decline; the projects assume more of a "service" nature; the leadership of artists, writers, and musicians give way to politicians and social workers; and each state project would exist at the pleasure of the state's relief administrator.

Through all of these machinations, thousands of project artists went about the work of creation free from interference. Spared the petty and paralyzing concerns of WPA decision-makers and directors, they practiced their crafts and many tried to reconcile art and life at the grass-roots. Indeed, WPA programs and administrators were to emerge from the recent fog of problems and the political storms of 1939 much more bruised and chastened than art and artists. Considering all the problems of organization and politics, WPA artists returned to the public an amazing quantity and variety of artistic objects and services.

[1] Stein, "Survey of the Federal Arts Projects," 3.

[2] *Ibid.*, 10.

[3] *Ibid.*, 8-9.

[4] Cahill to McMahon, Jan. 30, May 4, 1935, RG69/211.5.

[5] Cahill to Joseph A. Danysh, June 3, 1936, Cahill to Jacob Baker, May 13, 1936, RG69/FAP; Cahill to Edward Weston, March 12, 1936, RG69/651.315; "Cahill Reminiscences," 331.

[6] Cahill to Danysh, June 3, 1936, RG69/FAP.

[7] Cahill, "Record of Program Operation and Accomplishment," 38-39.

[8] Corrington Gill to Bureau of the Budget, Feb. 14, 1936, RG69/211; clipping from *New York Sun*, May 14, 1936, RG69/DI.

[9] *New York Times*, Dec. 5, 13, 1936; Einar Heiberg to Hopkins, Dec. 13, 1936, Dorthea M. Sawvelle to Hopkins, Dec. 1, 1936, RG69/210.4; Alice M. Sharkey to Olin Dows, Dec. 3, 1936, RG121/120.

[10] McMahon to Cahill, Dec. 31, 1936, Jan. 7, 1937, RG69/651.315.

[11] Donald S. Howard, *The WPA and Federal Relief Policy* (New York, 1943), 854-55; Samuel I. Rosenman, ed., *The Public Papers and Addresses of Franklin D. Roosevelt* (13 vols. New York, 1938-50), v, 571; clipping from *WPA Defender* (Jan. 2, 1937), AAA Reel NDA/HP4.

[12] Lewis Mumford, "Open Letter to FDR," *New Republic*, LXXXIX (Dec. 30, 1936), 263-65; Stuart Davis to Cahill, April 3, 1937, RG69/211.5.

[13] See Hopkins to Henry Morgenthau, Jr., Feb. 27, 1937, RG69/100; Daniel W. Bell to Roosevelt, Feb. 12, 1937, AAA Reel NDA/HP4.

[14] Stein, "Survey of the Federal Arts Projects," 20; V. Manning to Cahill, Oct. 25, 1936, RG69/651.315; John D. Millett, *The Works Progress Administration in New York City* (Chicago, 1938), 217.

[15] Clippings from *Pittsburgh Post Gazette*, May 15, 1937, and *New York Herald Tribune*, May 16, 1937, RG69/DI; *New York Times*, May 27, 1937.

[16] "Cahill Reminiscences," 458.

[17] *Ibid.*, 419, 459-60.

[18] Parker to McMahon, June 7, 1937, RG69/FAP.

[19] E. A. Stucklen to Theodore H. Popkin, June 22, 1937, RG69/651.3; clipping from *New York Herald Tribune*, June 23, 1937, RG69/DI.

[20] Clipping from *New York Herald Tribune*, June 24, 1937, RG69/DI; Popkin to Stein, July 6, 1937, RG69/651.3.

[21] Clipping from *New York Post*, June 25, 1937, RG69/DI; McMahon to Cahill, June 25, 1937, RG69/651.315.

[22] Clipping from *New York Post*, June 25, 1937, RG69/DI.

[23] *New York Times*, June 26, 1937; clipping from *Washington Herald*, June 26, 1937, RG69/DI.

[24] *New York Times*, June 26, 1937; telegram, Stein to Woodward, June 26, 1937, RG69/651.3.

[25] Cahill to McMahon, June 30, 1937, RG69/FAP; Woodward to Stein, July 7, 1937, RG69/651.315; Aubrey Williams to David Niles, June 28, 1937, RG69/651.3. A more detailed account of the role and strategy of the Artists Union is in Monroe, "The Artists Union of New York," 98-130.

[26] Clippings from *Philadelphia Record*, July 2, 1937, St. Paul (Minn.) *Pioneer Press*, July 21, 1937, RG69/DI; Marvin McIntyre to WPA, July 22, 1937, AAA Reel NDA/HP4; McMahon to Cahill, July 21, 1937, Cahill Papers.

[27] "Cahill Reminiscences," 408, 462.

[28] Roosevelt to Luther C. Stewart, Aug. 16, 1937, quoted in Woodward to Paul Edwards, Dec. 14, 1937, RG69/651.3.

[29] Stein, "Survey of the Federal Arts Projects," 19.

7

Relief Artists and the Fine Arts

Creative art, the work which established the reputation of WPA's art projects, engaged about 48 percent of the project workers so long as Washington retained control over technical affairs. Talented reliefers decorated schools, hospitals, and other public buildings with 2,566 murals and 17,744 pieces of sculpture. Easel painters contributed 108,099 works in oil, watercolor, tempera, and pastel, and graphic artists printed some 240,000 copies of 11,285 original designs in various print media.[1]

The freedom which with few exceptions characterized FAP units made for an almost infinite variety of art. The variety and its identification with the New Deal insured a lively if mixed public reception. In addition to providing work for artists in a free atmosphere, WPA intended to integrate art with daily life, and sought to do it by promoting art appreciation and art sales. The FAP theorized that appreciation would increase by allocating art to public institutions where it would receive broad public exposure. The scheme for increasing sales took the form of two national art sales weeks. The extent to which art became a part of daily life, despite heroic efforts, was far less than the intention, especially after the reorganization of 1939 and the subsequent emphasis on contributing to the military preparedness program.

Before 1939 the FAP administration, and the public generally, favored creative artists over workers in the practical arts. Workers rightly considered a transfer into a creative project a promotion and a transfer out a demotion. Through no quirk of fate the periodic purges required by WPA quota cuts usually reached only the weakest creative artists, yet eliminated entire practical art projects.

WPA artists reflected the aesthetic convictions of the 1930s. A few clung to imitation of academic or "classical" art and a few still preferred studio subjects. Another minority experimented with nonrepresentational art. But few in 1935 escaped the influence of Midwestern "regionalist" artists like Thomas Hart Benton, Grant Wood, and John Steuart Curry, or the "social realism" of such artists as Raphael and Moses Soyer, Joe Jones, Ben Shahn, Hugo Gellert, and William Gropper. Regionalists and social realists built their art on American themes and sought to register their message in the untutored American mind. The roots of these modes lay in the "country-wide revival of Americanism," Benton once speculated, that followed the defeat of President Woodrow Wilson's universal idealism at the end of World War I. As Benton explained history, and no social realist disputed him, adherents of "the new and effective liberalism" born of the depression locked in battle with "the entrenched moneyed groups," precipitating "a new and vigorous discussion of the intended nature of our society." Moreover, a flood of new historical writing during the decade called into question traditional images of America. Artists, flushed from elitist bastions by the depression and caught up in the debate by its dynamism, treated aesthetically what Americans everywhere seemed to be reassessing—the nature of American society. By focusing on questions which already engrossed much of the population, and by using terms understood by the man in the street, artists attracted an unparalleled audience. They also attracted unparalleled criticism because "the entrenched moneyed groups" understood all too clearly the message of artists identified with the new liberalism.[2]

The contemporary realist, whether regionalist or social realist, scrupulously avoided allegories, academic symbolism, tragic visions, eternal verities, and intimate topics. The major differences in the two views lay in the degree of nativism each embraced and the amount of social comment each thought appropriate. When a regionalist painted a farmer plowing under his crop, the social realist charged, somewhat unfairly, that the viewer could not tell whether the artist condoned or condemned it. The regionalists' rejection of anything foreign convinced some social realists that their colleagues were "congenial to fascism."[3] Yet the social realist, whatever his intellectual commitment to internationalism and contention that the American spirit embraced many nations, seldom strayed from the American scene. Like the regionalist, the social realist's art was impersonal and his forms and figures were clearly recognizable, but it focused more on the abstractions of politics and social justice. More strongly than the regionalist, the social realist commented on what he observed, intent on involving the viewer in the issue.

An artist's professional group or union, political party, reading material, friends, and colleagues obviously conditioned his comment. Not infrequently the combination produced art of calumny, anger, and detraction. These visual editorials of the contemporary scene had a more immediate than lasting appeal. By the end of the 1930s, when some of the earlier work lost its relevance, other ideas began to eclipse contemporary realism.

The concern for American themes and comprehension by laymen had interrupted the trend begun early in the century toward emulation of modern French artists. Throughout this American period "coteries of highbrows, of critics, college art professors and museum boys" loyal to the French modernists, to use Benton's categories, retained control of the art journals and of the best schools. These coteries, the contemporary realists charged, had a vested interest in "aesthetic obscurity, in high falutin symbolisms and devious and indistinct meanings."[4] Redirecting American art toward obscure and incomprehensible French models would reestablish those coteries as prophets. This explanation—Benton's—was perhaps too simple in that it ignored the evolution and honest conviction of American artists.

As the decade passed, more and more artists, especially New York City artists, tired of editorializing or illustrating the American scene. Perhaps the decline of the artists unions by the end of the decade, the disillusionment of collectivists with the Nazi-Soviet nonaggression pact, or logical evolution from the illustrative to something new influenced the change. In any case, the work of artists Henri Matisse and Pablo Picasso seemed more

106

47 Walter Quirt (FAP, NYC),
Obeisance to Poverty

contemporary and alive. More people began to speak out against the "putrefying particulars" of the realists. Some now reasserted that the world of the imagination was "violently opposed to common sense" and rejected presentism, contending that "only that subject matter is valid which is tragic and timeless." To Jackson Pollock and others inspired by French modernists to experiment with nonrepresentational art, the idea of an American art was as absurd as an American mathematics or American physics.[5] The waning influence of the "corn belt academy" and the "political cartoonists" began the filtering out of realistically portrayed objects on American canvases. The representational style of the thirties would yield to the influence of the Surrealists during the war years. By 1942 important foreign artists such as André Breton, Max Ernst, André Masson, Yves Tanguy, and Jacques

Lipchitz had taken refuge on the east coast of the United States. With other foreign artists of similar persuasion they stimulated more American artists to the belief that moral change was infinitely more important for man than political change. The shift in outlook of course resulted in changed art forms.

Art critics shared no greater consensus of what constituted good art than did the artists. At one exhibition of murals, six major critics lined up: two favorable, two hostile, and two hedging any position. Margaret Breuning of the New York Journal American spoke of "original conceptions" and Emily Genauer of the New York Herald Tribune of the "high level of work"; the New York Post's Jerome Klein thought the ideas unworthy and New York Sun critic Henry McBride considered the craftsmanship "not very good." In larger proportion than artists, critics resisted the style and message of the regionalists and social realists. The usual complaint of older and academic critics was that "a bleak drabness . . . a certain dry and hard rigidity . . . a wooden simplification" typified modern and federal art. Some critics said the style, so simple, encouraged mere technicians to presume the title "artist." Critics sympathetic to social themes in FAP work fulminated against abstract production as "loyal to the basic elements of a bean pole and pie plate superimposed, juxtaposed, enmeshed, and interlarded with . . . color." For them abstractions were unacceptable substitutes for the "boiling, turbulent, exciting material" of the times.[6]

Many critics allowed their views of the Roosevelt administration to dictate their assessment of New Deal art. The critic who taunted "the captious critics of boondoggling" that "this developing and nurturing of young talent . . . hardly makes the country safe for business" admired the whole output. The critic who railed against "the Rooseveltian idea of taking money forcibly from those who have it and throwing it recklessly to the improvident" abhorred it.[7] Judgment of federal art would have to await the dry light of the future and the passing of the contemporary zealots of aesthetic and political causes, or perhaps of the aesthetic and political causes themselves.

The FAP somehow maintained neutrality in the aesthetic controversy. Contemporary realists applauded the official description of FAP work which emphasized "a fresh poetry of the soil" and "art rich in social content." At the same time nonrepresentational art turned up on walls and easels "without undue censorship," its creators testified, and they acknowledged the FAP's "sincere efforts . . . to allocate and give it social currency."[8]

The variety in FAP murals attested the catholic taste of art's depression patron. The most comprehensive study of FAP murals, the work of Erica Beckh Rubenstein, exposes the influence of Mexican muralists, the tradition of the Italian Renaissance, French academicians and abstractionists, Oriental decorators, and commercial illustrators. Mrs. Rubenstein has noted that most work borrowed from many traditions and only a small part was entirely outside established modes.

People talked most about the Mexican "invasion" of American art. Leading Mexican muralists, such as Diego Rivera, David Alfaro Siqueiros, and José Clemente Orozco, worked in the United States and employed many American assistants. Most American artists considered study and travel in Mexico an essential part of their education. Among a certain artistic set, admiration of Mexican art took on something of the flavor of a religious cult. If a follower could not collaborate on a work by a Mexican master, he volunteered to grind colors or sat around the scaffolding watching the maestro. The probable reason murals painted by Mexican artists in the United States attracted so many politically radical artists is that their work projected an especially negative view of American life—an outlook held by most leftists. Mexican-inspired murals centered in northern California, New York City, and Chicago. In San Francisco, to the delight of Mexican devotees, the FAP supplied Rivera with assistants for a mural in a local college.[9]

Other artists consciously tried to resurrect the Italian Renaissance mural tradition. Since the United States lacked a mural tradition and many artists had their first opportunity to paint murals on the FAP, the work of Giotto di Bondone, Luca Signorelli, and Piero della Francesca served as models for artists not attracted to the Mexican school. The artists Lewis Rubenstein and Frederico Lebrun led an important "Italianate" movement in Boston and New York.[10]

Oriental traditions affected many of the murals on the West Coast. Some Oregon and Washington artists chose Japanese art. Much of the southern California work was the result of the strong personality and oriental prejudice of Stanton Macdonald-Wright, the supervisor of the Los Angeles project. Macdonald-Wright, according to his co-workers, insisted on designing many of the murals and assigned others to paint them.[11]

French abstractionists had their largest following in New York City and among a smaller group in Chicago. Parallel to the course of the FAP, a group called American Abstract Artists began to achieve respectability and acclaim. They made New York City, always sensitive to French trends, the center for abstract experiments. Moreover, the possibilities of abstract murals fascinated the FAP mural supervisor in the city, Burgoyne Diller, himself a leading abstractionist.[12]

Interspersed among the muralists were academicians, simple illustrators, and easel painters who never saw an essential difference between easel and wall painting.[13] While the bulk of the art could be described as contemporary realism, critics detected fleeting memories of everything from ancient art to contemporary French styles.

It followed that the source of inspiration would determine the subject of the murals. Mrs. Rubenstein found emphasis on agricultural life, on the union of man with nature. A large part of the mural production centered on history, especially on the pioneers. Another sizable group interpreted American "freedom," and yet another concerned cheering depression-generation children. "But above all," Mrs. Rubenstein concluded, there was "emphasis upon labor, upon the reward for a man's work, upon the dignity and right of a man to work."[14]

Cahill conscientiously refrained from interfering in style or subject. He often said that good murals were an integral part of an architectural scheme, that they contained large and simple

48 Stanton Macdonald-Wright (FAP, Los Angeles), *A Motion Picture Studio*, panel of mural for the Santa Monica Public Library, now transferred to the Smithsonian Institution

forms, clarity, carrying power, and rhythmic order that led the eye easily through the whole space. He admitted that the failure of many artists to conceive of murals as more than enlarged easel paintings, combined with lack of sufficient and competent supervision, produced much bad art. Cahill established a short-lived school in Boston to improve mural techniques, and for a while required mural sketches to be submitted to a committee of administrator-critics in his Washington office. At the same time the FAP director emphasized that the depression decade for artists, as for politicians and Americans in general, was a period of search rather than synthesis. The concern of artists for the "evil things which infect the social body" seemed to the FAP director a step toward the needed constructive self-criticism which would "reveal America to itself." Style and source of inspiration did not concern him. "American art is anything that an American artist does," he said. The administrator-critic committee, therefore, discouraged only obviously inferior sketches. It never forbade a sketch because of its unorthodox technique or social message. Finally, Cahill reminded critics that in "its great periods" mural art always had been associated with the "expression of social meaning, the experience, history, ideas and beliefs of a community."[15]

Mural painters did not always enjoy the freedom Cahill would accord them. The recipient of the art, having paid the nonlabor costs, more often than in the case of the nationally financed Section of Fine Arts, made bold to prescribe or forbid parts of WPA art works.

The combination of the anti-New Deal press and concentration of muralists inclined toward protest or realism produced the greatest embarrassment to FAP. The wide influence of Robert R. McCormick's anti-Roosevelt *Chicago Tribune* and the prominence in Chicago of Mexican-inspired muralists Mitchell Siporin, Edward Millman, and Edgar Britton made an especially volatile combination. In 1940 the *Tribune* carried a series of articles in support of the charge that WPA art in the "Windy City" was "wasteful, ugly and communistic." The reporter assigned to "investigate and write the facts" found three downtown gallery owners and the president of a large federation of women's clubs

to say what he wanted to hear. These "experts" singled out the work of Siporin and Britton, branded it "un-American in theme and design," in "poor taste" and possessed of "communistic influence." They warned that the murals might "exert an alien effect upon children and adults who view them." The same quotable experts obliged the reporter with descriptions of the body of FAP work as "full of tripe," "inane," "just daubs of paint," "just junk," "disgusting," "botches of colors smeared together" and "not art of any kind." Such assessments emboldened the school board of Chicago's Lucy Flower Technical School to plaster over Millman's six panels, "Woman's Contribution to American Progress." The board spokesman said that Millman's representation of Clara Barton and Jane Addams would not inspire young American womanhood. Instead the murals falsely suggested the "failure of our democracy to uplift its people."[16] That Millman and Siporin won a $29,000 Section of Fine Arts competition to decorate the St. Louis Post Office and Britton won a commission in the new Department of Interior building in Washington confirmed conservative suspicions of "the great conspiracy."

The Hearst press editorially enjoyed the charge of Des Moines Public Library officials that WPA artist Harry D. Jones's mural in the children's room was grotesque and distorted and frightened young library patrons. The conservative press carried other stories of conflict between artists and the receiver. In truth, there were ample cases to report because recipients of WPA art felt the murals reflected as much upon them as upon the artist.[17]

The receiver might prevent installation of the murals, remove them after they were up, or require some specific change by the artist. Citizens of Belleville, Illinois, forced the artist Arthur Lidov to take down a local mural depicting Abraham Lincoln because they thought the portrait looked like Nicolai Lenin. Mayor Frederick W. Mansfield of Boston stopped work on a mural illustrating relief activities for the city's Public Welfare Building. Mansfield considered the theme "the very worst of bad taste," and thought people resorting to the welfare office deserved something more cheerful to look at than caricatures of their own troubles. School officials of Fall River, Massachusetts, rejected as "unfit" two murals for the local high school because the paintings

49 Eitaro Ishigaki (FAP, NYC), with Chikenichi Yamasaki and Wolf Ubegi, detail of mural in Harlem Courthouse. Complaints were made about the way in which historical characters were portrayed

contained nude figures. And the principal of Brooklyn Industrial High School for Girls tried to get his school's mural removed because girls in it had "shoulders as big as Jack Dempsey's."[18]

New York City, whatever its reputation for tolerance of art tastes, reported many cases of interference. The artist Attilo Pusterla earned more than his share of notoriety for his murals in the New York County Court House. The first attack came from local Negro leaders who demanded that the artist explain just how the mural of a Negro child eating watermelon amid white eagles, wings spread, represented emancipation. Pusterla eventually re-

placed the child with Negro leader Frederick Douglass—without watermelon. Then Court Justice John E. McGeehan, a militant Catholic, heaped abuse on Pusterla for including Martin Luther in panels illustrating the history of jurisprudence. Across town at Harlem Court, lawyers and court attachés gave the FAP artist Eitaro Ishigaki a choice of retouching or removing his historical mural showing Abraham Lincoln "with Negroid features" and George Washington "as sour as old Scrooge." Artists mounted scaffolds to paint in Bellevue Hospital only after they agreed to the doctors' demands to paint no "items disembodied,

111

50 Moses Soyer (FAP, NYC), *Children*, mural in the Brooklyn Hebrew Orphan Asylum

51 Edward Laning (FAP, NYC), *Johann Gutenberg Showing a Proof to the Elector of Mainz*, panel of mural *The Story of the Recorded Word* in the New York Public Library

broken, angular, or incomplete," to use soft colors and portray restrained motion, and eliminate anything "remotely suggestive" in the placing or treatment of female figures. Other officials and civic-minded citizens in other cities meddled in the production of art offered for the cost of materials. Some had legitimate complaints. It took considerable tolerance, for example, to accept a mural of the signing of the Declaration of Independence showing George Washington in line for the signing.[19] The instances of interference, however, should not be overly emphasized, for the FAP could pair every malcontent with an elated customer and parade an impressive mass of award-winning artists.

Murals for children offset the effect of some of the controversial installations. Frolicking animals emerging two by two from Noah's Ark on the walls of a settlement house playroom, anecdotal panels in a hospital waiting room, a parade marching and dancing across nursery walls, bigger than life story-book characters in a library children's room, flashy abstractions in a housing development game room drew admirers of all ages. Mrs. Rubenstein found in many of the best children's murals "a gaiety, a freedom and experimentation, a decorative emphasis and freshness of color . . . often lacking in the murals designed for the general public."[20]

The FAP muralist to bring the most favorable publicity to relief administration art was probably young Edward Laning, whose first triumph was getting mural sketches for the dining-room of Ellis Island past Commissioner of Immigration and Naturalization Rudolph Reimer. The latter had amused the country in 1934 by rejecting the sketches of PWAP artist Hideo Noda because they showed Negro cotton pickers in turtle-necked sweaters and creased trousers and a draft animal more like a Percheron stallion than a Missouri mule. Then FAP artist Laning presented sketches showing the construction of the Central and Union Pacific railroads by Chinese and Irish laborers. Among other changes, Reimer made Laning adjust the height of boots on Army officers, paint the rail ties round instead of square and reduce the size of rails to that of the capacity of nineteenth-century rolling mills. Reimer's well-publicized demands for accurate detail, to which Laning acceded, drew attention to the work. All the

critics liked the results, among them Isaac Newton Phelps Stokes, president of New York City's Art Commission and member of the New York Public Library Board.[21]

Stokes admired Laning's work to the extent that he appealed to the Library Board to let Laning decorate the panels on the upper floor of the main building, panels designed for murals but unfilled since the building went up in the 1890s. Earlier library boards had considered John Singer Sargent and James Abbott McNeill Whistler for the job, which by the 1930s was probably the most prized in New York. FAP directors had tried to interest the library in murals by relief artists from the beginning; it took Stokes to convince the board that the 32-year-old Laning should do the work. With FAP paying Laning and his three assistants $23.86 a week, the work on a series of panels, "The Story of the Recorded Word," began in an abandoned church. From the church, shared with several rehearsing WPA theatrical groups, Laning moved to a warehouse and after nearly two years installed the panels depicting "words" from Prometheus to the mechanical typewriter on the library's third floor. Mayor LaGuardia unveiled the murals to an approving capacity crowd and the nearly 4,000,000 people who used the library each year.[22]

WPA muralists won a good proportion of national competitions and prizes. For all the criticism of FAP quality standards by the Section of Fine Arts, relief artists won a high percentage of the Section's most important competitions. In 1936 the Architectural League awarded FAP artist James Michael Newell its Gold Medal, described by Cahill as the "highest award for mural painting in the country." Eric Mose, another project artist, won honorable mention. By 1939 21 of the 29 muralists chosen to exhibit for the Architectural League were FAP artists. Muralists Philip Guston and Anton Refregier won awards for murals at the World's Fair in 1939. The Pasteur Institute of France purchased work from project artist Arthur Faber on the strength of his "Historic Concept of Disease" in New York's Willard Parker Hospital.[23] Other muralists gained experience on the project and escaped relief status by gaining private commissions.

In time murals became almost synonymous in the minds of many people with "government art." It is by no means certain, however, that federal patronage in the late 1940s or 1950s would have inspired murals for the hastily raised walls of the postwar building boom. Holger Cahill apparently thought not. His private opinion was that while some American muralists were good, "most of them are not," and that "the Mexicans aren't so good either." Moreover, he believed murals were simply the "style" of the moment. Professional art, in his view, "is the art of styles. It's the art of fashions, which may change rapidly. Some artist comes along and establishes another fashion, and then this old thing goes out—something like women's hats."[24] The FAP contributed to American art by providing conditions in which the mural style could run its course; by allowing the evolution of art and artists to continue uninterrupted.

Other FAP artists, receiving far less attention than the muralists, developed new materials and methods. In Massachusetts a paint testing laboratory and in New York City a technical division developed and put to use two of the most permanent types of synthetic resins, the alkyd and acrylic. The same technicians developed a noncrackable sizing for canvas which made movement of finished paintings less hazardous. FAP artists pioneered in a technique for painting directly on plastered walls by mixing a special glue with the paint. In California, where outdoor murals were popular, FAP artists by 1939 had installed 27 panels in mosaic tile. So strong was the demand that the Los Angeles unit trained 40 new men in the medium. Californians also developed the "petrochrome" mural. Petrochrome panels were thin slabs of concrete three or four feet square impregnated with marble chips and color oxides according to a design. When polished and affixed to building walls these blocks made economical and long lasting decorations. FAP "monumental" decorations also included a few stained glass windows. They ranged from the U.S. Military Academy's 12,000 fragment, 21 by 22 foot window showing scenes from George Washington's life, to the 200 fragment depiction of the USS *Tampa* in the American Legion Casino in Tampa, Florida's Plant Park.[25]

The FAP provided work for more easel painters than any other type of creative artist. At one point over 900 of them drew WPA checks. They treated almost any subject in whatever manner in-trigued them. A small group working with New York City hospitals attempted to solve "problems pertaining to the therapeutic value of art." Several others specialized in portraits. From school principals and ambassadors they turned to military officers; a portrait of Rear Admiral Alfred T. Mahan for the ship bearing his name, likenesses of officers departing from Hickam Field in Honolulu, and in the first months of 1942 oils of General Douglas MacArthur—three man-days per portrait. Most easels, however, reflected the immediate concern of the artist.[26]

Giving the easel artists *lebensraum* for artistic expression and development, as Mrs. McMahon conceived her mission, put her and other administrators in the position of seeking co-sponsors for some art which few people liked. Public institutions which paid something in order to receive art seemed to prefer realistically portrayed landscapes and flowers as subjects. The more avant-garde work which could not be placed went to the Washington exhibition unit or to storage.[27] In theory the paintings were safe because all of them remained the property of the federal government, property on long-term loan to the recipient. In reality, no one worried much that officials in Washington ever would demand an accounting.

Cahill and his state administrators occasionally worried about the quality of easel paintings. For a time the FAP field force considered the entire 24-man easel project in Salt Lake City "nothing short of miserable." When Mrs. McMahon scrutinized the easel output in New York after the organization phase, she insisted on a large number of transfers "to protect . . . quality." Other states solved the problem the same way. It pained Cahill to make judgments which might determine the future direction of a reliefer's life. He considered decisions based upon quality risky because "quality is a very hard thing to pin down." Besides, he believed that "You can't say to a man, 'You shouldn't do this any more. Why don't you find yourself another job?' "[28] Cahill encouraged, nonetheless, transfer of workers who were obviously inept, and in a short time FAP artists were claiming their share or more of awards and prizes in competition with artists able to support themselves without WPA.

More than 300 artists on the New York City project alone won

52 Jack Levine (FAP, Mass.),
The Feast of Pure Reason,
award-winning oil now on
extended loan to the Museum
of Modern Art, New York

awards. Most were easel painters. Success stories like John Edward Heliker's made FAP officers especially proud. The 31-year-old artist had only three months' formal art training, albeit from Thomas Hart Benton, in addition to his WPA experience when he walked away from the Corcoran Gallery's biennial exhibition of contemporary oil paintings with its Gold Medal and the $2,000 W. A. Clark Award. Before coming to the WPA, another young New Yorker, Robert W. Godfrey, rode subways all night because he did not have money for room rent. While he was on FAP rolls the Metropolitan Museum of Art noticed his "Portrait of My Wife" and purchased the piece for its permanent collection.[29]

The art world would begin to take more seriously the names of FAP workers and ex-workers in the 1940s and 1950s when they appeared on award certificates. Ivan LeLorraine Albright, late of the Illinois project, topped the list of FAP artists who swept a major exhibition of the New York Metropolitan Museum of Art in 1941. The $3,000 second prize went to the former Massachusetts project artist Jack Levine, and Marsden Hartley recently of the New York project took $2,000 for fourth. Aaron Bohrod and Raymond Breinen, formerly on the Illinois project, and Charles Howard from the San Francisco unit each took $1,000 in prize money and Philip Evergood, New York, and Mark Tobey, Washington, won $500. When the Museum of Modern Art organized a show of "18 artists from 9 states," 13 of the artists exhibited as veterans of FAP. Annual exhibitions of the country's best contemporary art at the leading art museums always included a respectable number of relief artists. Of the 115 exhibitors chosen by the Whitney in 1937, 28 were project workers. The next year FAP artists numbered 72 among the 200 selected. The Pennsylvania Academy of Fine Arts included the work of 50 project artists in its 1938 exhibition, about one-fourth of the total, while other art museums selected a proportionate number. As for winning top honors, WPA veterans in 1942 took 50 percent of the prizes at the Virginia Biennial, 60 percent at the Pennsylvania Academy's 137th Annual, and 100 percent at the Chicago Art Institute Annual. From 1935 through 1943 FAP artists appeared on every roster of Guggenheim fellowship winners and in 1941 half that

foundation's awards to artists went to former WPA employees. Scores of FAP graduates won Carnegie Endowment fellowships which made them instructors of art for a year at colleges and universities. Many Carnegie fellows stayed on as permanent staff. And at least one new art school consisted of a former project supervisor and crew.[30]

Few easel artists, although they appreciated the opportunity to work, learned to live comfortably with the frustrating rules of WPA. Most preferred to work at home or in their own studios and at times of the day and month of their own choosing. In the smaller state projects such as Alabama, Connecticut, Louisiana, Montana, and experimentally until 1939 in many other states such as Illinois, New York, New Jersey, they did. Most states used a production quota system. Typically, the project required the artist to turn in a watercolor or gouache in three weeks and, depending on size, an oil in four to six. Graphic artists, muralists, and sculptors worked under adjusted timetables. Administrators took the artists' word that they spent the required hours on the job and settled for periodic checks in the studios. Only in the metropolitan centers, where more than any other WPA activity the arts projects symbolized New Deal boondoggling, did nervous administrators demand a system of guaranteeing a full 90 hours work each month and submission of current work—not uncloseted pieces from student days. One by one the large projects turned to central workshops with individual cubicles for painters. Like other reliefers, artists checked in and out with a timekeeper each day, and supervisors frequently scrutinized their work.[31]

Cahill admitted the workshops satisfied the demands of administrative procedure, but he believed they caused deterioration in the quality of the output. No creative artist worthy of the name, the FAP chief argued, would stop at a given time if the work was going well or if stopping meant losing continuity. Occasions did arise where an artist volunteered 20 hours overtime in the interest of his work, and then because of accident or fatigue lost pay for being five minutes late. Some artists had their inspirations and produced their best work off the project site and at odd hours, traits incompatible with factory conditions and art by the clock. Moreover, many artists resented the system they felt impinged upon their creative independence and protested that travel to a workshop consumed the precious morning light and period of greatest productive energy. Finally, maintaining the workshops did increase project costs. Cahill preferred the production quota system and asked his superiors to exempt the FAP from WPA timekeeping regulations.[32] Nothing came of the appeal and conditions continued to vary according to personalities and each state's administrative and political climate.

Workshops seemed not to concern graphic artists and sculptors so much as they did easel artists. The association of over 200 print makers brought new techniques and unexpectedly high production. Project artists prepared designs on four or five different stones to produce lithographs in as many colors. They made six-color wood block prints according to the same principle; one die for each color, the paper carefully pressed to each die to add the colors. In Philadelphia the Negro artist Dox Thrash and co-workers Richard Hood, Michael Gallagher, Roswell Weidner, and Hubert Mesibov talked the Carborundum Company, makers of silicon carbide abrasive, into providing material and technical data for experiments. From their efforts came the carborundum print. In the New York City graphics unit a group led by the artist Anthony Velonis pioneered in making a fine arts medium out of the silk screen process. The FAP sheltered practitioners of every known branch of the graphic arts and offered work to co-sponsors which compared in quality with FAP easels.[33]

FAP print makers won scores of honors. Some received Guggenheim fellowships and others were among the 100 selected to participate in the International Exhibition of Lithography and Wood Engraving. The Print Club of Philadelphia, the Wichita Art Association, the San Francisco Art Association, and other

53 Samuel Green (FAP, Mass.), *Joppa Flats*, drypoint

54 Yasuo Kuniyoshi (FAP, NYC), *Trapeze Girl*, lithograph

clubs tendered their top graphic art prizes to project workers. Probably the highest of the many honors was the inclusion of 10 FAP print makers in the prestigious British publication *Fine Prints of the Year* in 1937. That year FAP artists numbered nearly one-fourth of all the Americans included.[34]

While print makers on relief paid the FAP homage for opportunities presented, many individuals lamented the opportunities that the FAP missed. Despite the effects of the occasional critic who protested the "extraordinary scarcity of names of Anglo-Saxon origin" among print makers, or the junior high school principal who found barely 10 of 100 prints "fit to even hang in the halls of a school building," graphic artists had the greatest potential of integrating art and daily life. The nearly 240,000 prints which they produced eventually found their way to schools, colleges, libraries, and government offices.[35] If the public, the acquisitive and status-conscious American public, could have purchased them or kept them at home even temporarily, what greater effect might they have had?

FAP artists knew how to make prints so reasonably priced that they were available to the general public. Using the project-developed silk screen technique, a print maker could turn out upward of 1,000 prints of a single design with simple and inexpensive equipment. The artists unions believed the sale of prints, with the weight of WPA behind a marketing scheme, would make the project self-supporting, and, by stimulating demand, eventually self-liquidating. Florence Kerr and other WPA underlings suggested the idea once or twice, but neither Harry Hopkins nor his successor, Francis Harrington, seriously considered letting WPA workers sell what they produced on government time.[36] Loans through local libraries, the other possibility for bringing art into depression homes, also failed to win administrative sanction.

Without approval from Washington the northern California project installed 317 mounted lithographs in an exhibition room at the Berkeley Public Library and allowed each library card holder to borrow one print for 30 days. Of the first 206 people to wander into the exhibition room 95 took out prints. Some hesitated on their first visit, fearing loss or damage and consequent fine, and then came back ready to take the chance. The library reported no losses and little damage to the prints. Soon requests for details of the experiment were coming in from other states. In New York the circulation division of the impressive New York Public Library sent in a request for prints it could loan. By the time FAP administrators got around to a policy decision, in the spring of 1939, Congress had the WPA running scared. No one needed to guess the reaction of the Appropriations Committee if it learned that people were taking something home free that had cost the government a considerable sum of money to produce. Assistant FAP administrator Parker reminded the librarians of the policy to make allocations only to institutions which defrayed the material and other nonlabor costs. No library had made an offer of payment, he noted, and expressed concern that the scheme "would only increase the expenditure of nonlabor funds of the project." All considered, he thought it not "wise" to approve lending to private individuals.[37]

As with murals, easel work, and graphic art, the range of media and subjects in FAP sculpture almost defied description. Sculptors on the New York City project developed a plastic product called magnacite for small sculptures and mosaic work. Modernists used the welding torch to create forms impossible to cast or carve. Project artists cast pieces in aluminum as well as bronze and sometimes achieved special effects by electroplating other metals to the casts. Stainless steel and copper sheets served some artists' purposes. FAP sculptors found time to work with traditional marble, granite, and limestone, but the high material costs of sculpture and WPA's insistence that the receiver pay for everything except the labor encouraged wider use of precast concrete.

The subjects of FAP sculpture, like FAP murals, usually depended on the character of the places receiving them. Schools in Ohio received a series entitled "Alice in Wonderland," carved animals went to the Brookfield Zoo in Chicago, and the U.S. Housing Administration cemented bulky, indestructible story book figures into housing project playgrounds. Stone fountains were popular for hospitals, parks, and botanical gardens. The number of traditional statues of local heroes erected on city building lawns, town squares, and in armories mounted into the hundreds. FAP also worked to make sculpture a part of new WPA and PWA buildings. Thus FAP sculptors joined construction workers at the Jamaica, New York, sewage treatment plant, and installed two bas-relief panels symbolizing chemistry and engineering; at the Bowery Bay plant they erected four panels depicting men and machines constructing a sanitary system; and so it went across the country. Whoever tried to find a common denominator in FAP sculptures had to deal with activity ranging from restoration of time-worn carvings on headstones in Hartford's Center Church Cemetery, to casting of bronze busts of Civil War generals for a new crypt in Ulysses S. Grant's tomb, to molding paperweight-sized pieces for bureaucrats' desktops.[38]

During the depression few Americans reacted with more than half-interest to impressive statistics or complementary professional judgments about government operation. National attention was much more certain to linger over a bureaucratic embarrassment. In the course of the FAP one incident brought considerable attention, of dubious value to the project and to sculpture and illustrated again the problem of reconciling multiple tastes and interests. The incident grew out of San Francisco's desire for a harbor statue comparable to New York City's Statue of Liberty.

Early in 1937 local politicos, the San Francisco Art Commission, and the FAP agreed to erect a gigantic figure representing the spirit of San Francisco on Christmas Tree Point. They chose the sculptor Beniamino Benevenuto Bufano to design and supervise the work. Bufano, colorful and profane and slightly crippled from a wound self-inflicted to avoid war service, proposed to raise a modernistic portrayal of Saint Francis of Assisi 156 feet tall made from sheets of copper silicate alloy. When a citizen's committee reproduced his sketch in newspapers to raise funds for the materials, they drew a barrage of criticism which reflected varied mixtures of religion, politics, and aesthetics. Archbishop John Joseph Mitty approved of the design, but leaders of the Franciscan Order called it a "Mephistophelean monstrosity." More unsettling, Protestant patriots refused to tolerate a publicly constructed monument of a Catholic saint 5 feet taller than the Statue of Liberty. John H. Cowles, Grand Commander of the Scottish Rite, charged WPA with endorsing "a scheme to minimize the Statue of Liberty" which violated the principle of separate church and state. The American Protestant Defense League immediately demanded a matching statue in the harbor of Martin Luther or some other Protestant.[39]

Columnist Westbrook Pegler called the attention of his readers to the stark figure which offended him aesthetically as much as the New Deal offended him politically. He described Bufano's model as "a figure with . . . pointed beard, inclosed in an aviator's helmet and having, beneath the chin, a sort of bib or drool cloth. The hands are upraised in the standard posture of the guest of honor at a stickup and the figure then declines, round, rigid as a concrete pipe and innocent of fold or human line to the waist, where it disappears into a barrel." Pegler said he would sculpt something better, and with photographer present donned smock and beret. He "created" something called "Mrs. George Spelvin" which included cornucopia, gear wheel, and dangling mouse. Bufano then parodied Pegler's parody for eager photographers. It was good fun for Pegler and Bufano, but not for WPA, the San Francisco Art Commission, or the citizens' committee trying to raise $15,000 privately and $22,000 from the city government.[40]

At one point donors sent copper sheets worth $2,500, but the WPA returned the sheets in October 1939 because politicians, bureaucrats, and sculptor had failed to agree on a final design. The next spring the California art project rid itself of Bufano when it learned the playful sculptor had used CIO leader Harry Bridges, accused of Communist activity, as a model for a frieze depicting athletics in a local high school.[41]

Doubtless the state of sculptural art was better served by more sedate producers and recipients. Instructions went out to New York City sculptors not to create "pot boilers" and not to worry about the problems of allocating what they produced. "The one thing the project requires is that you do your best work," supervisor Gerolamo Piccoli told them. Almost all did. Names soon to be well known—such as David Smith, José de Rivera, Concetta Scaravaglione, Ibram Lassaw, and Robert Cronbach—developed their individual styles on the project. A fair share of project

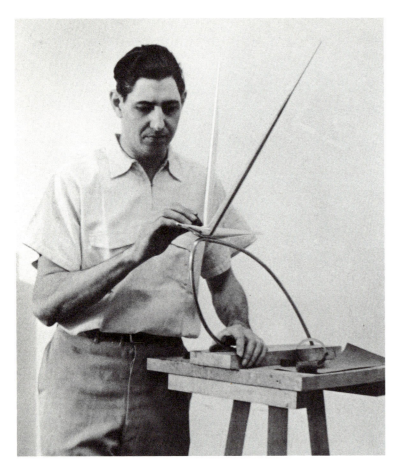

55 José de Rivera (FAP, NYC), with *Flight*

56 Concetta Scaravaglione (FAP, NYC) at work on the plaster model of *Girl with Gazelle*

sculptors won showings and prizes, and success stories like that of Thomas Lo Medico kept morale high. Lo Medico had counted pennies to pay for his breakfast earlier in the day that he won $8,000 in a competition sponsored by Metropolitan Life Insurance Company. The FAP enabled sculptors, one careful student wrote in 1970, "not only to sustain their talents . . . but also to prepare by their experimentation and their group efforts, for a new phase in American sculpture."[42] Federal subsidies, to repeat, permitted the evolution of American art to continue without the disruption the depression otherwise would have caused.

The evolution toward increased appreciation of art by the public was slow. There was little to indicate that the work of the creative artists was more integrated with daily life in 1940 than in 1935. A population of 130,000,000 spent less than $500,000 a year

120

on contemporary art, and barely 150 American artists earned as much as $2,000 annually from the sale of their work.[43]

With the full-time practice of art still almost impossible, and with Congress more disposed to economy than art subsidy, Roosevelt, in January 1940, suggested a new plan for persuading individual Americans to buy creative art. The President believed people outside the larger cities who rarely saw art would buy it if they could get it and if somebody promoted and priced it sensibly. He suggested that local artists exhibit for a week or two each year in the county court house or principal high school of the nation's 3,000 rural counties. WPA modified Roosevelt's idea to fit its administrative machinery and sent it back to him in the form of a proposal for an Art Week organized by WPA. The President liked the plan and appointed himself honorary chairman of the event.[44]

WPA's Community Service Division, the new name for Florence Kerr's Women's and Professional Division, zealously promoted the scheme. Mrs. Kerr reasoned that the national art audience already included about a third of the population. She cited art museum attendance, 20,000,000 a year; WPA art center attendance, some 3,660,000 a year; WPA Recreation Project and National Youth Administration and 4-H Club art programs, involving 500,000 a week; and the profitable publication of art books, 250 titles the previous year. Hundreds of coordinated sales exhibitions would "dramatize the fact that good work . . . appropriate for the home and for places of business and pleasure" could be had "at a price within reach of the average consumer." The WPA assistant administrator aimed to sell $5,000,000 worth of art for WPA and non-WPA artists during Art Week.[45]

Because Art Week, November 27–December 3, would benefit all artists, the WPA emphasized that preparations had to be a joint private-government enterprise. Mrs. Kerr arranged for Roosevelt to invite Francis Henry Taylor, director of the New York City Metropolitan Museum of Art, to chair a national advisory committee. Civic and cultural groups could join the effort by filling in appropriate blanks on mimeographed resolutions sent out by WPA. Many did, including the General Federation of Women's Clubs, the Association of Junior Leagues of Ameri-

ca, and the American Association of University Women. In all, the WPA public relations division announced, some 210 government agencies, 780 art organizations, 650 museums and art schools, and 4,300 commercial houses stood behind the effort. Local WPA art project supervisors and Community Service directors organized upwards of 6,000 museum directors, women's club leaders, sales people, artists, officials, and prominent citizens into 507 state and local committees to plan and conduct the sales. Washington furnished "Service Help Bulletins," telling the committees when and where and how to make announcements and solicit exhibition space and contact artists. In support of the theme, "American Art for Every American Home," advance stories, instructions for conducting press events, scripts for radio spot announcements, and "interviews" flowed from WPA headquarters. While WPA employees could not staff the sales exhibitions or market what they produced on government time, WPA labor readied many exhibition sites and project supervisors urged artists to offer the art they produced off duty.[46]

The local committees showed surprising initiative. In Chicago a speakers' bureau addressed 175 meetings. Sales committees in New Jersey and Connecticut encouraged Rotary Clubs, Kiwanis, Lions, trade unions, and country clubs to buy art. Kansas and Nebraska committees made trucks ready to carry exhibitions from town to town. Persons boarding a streetcar or bus in New York City, Chicago, or Washington confronted posters and window stickers heralding Art Week. Stamford, Connecticut, department stores sent out Art Week announcements with the monthly bills while notices reached urban Nebraskans with dairy deliveries. Girls in Chicago made sandwich boards to parade around the city's downtown "loop." Radio programs, including one featuring Mrs. Roosevelt, and teas and "arty-parties" drew attention to the coming event. By the time it arrived the committees had set up 1,641 sales exhibitions and received 134,255 items to sell from 31,403 artists and craftsmen.[47]

Such widespread enthusiasm and generosity moved Taylor to proclaim at the official opening that this effort to offer art "within the range of the most modest pocketbook" could well prove "one of the most significant events in the history of modern art and in

57 Art Week in Milwaukee, 1941

the history of our American civilization." The crowds that turned out for the sales exhibitions made Taylor's optimism plausible. Past $10,000 sculptures and $2 prints, baby shoes of Angora rabbit skin, wrought-iron foot scrapers, little figurines of wood and plaster, Indian blankets and more, they nudged and shuffled—by the end of the week 5,000,000 people had attended the exhibitions. Even before Art Week 1940 ran its course Roosevelt proclaimed Art Week an annual event under the sponsorship of the President.[48]

To reach the sales goal, each of the 5,000,000 patrons needed to spend a dollar. Each spent an average of two cents. Balancing the time and effort invested against the $100,018.45 income, Art Week flopped. By conviction or in defense WPA argued that the low sales figure meant less than the "general public interest which gave promise of future support," and the fact that over 90 percent of all purchases were of items priced at $25 or under. That, plus the distribution of sales, the official report said, "would

suggest that buying publics in the middle and lower income brackets have been reached." Advisory council chairman Taylor rejected the WPA report as "flamboyant and uncritical." Obviously something was wrong. In view of the frightening diversions of flaming Europe and Asia and the need to study the potential of future art sales weeks, he advised postponing Art Week 1941.[49] But WPA already had plans in motion, plans based on the lessons of 1940.

In 1941 WPA intended to organize the potential art buyers as well as the sellers. For advisory council chairman they chose Thomas J. Watson, the president of International Business Machines Corporation and a prominent collector. WPA revived the local committees and charged them to consider permanent art sales machinery while they planned the 1941 sales exhibitions. Watson organized businessmen's committees in most states and offered to speak before any art-buying group. Hoping to set a precedent and good example, he announced that he would buy a piece of sculpture in every state and easel works for each of the 88 street-level IBM offices in the country. Frank M. Mayfield, vice-chairman of the national advisory council and president of a major association of department stores, encouraged the stores to accept and sell art on commission. Everyone seemed convinced that plans had "developed along practical and merchandising lines."[50]

When Art Week 1941 began on November 17, under the slogans "American Art for American Homes" and "Buy American Art," a thousand outlets offered 130,000 pieces from 30,000 artists and craftsmen. Again the patrons turned out. Again they looked and commented and left without buying much. The tenseness and uncertainty of those unhappy days immediately preceding Pearl Harbor undoubtedly affected the attitude of many viewers toward art purchases. Reporting sales in Louisville, at about half the 1940 figure, the WPA organizer concluded that "the people of Louisville are more interested in defense, at the present time, than in art activities." In the urgency of redirecting WPA after December 7, 1941 no one bothered to make a public report of Art Week tallies. Even the records disappeared. Art Week's most optimistic friends estimated that sales exceeded those for the year 1940 by a mere $30,000, and Watson spent well over $25,000 of that. No one seriously tried to put together an Art Week for 1942.[51]

Why had two national art weeks grossed less than $250,000? In the first place Mrs. Kerr's contention that the art audience numbered one-third of the population was ill-founded. When art museums reported 20,000,000 in annual attendance it did not mean 20,000,000 different people. More likely it meant that a small clientele visited frequently. Probably, too, that same clientele bought the art books, journals, and augmented WPA art center attendance. Nothing indicated that contemporary art particularly interested that audience. The museums they visited consistently emphasized the Old Masters.

Secondly, "the most modest pocketbook" Art Week aimed to tap was modest indeed. With half of the American people earning less than $1,000 a year, 85 percent under $2,000, who had money for refinements?

Finally, many artists declined to support Art Week. Some on WPA feared their Art Week sales would invalidate their relief certification and end their steady jobs. Others believed Art Week organizers expected the impossible, serious art at cheap prices. To make $3,000 a year an easel artist had to sell a painting every ten days for $150 (one-third going for dealer's commission). A sincere artist might consider himself capable of creating 12 or 13 good easels a year, but not 30 or 50. To make a $3,000-a-year-living by selling at $25, as Art Week organizers requested, he needed to paint 160. Still other artists by 1940 and 1941 disdained "pictures for the home." Many, especially in New York City, defended a new art which spoke only to those "who have had the opportunity and the will to cultivate it." Since understanding of their work depended upon "a consummated experience between picture and onlooker," these advanced artists concluded that their work "must insult anyone . . . spiritually attuned to interior decoration . . . pictures for over the mantel, pictures of the American scene."[52] Significantly, New York City Art Week offerings and sales trailed Washington and Los Angeles.

WPA efforts to increase art appreciation through sales failed to achieve the expected result; and so did the effort to increase ap-

preciation through large allocations to public institutions. While the effect of the art the public did view is impossible to assess, doubtless it was less than it might have been. A sizable part of the easel and graphic work found its way to offices infrequently visited by the average citizen. Other pieces intended for display ended in library and school art files. Somehow the strong sense of community ownership that the art officials had hoped for failed to develop. Many friends of nationally subsidized art believed that in time critics would recognize greatness in many WPA artists and that curiosity and pride would draw people to inspect the work. In time, too, the sheer volume of WPA art would overflow the offices and files and people would see more of it. The erosion of creative art production by the WPA war effort understandably saddened friends of nationally subsidized art. These friends had yet to bear a final disappointment, the careless disposal of art when WPA disbanded.

After the WPA art project turned almost exclusively to war work Cahill set up a Central Allocations Unit in Chicago and encouraged states to send their undistributed creative art to it. The unit routinely handled the "sponsor's contributions" (fees from receivers), multi-copied forms, stickers, and brass tags that allocation involved. Then, when word arrived of WPA's certain demise and the state projects closed, officials in charge of liquidating the projects smothered the Chicago unit with long-stored art. WPA wanted all books in order by April 30, 1943. To speed distribution, officials in Washington quit requiring a contribution from recipients and sent the directors of WPA Service Projects in several states confidential letters asking them to select discreetly one or two public institutions and tell them they could have unframed art for the shipping cost. Even museums, which regulations formerly excluded to prevent competition with private production, now received invitations to apply. Not surprisingly the allocations unit "moved" 15,000 items in one three-week period.[53]

The hasty liquidation alarmed the officers of the rival Section of Fine Arts. Edward Rowan, assistant Chief of the Section, hurried to acquire WPA work for future use by the Public Buildings Administration. In New York he laid claim to 500 items, passed through New Jersey and Pennsylvania making selections, and in

Chicago set aside 7,500 prints, 500 paintings, and a small group of sculpture, ceramics, and textiles. He agreed to take whatever the Chicago unit had left on April 30. Rowan returned to Washington convinced that WPA art comprised a valuable social record and included pieces by geniuses and first-rate artists as well as "junk." "Unless we want to risk throwing away the geniuses," his colleague Forbes Watson warned, "we'd better be careful and not treat this production with disrespect and ignorant haste." The Section of Fine Arts wanted the record preserved and examined "item by item by a body of cool, unprejudiced, understanding experts." If they failed to do it, the former critics of WPA concluded, "we shall deserve all the names a more advanced posterity will heap upon us."[54]

The Chicago unit closed before all the projects assembled their art; departing administrators left confusion in their wake; with the result that some art had to be disposed of in other ways. A shocked art public learned a few months later from a story in *Life* magazine that a New York City junk dealer had purchased several mildewed bales of canvas—which turned out to be WPA art—for 4 cents a pound in an auction at the federal warehouse in Flushing. The junkman turned up one day at Henry C. Roberts's secondhand bric-a-brac shop in Manhattan, and Roberts bought the lot, cheap. Herbert Benevy, a framer and restorer, was among the first to stumble on to the cache. He took out a loan and bought 300 of the best canvases for about $5 each. Benevy walked away with three pieces by Jackson Pollock, several by Mark Rothko, and others by Adolph Gottlieb and Ben Benn. Another early purchaser, the artist Michael Zaga, bought 400 in the $3 to $5 range. Many artists rushed to buy their own work and others pooled their money to buy in quantity. Soon buyers packed the little shop, crumpling and trampling the canvases that fell from the long tables. The murals that lay limply across furniture and stacks of books brought $25, the rest $3 to $5.[55]

Cahill, "plenty infuriated" at this scandal which eclipsed any other embarrassment during the FAP's history, spread the blame between the author of the article, Mrs. Kerr, and Mrs. McMahon. He had "a terrible row" with *Life*'s writer, and always believed

58 Jackson Pollock (FAP, NYC), *Abandoned Mill*, one of the canvases which the WPA disposed of as surplus property. A secondhand store in Manhattan sold them in 1943 for about $5 each

that she had made the error seem worse than it was because she had failed to "make the grade" as an applicant to the FAP. Mrs. Kerr had contributed by her lassitude in issuing the letters and orders to allocate the art in the last weeks of the project. She had declined to act until Mrs. Roosevelt decided whether federal dormitories (with appropriate art) should be established for girls coming to Washington to work in war agencies. Mrs. Mc-Mahon had been promoted to another job, and what with the way "a lot of things were shabbily done on the New York project," a warehouse of art had been "forgotten." Cahill knew nothing of the warehouse. New York administrators feared he would appropriate the good art they could not allocate, he concluded after the fact, and therefore they kept him from seeing it.[56] In the emotional heat of the need to assign fault, the former national director and the former New York project chief exchanged words for which neither could completely forgive the other.

Cahill's sense of propriety and loyalty was too highly developed to air publicly his belief that Mrs. Kerr and Mrs. McMahon were partly responsible. He defended the projects by attacking *Life*. The magazine's editors "were on the bearish side," he said, in playing up the fate of a fraction of 1 percent of WPA art and in failing to balance it with the achievements of depression art programs. True, the work of some well-known artists turned up in the secondhand shop. But much of it was "scaffolding" work, preliminary sketches, and full-scale details for work later repainted by muralists. No one ever intended those for allocation. Many of the easel canvases were unfinished pieces which artists turned in when they left the projects. Others were trial paintings by applicants, work rejected by project supervisors. The junkman, Cahill publicly admitted, also had served as pallbearer for some work returned late from exhibition. Such work unclaimed by sponsors became surplus property and what happened to it was "mandatory in law and in government regulations." *Life* would better serve art if, rather than focus upon the few pieces that slipped away, it stressed the project's objective of providing employment and the remarkable by-product of placing so much work in high-ranking institutions.[57]

Time only partially proved the soundness of Cahill's admonition. Artists credited WPA, whether fondly or grudgingly or bitterly, with enabling them to continue the work they loved. America's galleries, dealers, universities, art schools, and position in world cultural affairs were better for it. Still, the lack of stress

59 Morris Graves (FAP, Wash.), *Wheelbarrow*, oil now transferred to the Smithsonian Institution

on preservation and failure to provide for continuing evaluation encouraged in the receivers of WPA art variously apathetic, cynical, and cavalier attitudes. Twenty-five years after the WPA, most high schools and universities had lost or destroyed their federal art. Countless murals had disappeared behind institutional green paint while easels went home with bureaucrats, to dank storerooms, or to incinerators. The General Services Administration, successor of the Public Buildings Administration, had in the early 1970s located but a fraction of the mass of WPA art Rowan had anxiously collected.[58]

Despite much that was clearly "junk" both as art and social document, much was precious. No one could accurately assess the monetary worth of WPA art when it was 30 years old, but

Roger Stevens, head of the National Arts and Humanities Foundation, in 1966 thought that New Deal art was then "conservatively valued at around $50,000,000." The best estimates of the amount spent on WPA art are about $35,000,000. In 1965 critics believed one of Stuart Davis's WPA murals, which cost taxpayers $245, would sell on the open market for perhaps $100,000. In the same year the Smithsonian Institution valued the WPA easel paintings of the artist Morris Graves at $10,000 or more each. Francis V. O'Connor, a leading student of the art of Jackson Pollock, speculated in 1967 that the taxpayers received close to $450,000 worth for the $7,800 they paid Pollock between 1935 and 1943. Unfortunately, most of Pollock's project work has been lost. The value of work by artists who later achieved renown easily would equal the amount of money spent on the projects.[59] Financially, at least, New Dealers had made a good investment.

New Dealers should have anticipated the need for better safeguards for the art and for some scheme to assure its periodic appraisal. They could not anticipate, however, that so many artists would obscure and even deny their tenure with WPA. In the context of the spiraling affluence which followed World War II, it somehow seemed to most artists that the less talk about prewar days on relief the better. And so it seemed to the postwar American government. The unfortunate result was that individuals of the next generation who believed that government should improve the quality of national life, and who assumed that appreciation of the visual arts was both means and result, knew too little about the New Deal precedent to invoke or learn much from it.

[1] *Final Report on the WPA Program*, 133. Reports of WPA production vary. By Oct. 1941, according to a report FAP supplied the *American Art Annual*, graphic artists had produced 239,727 reproductions of over 12,581 original designs. Erica Rubenstein computed graphic production of over 2,000,000 copies from 35,000 original designs. See Florence S. Berryman, "Three Years in Art," *American Art Annual*, XXXV (1941), 16; Rubenstein, "The Tax Payers' Murals," 59. Practical arts projects occupied 29 percent of FAP workers before 1939, another 17 percent provided educational services, and technicians and coordinators made up the remaining 6 percent.

[2] Thomas Hart Benton, *An Artist in America* (New York, 1951), 314-15.

[3] Saul Schary, "Tendencies in American Art," in American Artists' Congress Against War and Fascism, *First American Artists' Congress*, 62.

[4] Benton, *Artist in America*, 316.

[5] *New York Times*, June 13, 1943. See the discussion of depression art in Lloyd Goodrich and John I. H. Baur, *American Art of Our Century* (New York, 1961), 84-118, and in Oliver O. Larkin, *Art and Life in America* (New York, 1960), 405-61.

[6] *Art Digest*, XIV (March 15, 1940), 8; clippings from *Washington Post*, Oct. 18, 1936, *Washington Evening Star*, May 13, 1937, *Boston Herald*, April 7, 1940, RG69/DI.

[7] *Art Digest*, XIV (March 15, 1940), 29; clipping from *New York World Telegram*, May 20, 1936, RG69/DI.

[8] Cahill, *New Horizons in American Art*, 33-35; Benson, "The Accomplishments of the WPA Federal Art Project"; Stuart Davis, "What About Modern Art and Democracy?" *Harper's*, CLXXXIII (Dec. 1943), 22.

[9] Rubenstein, "The Tax Payers' Murals," 95-115. The Rivera mural was painted at the Golden Gate International Exposition of 1940 for the City College of San Francisco.

[10] *Ibid.*, 116-24.

[11] *Ibid.*, 125-29; Los Angeles, California, Branch of American Artists' Congress, "Report on Southern California Art Project," typescript, nd, RG69/651.315.

[12] Rubenstein, "The Tax Payers' Murals," 131-34.

[13] *Ibid.*, 136-66.

[14] *Ibid.*, 217-19.

[15] Holger Cahill, "Mural America," *Architectural Record*, LXXXII (Sept. 1937), 63-68; Federal Art Project, *Federal Art in New England*, 13; Cahill to Mary R. Beard, Oct. 26, 1937, RG69/211.5; see also typed press release, "WPA Muralists Paint for the Public Schools," nd, RG69/DI; "Cahill Reminiscences," 328.

[16] Clippings from *Chicago Tribune*, Dec. 19, 20, 22, 1940, *Chicago Times*, Nov. 4, 1941, RG69/DI.

[17] Rubenstein, "The Tax Payers' Murals," 261; clipping from *Chicago Tribune*, Jan. 11, 1941, RG69/DI.

[18] Clippings from *Chicago Times*, Oct. 16, 1941, *New York World Telegram*, Sept. 10, 1936, *Boston Globe*, March 4, June 9, 1937, *Boston Evening Transcript*, March 4, 1937, RG69/DI.

[19] Clippings from *New York Times*, March 26, 1937; *New York Journal American*, April 1, 1938, *New York Post*, Dec. 1, 1936, *New York World Telegram*, Oct. 17, 1936, *Los Angeles Times*, June 9, 1941, RG69/DI.

[20] Rubenstein, "The Tax Payers' Murals," 169; clipping from *Miami Herald*, Sept. 6, 1936, RG69/DI; *New York Times*, Dec. 25, 1936.

[21] Clipping from *New York Post*, Aug. 25, 1937, RG69/DI; *Time*, XXIX (Sept. 16, 1935), 30.

[22] Clipping from *New York World Telegram*, July 9, 1938, RG69/DI; *New York Times*, April 23, 1940; *Time*, XXXII (July 18, 1938), 23; *Life*, IX (Sept. 30, 1940), 64-66. Laning's account of his experience is in Francis V. O'Connor, ed., *The New Deal Art Projects: An Anthology of Memoirs* (Washington, 1972); see also *American Heritage* (October 1970).

[23] New York City WPA Public Information Section Press Release, Nov. 1, 1939; Cahill, "Record of Program Operation and Accomplishment," 48-49; "Progress Report . . . Nov. 1937-April 1, 1938," Cahill Papers.

[24] "Cahill Reminiscences," 224, 291.

[25] Southern California Art Project, *Southern California Creates*, (np, nd) in National Gallery of Art Library; *Art Digest*, XIV (Sept. 1, 1940), 18; Ruth Reeves, "Murals," *Architectural Record*, LXXXVIII (Oct. 1940), 73-76; clipping from *New York Herald Tribune*, April 16, 1936, RG69/DI; Thomas C. Parker to A. W. von Sturve, Aug. 2, 1938, RG69/651.315; clippings from *Tampa Tribune*, Jan. 5, 6, 1938, RG69/210.1.

[26] New York City WPA Public Information Section Press Release, Nov. 1, 1939, clipping from *Los Angeles Times*, March 21, 1942, RG69/DI; *New York Times*, Jan. 23, 1938.

[27] See, Connecticut WPA Art Project, "Allocations of Non-Sponsored Work, Nov. 20, 1935-Dec. 31, 1940," Cahill Papers; O'Connor, *Federal Support for the Visual Arts*, 47; "Cahill Reminiscences," 452.

[28] Donald Bear to Cahill, April 23, 1937, McMahon to Cahill, Dec. 18, 1936, RG69/211.5; "Cahill Reminiscences," 182, 226.

[29] Cahill, "Record of Program Operation and Accomplishment," 48-51; Cahill to Maury Maverick, Aug. 28, 1936, RG69/211.5; State Final Report: New York; *Time*, XXXII (Jan. 3, 1938), 38; clipping from *Washington Star*, March 30, 1941, RG69/DI.

[30] Cahill, "Record of Program Operation and Accomplishment," 48-51; "Progress Report . . . Nov. 1937-April 1, 1938," Cahill Papers; *Art Digest*, XVII (Jan. 1, 1943), 27.

[31] See RG69/State Final Report file, esp. New York City and New Jersey.

[32] Cahill, "Record of Program Operation and Accomplishment," 36-38; Cahill to William Nunn, April 2, 1936, RG69/FAP.

[33] Florence Kerr to Charles Knupfer, Jan. 29, 1941, RG69/211.5; State Final Report: New York, Pennsylvania; New York City WPA Public Information Section Press Release, March 4, 1940, RG69/DI.

[34] Woodward to Hopkins, March 28, 1939, RG69/211; New York City WPA Public Information Section Press Release, Nov. 1, 1939, RG69/DI.

[35] Frederick B. Graham to Federal Art Project, Dec. 18, 1936, RG69/651.315; clipping from *Washington Star*, Oct. 16, 1938, RG69/DI.

[36] When Harold Stein proposed that artists on relief be permitted to sell their project production, or a part of it, the WPA finance office could think of no way of arranging a procedure which would be "adequate or at all likely to be approved by our Administration, by the Treasury, or by the General Accounting Office." Even Cahill, for bureaucratic reasons, opposed the sale of project art. Confidential memorandum, Julius Davidson to Lawrence Morris, Feb. 5, 1938, Cahill Papers.

[37] [California] *Federal Art Project Bulletin*, mimeographed, nd, in Cahill Papers; Romona Javitz to McMahon, Feb. 12, 1939, Parker to McMahon, April 8, 1939, RG69/211.5.

[38] Federal Art Project, *Federal Art in New England*, 14-15; New York City WPA Public Information Section Press Release, Nov. 1, Dec. 5, 1939, April 28, 1941; WPA Information Section Press Release, nd, clipping from *Washington Post*, Sept. 1, 1940, RG69/DI.

[39] John H. Cowles to Woodward, Aug. 19, 1938, Thomas E. Little to Hopkins, Aug. 22, 1938, RG69/651.315.

[40] See *Time*, XXXII (Aug. 29, 1938), 28; *New York Times*, July 28, 1938.

[41] William R. Lawson to William H. Brummett, April 25, 1940, RG69/651.315; *Art Digest*, XIV (April 1, 1940), 13.

[42] Eleanor M. Carr, "The New Deal and the Sculptor: A Study of Federal Relief to the Sculptor on the New York City Federal Art Project of the Works Progress Administration, 1935-1943" (unpublished Ph.D. dissertation, New York University, 1969), 72ff., 128.

[43] Francis Henry Taylor, "National Art Week and the Museum," *Bulletin of the Metropolitan Museum of Art* (Nov. 1940), Section II, 3-4.

[44] Roosevelt to Bruce, Jan. 23, 1940, AAA Reel NDA/HP1.

[45] Kerr to Harrington, July 24, 1940, Service Help Bulletin No. 1, RG69/211.5.

[46] Dornbush to William D. Hassett, Nov. 27, 1940, AAA Reel NDA/HP1; "National Report: Art Week," mimeographed, 1941, p. 8, resolutions filed in RG69/211.5.

[47] Service Help Bulletin No. 6 A, George Thorp and Leonhard J. Nederkorn to Robert I. McKeague, Nov. 10, 1940, RG69/211.5.

[48] Taylor's speech on NBC radio, Nov. 25, 1940, RG121/141; memorandum for Archibald MacLeish, Nov. 16, 1940, RG121/140; clipping from *Washington Daily News*, Dec. 1, 1940, RG69/DI; "National Report," 11.

[49] "National Report," ii, 8; *New York Times*, July 6, 1941.

[50] National Council for Art Week Headquarters Press Release, Nov. 16, 1941, Summary of Information on Art Week 1941, in RG69/211.5.

[51] Kerr to Community Service Program directors, Nov. 26, 1941, Earl D. Hale to Walter M. Kiplinger, Dec. 4, 1941, RG69/211.5; *Time*, XXXVIII (Dec. 8, 1941), 44.

[52] Davis, "What About Modern Art and Democracy?" 17; *New York Times*, June 13, 1943; Francis Henry Taylor to Roosevelt, Oct. 8, 1940, Office Files of Bureau of the Budget.

[53] Field Trip Report by Cahill, Dec. 19, 1942, Mildred T. Law to Service Project directors, nd, RG69/211.15. Federal art went to some nontax supported museums. The Museum of Modern Art, for example, received FAP work on "long-term loan" from the tax supported Brooklyn Museum. See "Cahill Reminiscences," 535.

[54] Field Trip Report by Cahill, Feb. 10, 1943, Forbes Watson, "The Significance of the Painting and Sculpture Created Under the WPA Art Program—As Art and as a Lasting Record," typescript, 1943, RG69/211.15.

[55] *Life*, XVI (April 17, 1944), 85-86; *Art Digest*, XVIII (Feb. 15, 1944), 7. Rumor persisted in California that some paintings on hand in San Francisco when the project ended were taken to a dump at night and burned. See Mary Fuller, "Emblems of Sorrow," *Artforum*, II (Nov. 1963), 34-37.

[56] "Cahill Reminiscences," 536-40.

[57] Holgar [sic] Cahill, "A Defense of the Art Project," *The League*, XVII (Winter, 1944-45), 12-13.

[58] By 1970 there were two government-sponsored projects to locate and preserve the New Deal art. The Research Program of the National Collection of Fine Arts had established a "Register of New Deal Art." Depending largely upon voluntary reporting by organizations and individuals interested in art, the "Register" was intended to locate, catalogue, help preserve, and publicize FAP and Section products. In addition the General Services Administration had begun what one official thought might be "the biggest detective story the art world has ever seen." Through a "fine arts inventory project," the GSA announced, it hoped to find and catalogue some 100,000 pieces of federally owned art and "bring the history of WPA and Treasury art up to date."

[59] *New York Times*, August 18, 1965; *Christian Science Monitor*, March 13, 1965; *Wall Street Journal*, Dec. 21, 1967; Roger L. Stevens, "The State of the Arts: A 1966 Balance Sheet," *Saturday Review*, XLIX (March 12, 1966), 25. The exact cost of the WPA creative art program cannot be determined. WPA reports never distinguished between allocations for creative projects and allocations for practical art projects. Moreover, in 1941, WPA consolidated its museum and visual aid projects with the art program. According to the *Final Report on the WPA*, taxpayers spent $69,578,055 for all "art and museum" projects. "Sponsors" contributed an additional $9,230,646 bringing the total expenditure of public funds for WPA art and museum work to $78,808,701. In January 1942, by which time the arts projects were described as in "suspended animation," Cahill computed the cost of FAP, together with the cost of the museum projects from July to December 1941, at $38,849,934. Sponsors' funds for the art project and 6 months of the museum work amounted to $3,433,191. In the Treasury Department, PWAP cost $1,312,177.93; TRAP cost $735,784; and the Section of Fine Arts cost $2,571,267. Totaled, the Treasury spent $4,619,228.93 on art. Responsible writers have estimated the cost of the art projects alone to be between $35,000,000 and $43,000,000. The careful study by Francis V. O'Connor, *Federal Support for the Visual Arts*, estimates a little more than $39,717,000. The federal outlay for creative art was less than half of any of these figures. See *Final Report on the WPA Program*, 122; Cahill to Julian S. Huxley, May 13, 1942, Cahill Papers; Dows, "The New Deal's Treasury Art Programs," 52; Erica Beckh, "Government Art in the Roosevelt Era," *Art Journal*, XX (Fall 1960), 4; Pietan, "The Federal Government and the Arts," 126; Thomson, "Peggy Bruce: Of Art and Salty Memories," 48.

8

Relief Artists and Socially Useful Projects

Unlike the more conservative academicians and purists, Holger Cahill and the WPA never defined an artist simply as a creator of murals, sculpture, easel painting, or graphic art. Training and talent (because it was meager or specialized), temperament or interests disqualified some individuals as masters of those art forms, and yet, by virtue of skills and knowledge, they were artists nonetheless. When these persons found themselves on the relief rolls, the FAP offered them work. Cahill asked only that projects not classed as "fine arts" be "socially useful." Thus, from the beginning FAP "practical" art projects undertook a wide variety of work, including poster-making, photography, recording traditional American designs, craftwork, and model making. At the same time the FAP inaugurated an art teaching program with beginning and advanced courses in practical and creative arts. The proportion of WPA artists on noncreative projects steadily increased, especially after the reorganization of 1939. By April 1940, over 4,100 of the 5,818 workers on WPA art programs worked in these practical endeavors, and the percentage increased as WPA defense projects got under way.[1]

Most of the WPA workers in the practical art and art teaching programs worked on the Index of American Design or in the WPA Community Art Centers. But there was other work, nowhere more imaginative and varied than in New York City. Many of these projects dissolved with the 25 percent cut in 1937

60 FAP traveling workshop, from which instruction in arts and crafts was given to Civilian Conservation Corps camps in New York State

and few survived the reorganization of 1939. Of the noncreative work in New York City probably none had greater impact on the city than the art teaching division.

The first summer that FAP operated in New York City, Mrs. McMahon assigned some 465 art teachers to augment the programs of 180 settlement houses and social agencies. Many of the teachers had been transferred from easel or graphic projects "to protect quality," others were beginners hoping for promotion to the creative projects, and many were long-time teachers doing what they knew best. An exhibition of the teachers' own art, one competent critic reported, showed "as broad a stratum of talent, and one as varied in its ingredients, as that represented by artists . . . in various creative assignments." Seminars on such subjects as "the therapeutic aspects of art teaching to underprivi-

leged students," "techniques," and "pedagogical methods" gave some uniformity to the classes. For a short time FAP held refresher and advanced courses for its teachers.[2]

That first summer 80 percent of the New Yorkers reached by the art teachers were children. Instead of embarking on a course of formal instruction, FAP supervisors decided, teachers should become first of all "guide and friend" to the youth. "We are not particularly interested in developing what is known as art appreciation," Cahill said, "We are interested in raising a generation . . . sensitive to their visual environment and capable of helping to improve it." The classes scattered throughout the city's five boroughs organized trips to the zoo, waterfront, parks, and nearby countryside. On the theory that no one fully appreciates what he does not have to pay for, some locations charged children 25 or 50 cents which could be worked off, if need required, by sweeping up or doing other small chores. In boys' clubs, girls' service leagues, orphanages, day nurseries, hospitals, churches, and settlements, FAP art teachers showed youngsters how to secure "canvases," usually pieces of brown wrapping paper, and mix their paints in muffin tins. Students seemed to like it, for at the end of the first year FAP boasted that in New York City and its vicinity 50,000 children and adults were being reached weekly through the teaching force. After the quota cuts of 1937 and 1939 fewer teachers reached fewer students. The statistics showed an average weekly attendance of 30,000 in 1938 and 10,000 in 1940. Of course the five Community Art Centers established in the city in 1937-1938 absorbed some of the participants.[3]

The New York teachers offered an appealing variety of services. One unit trained 63 reliefers to teach art and crafts out of traveling workshops in 54 New York State Civilian Conservation Corps camps. Another prepared exhibits and descriptive literature for use by public school teachers. It volunteered to send in artists to demonstrate lithograph or silk screen presses or lead discussions on design, using FAP products as stimulants. Evening classes, frankly aimed at taking young people "from the frequently disastrous influences of the streets," proved so successful that administrators could show that juvenile delinquency declined in areas around teaching locations. Letters in the files applauded

130

61 The Design Laboratory, a school of industrial art, was maintained by the FAP in New York City until 1937

FAP classes in hospitals for their recreational and inspirational value and their usefulness in diagnosis and treatment of the mentally disturbed and retarded. By 1941 the WPA art curriculum included 23 subjects, from photography to fashion illustration to ceramics. As months passed, more adults enrolled in the courses. According to one accounting, they increased from 20 percent in 1936 to 35 percent in 1940. By WPA's counting method a total of more than 2,000,000 students attended classes held in 160 locations. Perhaps half a million students "graduated" from the New York City WPA art courses.[4]

Until the cuts of 1937, a teaching project in New York City operated the Design Laboratory, a school offering professional level courses in industrial design. Based on the philosophy of Walter Gropius's design academy in Germany, the Bauhaus, the Design Laboratory aimed to apply the principles of the fine arts to industrial production. It accepted the Bauhaus view that the basic principle of industrial design was "functional rightness," not ornament; that a chair was first something to sit in and only second a decorative piece of furniture. To instill that idea in students the school coordinated studies in aesthetics, industrial products, machine fabrication, and merchandising. Requirements for the school's three-year diploma in industrial design, textile design, advertising, or photography included courses in the fine arts, both two and three dimensional, and machine shop taught from the point of view of mass production. Students became masters in neither, but co-director Gilbert Rohde explained that for a designer only a modicum of artistic and engineering ability was required. It was the combination that was important. The faculty of the Design Laboratory fluctuated between 25 and 35, including several capable artists who worked simply for the sake of the experiment. They worked with 300 to 400 students. When 14 students found commercial jobs as the result of an open house at the end of the first two semesters, prospects seemed bright.[5]

Co-directors Gilbert Rohde and Josiah P. Marvel saw in the Design Laboratory an educational institution deserving of encouragement and funds for expansion. Cahill, acutely aware of the WPA college's base of support, viewed it as a relief project. For the school administrators, WPA regulations meant short-term planning, limited space, a minimum of equipment, practically no library, and paltry salaries. Serious problems developed in December 1936. News came that WPA anticipated layoffs and monetary cuts, thus reducing the program by one-third. Marvel sent out form letters to individuals he believed to have influence in the government asking them to intervene. At the same time he appealed to Hopkins for a "more favorable attitude" and more money. Mrs. McMahon pronounced Marvel's attempt to save the project in "very poor taste," a violation of procedures established for official communications to the Washington headquarters, and suspended him for a week. Although no other institution in the country offered a comparable course of study, WPA's regulations concerning competition with private enterprise made students who could afford to pay elsewhere in-

62 FAP posters produced for the New York State Department of Health and the New York City Housing Authority

Several collections bearing such titles as "Coney Island, Playground for New York's Millions" traveled the FAP exhibition circuit. Another unit made motion pictures. One film, "The Technique of Fresco Painting," recorded James Michael Newell painting "Evolution of Western Civilization" in the library of Evander Childs High School. A second two reeler showed "Sculpture for Today," and another, "From Hand to Mouth," explained bacillary dysentery. Work prints for two additional motion pictures were on hand when the unit disbanded.[7]

Poster-makers, together with photographers, enjoyed some stability. Except for posters "to inspire the youth of America to bear arms in aggressive warfare," which the unions forbade their members to make, the unit stood ready to give dramatic presentation to practically any subject. Every division of WPA needed posters as did the departments of the city government. Promoters of fire prevention, obedience to the law, prenatal care, noise abatement, reading books, or treatment of congenital syphilis eagerly sought the eye-catching, silk-screened creations the poster division could supply at less than a dime apiece. So many people recognized the bargain that the division had to gear up for production of 750,000 posters a year.[8]

Most other projects classed as practical art were small and relatively short-lived. The creative home planning division was one example. The 20 or so artists of the unit built models of apartments with interchangeable walls and furniture with various coverings to demonstrate arrangements and color effects. They offered free instruction in choosing and using curtains, furniture, colors, rugs, and lampshades. They gave shopping advice and conducted shopping tours. To prove what they could do, they rented and furnished a three-room apartment for demonstration purposes at a total cost of $60. Enough housewives were sufficiently convinced that they filled up classes for making hooked rugs, lampshades, slipcovers, curtains, and quilts.[9] The creative home planning unit, whatever good it may have served, was a casualty of the quota reduction in 1937.

The costume design unit followed a similar course. A spokesman for its two dozen workers explained that they taught "the art of costume design, embracing figure drawing, anatomy, line,

eligible to enroll in the Design Laboratory. The directors enrolled many students with money anyway. "It was mainly for that reason that we terminated the Design Laboratory," Cahill explained after the retrenchment of 1937.[6] Probably personality clashes had something to do with it too.

Among the practical art projects in New York the one for photographers enjoyed greatest popularity inside the government agencies. Photographers on relief served all the projects of Federal One, most departments of the New York City government, and sometimes furnished WPA construction projects with progress photos and publicity pictures. The New York photographic division released over 170,000 prints during the federal period. A "creative unit" of the division made photo murals, photo posters, and exhibition prints. The FAP arranged book publication of photographer Bernice Abbott's film documentary of commonplace and spectacular scenes of the city, *Changing New York.*

63 *Chronic Illness*, model by the New York Scenic Designers and Model Makers project for a public health display

form, and color and historical costume, so that the pupils have the fundamentals of art, in addition to equipping them for the industrial field—also keeping them interested in constructive work under good social influences." In more simple terms the project taught to girls who might otherwise be on the streets the elements of contemporary style and taste and its economical application. In early 1937, 2,500 girls flocked to 30 locations for this instruction. The petition of 27 welfare houses could not save the unit when the cuts of 1937 abolished it.[10]

Model makers and scenic designers operated other small projects. Their number fluctuated between 15 and 50 and their duties

from contructing three-dimensional models illustrating flood prevention by the Tennessee Valley Authority to painting stage curtains at the New York Women's House of Detention. The 1930s vogue for visual education through dioramas kept the model makers busy. City museums took advantage of the low prices to acquire architectural models made from original blueprints, theater scenes, and interior cross-sections of buildings. Requests from the other large Federal One projects in New York City consumed much of the designers' time. They illustrated many of the guidebooks and catalogues for the writers project, and for the theater and music projects made special posters, programs, and

133

64 The Department for Lettering, Signs, Project Markers and Miscellaneous in Chicago, run by the Allied Arts Department of the FAP, Illinois

brochures, provided backgrounds for some stage productions, and even animated a strip of film for a federal play.[11] Because they served other agencies, the model makers and scenic designers enjoyed a longer tenure than workers in most of the peripheral projects.

Special practical art and peripheral projects grew up in many parts of the country. The rich human and physical art resources of New York City simply made such projects more varied in the metropolis. In what other city could the FAP create an eight-man project to clean, retouch, varnish, and treat blisters on city owned art or maintain a group to give lectures and free tours of city art galleries to almost anyone who wanted them? Still, more than 180 FAP art teachers across the country, not counting those in WPA art centers, tried to transfer the satisfaction gained from

self-expression to the people of their communities. WPA provided the first technical art instruction for Negroes attending New Orleans' segregated schools and for students in the schools of rural Vermont and Florida. For middle-aged workers in the lodginghouse district of Boston's South End, FAP teachers brought a stimulating alternative to idleness or grousing and an atmosphere of sympathetic fellowship. Detroit, Minneapolis, Cleveland, Boston, St. Paul, and Philadelphia operated poster projects. Chicago's group was for a time larger than that of New York. Model makers in several areas made relief maps and dioramas for local education and publicity, raising the FAP total of dioramas and models to 925 and maps and diagrams to 39,125. In most states FAP serviced the Writers Project with drawings for use as chapter heads and tail pieces and with other art work for Writers Project publications. After the states assumed most responsibility over the projects, Illinois established a design unit reminiscent of the New York Design Laboratory. The main differences were that the Chicago project offered no public courses and directed its energy to designs for WPA craft projects instead of industry. One of the original members of the Bauhaus faculty donated full time to the work and about half the designers worked "in close collaboration" with Laszlo Moholy-Nagy, head of the American School of Design—the American Bauhaus. The Massachusetts FAP developed a paint testing laboratory in 1937 as a project service. A Bureau of Standards code of minimum specifications for artists' materials resulted from the union of art and chemistry. FAP photographers outside New York learned to make photo murals and produced, together with the New York unit, a total of 495,620 photographs and 15,300 slides. California photographers completed at least half a dozen short motion pictures and left unassembled film footage for others. They focused on wood and stone sculpture, pencil drawing technique, the mosaic process, and the making of petrochrome panels.[12]

Other art projects across the country lent talent to tax-supported museums, and some developed unusual specialties: wrought iron in Oregon, textiles in southern Illinois. "Craft work" belonged to special FAP units when the intended result was to be primarily distinctive or decorative. In cases where "utility" was the object, WPA Welfare and Production projects made the craft items.[13] If some of the work seemed unnecessary, the variety bewildering, and the fragmentation inefficient, the FAP justified it on grounds of preserving and developing skills during the depression.

Commercial artists constituted one of the largest and most desperate groups under FAP jurisdiction. Many found work in the projects discussed above, but one nationwide project, the Index of American Design, busied some 300 individuals for six years. The FAP undertook to find the main types of American decorative art from the colonial period through the Gilded Age and to record them in a colossal Index of American Design. Project artists were required to examine furniture and household items, quilts and clothing, ship figureheads and cigar store Indians, weathervanes and toys, tavern signs and baptismal fonts, bootjacks and finger-bowls—an unending variety of hand-produced products. A full record of design indigenous to the United States would take indeterminant time, certainly longer than the project could expect to last. The FAP, though, could make a beginning. Project spokesmen explained that "the groundwork could be done only by such a far-reaching agency as the Federal government." No other organization had the manpower or such far-reaching geographic expanse. The Index project aspired to "map out the ground plan" and complete the preliminary work on the massive inventory "for whomever [sic] may be destined to complete it."[14]

The idea for the Index grew out of discussions between Romona Javitz, head of the New York Public Library's picture collection, and artists who came in to do research. No comprehensive source collection for American design existed and they desperately needed one. Ruth Reeves, an artist and participant in the discussions, became a missionary for the creation of a source collection, and took the problem to Edward Bruce of the Treasury and Frances Pollak, second in command in New York City's early art relief programs. Bruce and Mrs. Pollak immediately saw in the Index proposal a solution for unemployment among commercial artists. Bruce was not otherwise interested in the undertaking; however, Mrs. Pollak, soon to be on the FAP staff, was intrigued by the idea and supported it. Cahill proved immediately receptive. He knew from his museum days and the project to restore Colonial Williamsburg how rich the country was in indigenous design. In early 1936, after the main units of the FAP were in operation, Cahill directed his staff to work out a plan for the Index.[15]

Cahill expected the Index to preserve a rapidly disappearing part of Americana and to inspire contemporary design. He explained to the public that the project would "clarify our complex heritage for the expert" and "recreate the past in human symbols for the average citizen." He admitted that much of the material in the Index would be useful simply as a record, but he also expected to publish a large group of plates for free distribution to any tax-supported repository that would make the portfolios available to manufacturers, artists, and designers. That was not to say he meant to exhume designs and suggest that manufacturers and craftsmen of the 1930s copy them. He believed that somehow machine technology had developed in the United States outside the sphere of craft design. A new examination of America's craft traditions should provide designers with "admirable suggestions." Designers and manufacturers should use Index designs, he contended, "not as things to imitate, but as pollen —or what you please—with which to fertilize contemporary design."[16]

Cahill appointed Ruth Reeves national coordinator of the Index. She guided the work of the state Index projects, preventing duplication of effort, determining the locale of the best examples for recording, and setting up priorities. A small research staff checked the accuracy of the state research and the quality of the renderings. At the outset the national staff decided to limit the Index to practical, popular, and folk art of Americans of European origin. Indian design belonged to the ethnologists, and architecture concerned two other New Deal projects, the Historic American Buildings Survey and the Historic American Merchant-Marine Survey. Regional and local crafts received preference: the workmanship of Germans in colonial Pennsylvania, the Spanish in the Southwest, the Mormons in Utah, the pioneers of the Midwest. Miss Reeves helped state administrators who employed large numbers of artists set up research staffs which sur-

65 Magnus Fossum (Index of American Design, Fla.) recording the design of an 18th-century coverlet

veyed the local material, selected the items for artists to record, and checked their history and authenticity. One or two project supervisors handled the research and selection in states where FAP employment was small.

The Index contained little to make the FAP proud during its first year. Washington had asked local Index artists to abide by principles of "strict objectivity, accurate drawing, clarity of con-struction, exact proportions, and faithful rendering of material, color, and textures so that each Index drawing might stand as surrogate for the object." Commercial artists and rejects from the creative projects often lacked the ability to comply with such challenging standards and local researchers the expertise to se-lect objects worthy of copy. Moreover, the first traveling repre-sentatives from the national office lacked the inclination and perhaps the ability to force improvements. A state FAP supervisor whom Cahill respected looked at the first year's collection of plates and came away impressed with its worthlessness. Drawings of textile designs made in California, Minnesota, Wisconsin, New York City, Delaware, Indiana, and Florida during the year, he reported, "can practically be thrown out." Drawings from Louisiana were "never finished." Artists in Kentucky, Ohio, and Pennsylvania needed help. And the whole unit in the state of Washington was "just ignorant of the result desired." Assistant FAP director Parker told the New York City project that its production was "very irregular" and at times did not justify "the tremendous financial outlay and large personnel."[17]

The evidence of poor work prompted frequent objections from those who argued that the camera offered a better medium for the design project. Cahill and his staff continued to reply that their reasons for drawing the objects instead of photographing them were not merely the result of an unemployment problem. Photographs did not assure accuracy and they lacked the spark of life inherent in the original. A good artist could better render undercuts and high relief, colors, and the subtle interplay of form, color, and texture. "A careful, accurate drawing, in other words," said project spokesmen, "is frequently nearer the truth than a photograph."[18] Instead of changing to photography, Index administrators moved to improve the quality of the drawings.

In spring 1936 Ruth Reeves stepped down and by early 1937 her replacement, the forceful, young C. Adolph Glassgold, was presiding over a thorough reorganization, the most important part of which was in the instruction and supervision of the recording artists. Glassgold stressed a meticulous technique of documentary painting in watercolor worked out by Joseph Lindon Smith on an Egyptian expedition. The technique rapidly spread through New England and New York and, where intricate WPA travel regulations could be manipulated or subverted, experts on the "Egyptologist's technique" taught it in other parts of the country. Other groups devised their own precision methods. Most used watercolors but some Michigan and Pennsylvania artists developed an oil technique and others in New York and New Jersey pricked lines into specially waxed and painted paper to

bring out fine detail. When color was not important artists used pen and pencil, and photography proved best for a number of items. Whatever method the artists used the national office insisted on professional results. Imperfect plates began coming back to the project sites for correction or redrawing. Accompanying them was word that henceforth the Index would be "a scholarly, artistic, workman-like program and that the portfolios of plates eventually to be formed must equal or exceed in quality the finest publications in design ever produced."[19]

By 1938 the FAP proudly included collections of Index plates on an exhibition circuit of leading department stores, Community Art Centers, and interested private groups. It had overcome the worst difficulties not only of incompetence, but also of reluctant state WPA administrators, bored artists, and suspicious owners of the items artists recorded. Problems with the state WPAs existed because of the national demands for local contributions in cash or kind and the states' hesitancy to support a project that sent its products straight to Washington. The problem became acute in 1939 when Congress required 25 percent of the costs from the state. In the end, state pride usually convinced administrators to participate. The WPA administrator of Texas, who regarded the FAP as such a waste of money that he refused to permit other art projects in the state, welcomed an Index unit. Field workers concluded that the Index "fit in perfectly with the desires of the Texan mind because it glorifies and advertises their local cultural development." Eventually 35 states had Index projects. At first the best artists assigned to the Index regarded their task as "dead copying." The new techniques and self-confidence led many to see a place for creativity. Assignments with different subject matter reconciled others. The FAP director of Utah trained some gifted cowboys to record leatherwork and spurs and such. "They were the saddle and spur type," he wrote, who "wouldn't be caught dead doing a textile, but you could certainly keep them out of trouble with something of the Old West." Finally, private collectors and museums needed assurance that they could trust relief artists and that the motive of Index officials was design preservation, not politics. *Antiques* magazine allayed apprehensions through its sympathetic articles as did the frequent speeches of Constance Rourke, the well-known writer who was an "editor" of the Index.[20]

State Index artists eventually sent 22,000 plates to Washington. A small number of duplicates went to state libraries and schools. Pennsylvania mass produced portfolios of German inspired designs, as did southern California of Spanish inspired designs. New Mexico distributed hand-drawn portfolios of Spanish, Colcha, and Indian blanket designs; New York City, cast iron toys and Hadley and Hartford chests; Connecticut, wall decorations; Ohio, folk painting; Utah, Mormon quilt blocks. Most of the hand-drawn duplicates were the work of new trainees on the local projects. Cost-conscious administrators discouraged duplications by skilled workers. Artists in training took four to six weeks to complete each of the 12 watercolors in a New York City portfolio—a labor investment of about $1,175. The school that received it paid a "sponsor contribution" of $25. Besides the cost, WPA headquarters had other reasons for not encouraging hand reproduction. The Index of American Design, Cahill asserted, should be placed in every school, library, museum, and art center in the country, and should be a standard reference work for art schools, craft groups, design studios, manufacturers, art shops, clubs, and organizations of all kinds interested in education and culture.[21] Of course, WPA could distribute the Index only by publishing it, and in 1939 Cahill and his staff confronted that task.

Cahill set high standards for publication of the Index. Faithful color reproduction in the 1930s was difficult, time-consuming, and expensive. Commercial publishing houses balked at the heavy initial outlay a series of Index volumes required. Cahill needed an underwriter to assure prompt publication of the sort he wanted, and for a while it appeared he had found one in the Progressive Education Association. The Association proposed quarterly publication of 20 or 30 plates for an annual subscription of about $15; but as it turned out the Association could not put up the money. Mrs. John D. Rockefeller, Jr., patron of the Williamsburg restoration, was greatly interested in the kind of Americana represented by the Index and she could well afford to back the publication. Cahill asked his close acquaintance to risk $20,000; but her conservative politics had already jaundiced her view of government art. "She just wrote back," Cahill reported, "Let the Government do it." Cahill told the house of Little and Ives that he was "dubious of the wisdom" of their proposal to photograph many of the plates and publish the photographs in small books. The company had promised immediate production and national distribution without an underwriter. Nor would the federal administrator entertain the request of publisher J. J. Augustin, Inc. for an exclusive option to publish all Index material in return for the risks of producing the first volumes.[22]

While these discussions were in an early stage, the American Council of Learned Societies granted $1,475 to the American Documentation Institute for the purpose of making colored film strips of the Index. The Institute won Cahill's blessing. The strips, he believed, would publicize the Index and enhance chances for publication. Index officials selected plates for the first 75 strips of 35 frames each on subjects from music boxes to hearth tools. They mimeographed for distribution a list of titles and an invitation to purchase them from the Institute at $1.75 each. The Institute produced no more than three films, all of which Cahill found unsatisfactory. Seemingly the poor fidelity of the Dufay process used by the Institute caused Cahill to stop the work. He wanted the record in Kodachrome, but that would cost about twice the amount the Institute had to spend for the project.[23]

Before 1939 ended, the question of publication became tangled with the question of the ultimate disposition of the original Index plates. When Congress nipped off federal control of the arts projects and fixed state financial responsibility, Archibald MacLeish, the Librarian of Congress, assumed that the projects would wither and that their materials might be dissipated or lost unless they were collected promptly and deposited in the Library of Congress. MacLeish wanted the Index plates for safekeeping and for public use.[24] WPA even approved the Library of Congress's request for money to pay the employees and for accession of materials from Federal One. Although most of the art projects and Index projects did not collapse as expected, MacLeish continued

66 A. L. Davison II (Index of American Design, Pa.), copy of ceramic plate from Montgomery County, Pennsylvania

67 *Teddy and the Bear*, early twentieth-century toy bank recorded by the Index of American Design in California

to press for the Index plates on hand and an agreement for future acquisition of those on tour and in the states.

Cahill refused to concede an end of state Index projects, and, indeed, sought to use the Library of Congress to insure their future. Index workers had completed less than one-half of the 50,000 plates the director felt would offer an "adequate picture" of American design. He doubted that the states would continue Index projects if all the output went directly to a depository such as the Library of Congress. Cahill wanted MacLeish to arrange the publication of all designs as WPA made them available and forthwith return the plates to WPA for further exhibition. Then, much later—and after extensive publication—the original plates could be deposited in the Library. The publications and continued exhibitions, Cahill reasoned, would encourage states to press on toward an "adequate" record of designs and encourage sponsors to keep up their contributions.[25]

Cahill's concern, then, was for publishing the plates and continuing the projects; MacLeish's was for collecting the materials. For nearly two years each side repeated its "purpose" and "intent."

One cold day in January 1941 Mrs. Kerr, flanked by Cahill and other ex-Federal One officials, trooped into MacLeish's office to thresh out the future between the Library of Congress and the WPA. After all the polite exchanges, the relief administrators came away believing the WPA unit in the Library of Congress would receive selected Index plates on temporary loan and thoroughly research and edit background material for them "looking toward publication and eventual repository of the original plates in the Library of Congress." MacLeish came away with a different understanding. He denied that the purpose of WPA employees in the Library of Congress was to publish the Index. "It cannot be stated too emphatically," the Librarian shot back when he learned WPA's interpretation of the meeting, "that the prime purpose of the WPA project in the Library of Congress is to secure the products of the WPA arts projects, to add them to the collections of the Library for the use of the people of the United States, and that publication, however earnestly desired and eagerly sought, is incidental to that prime purpose."[26] With that blunt statement MacLeish wrecked his chances. He continued to appeal, but Cahill insisted the plates were more useful on exhibition than languishing unpublished in the Library of Congress. If MacLeish got the Index, Mrs. Kerr believed, he would "forget" all past WPA services, ignore Cahill completely, and move on to some other "urgent demand." "The gentleman," she assessed the situation for her own superiors, "has a bad case of the 'gimmees.' "[27] In their zeal to publish the Index Mrs. Kerr and Cahill next tried a scheme involving the President himself.

In autumn 1941, while the nation slipped toward war, a well-publicized exhibition of Index plates opened in the museum of the year-old Franklin D. Roosevelt Library at Hyde Park, New York. Mrs. Kerr and Cahill took advantage of the President's attention to propose that the library sponsor Index publications. They felt the Library's name would lend "special distinction . . . insure the success of the effort," and thereby enable them to assemble a wealthy committee to underwrite nonprofit publication. In a flattering prospectus Mrs. Kerr wrote for the President, she suggested that history would link his name with Thomas Jefferson "as one who has exerted a profound influence upon the art and culture" of the country. It was fitting that the Index, "documents representative of the contribution to the peaceful arts of the home and community," be associated with the Roosevelt Library.[28]

Roosevelt did not reject the proposition out of hand, but preferred that WPA investigate sponsorship by the Library of Congress or the Archivist of the United States. The Archivist, the harassed chief executive scrawled to an adviser, "could have the work done and published through the FDR Library which is under him anyway." Before WPA responded, the war broke out. The publication project was among the first casualties. Anticipating difficulty in securing copper plates and paper, WPA postponed the multivolume Index for the duration.[29]

War meant an end to state Index projects and new concern for the destiny of the completed plates. The Library of Congress again promised "to give serious consideration to the possibility of full color publication of a significant portion of the product of the Index" should it become Library property. Now, however, the Library of Congress found itself vying with the New York Metropolitan Museum of Art for WPA favors. Vice-director of the Metropolitan Horace H. F. Jayne got on with Mrs. Kerr better than did MacLeish. He presented a detailed program the Metropolitan would undertake in return for the Index. For this "extraordinary corpus of material," as Jayne was wont to call it, the Metropolitan would store and continue to organize the mass of material, make it available to the public, exhibit it in New York and on the museum circuit, and develop a publication, filmstrip, and slide program. Mrs. Kerr, applauded by Cahill, offered the Index on long-term loan. Metropolitan director Francis Henry Taylor lightly protested that it should be a permanent allocation, but on May 5, 1942 Jayne and Mrs. Kerr signed the loan papers.[30]

For a year the Metropolitan faithfully kept its agreement. The museum's Index Study Room received artists and designers, its exhibition staff arranged displays and 12 out-of-town showings, its publications division printed a portfolio of "Folk Art of Rural Pennsylvania" and two small "picture books," one of patriotic emblems and insignia and one of nineteenth-century house interiors. However, when Roosevelt dictated the end of WPA and ordered its goods and chattel divided, government lawyers ruled that some federal agency must receive title to the federally owned Index.

To prevent the Library of Congress from acquiring the Index, Cahill—for reasons rooted in the clash of personalities as well as the conviction that the Library did not "handle . . . art very well"—asked Harry Hopkins to intervene. With Hopkins arguing that the FAP had created the Index and therefore the FAP should be permitted to dispose of it, arrangements began for the transferal of ownership to the National Gallery of Art. MacLeish dutifully acceded. He wrote to General Philip B. Fleming, the officer who presided over WPA's dismantlement, that "the claims of the National Gallery are, perhaps, more immediate and direct than those of the Library of Congress, since the Index is . . . essentially museum material." In May 1943, Fleming offered the National Gallery title to the Index and the Metropolitan a five-year loan of the material. Metropolitan director Taylor did not want to invest further museum resources in the collection if the museum never could own it. Taylor asked the National Gallery to take the collection off his hands in September.[31] Eventually the National Gallery opened a basement room for artists and designers who wanted to use the Index. Occasionally the Gallery exhibited a few of the plates, but, except on postcards for the souvenir shop, it never published the plates as Cahill had hoped.

Perhaps from the perspective of the postwar world the plates were unworthy of publication. Unfortunately only a part of the art "establishment" was in a position to make that judgment since so few knew about the accessibility of the Index and fewer had examined it. If for no other reason than its size, consumption of man hours, and cost, the Index deserved review by the wider audience that only publications reached. Possibly the Library of Congress would have tried harder; it could hardly have done worse.

The broad purpose of the Index of American Design was the same as that of the Community Art Center program. Project directors had conceived both as devices to use the diverse skills of the unemployed and to provide alternative work to the creative art projects. Directors also intended both to integrate art with the workaday world and to affect American life after WPA ended. In a sense the art centers had a better chance because they reached more people.

Thomas C. Parker, who spent most of his time taking in and sending out the FAP's bureaucratic laundry, was particularly eloquent in explaining the Community Art Centers. When he had a chance to philosophize, as before the conventions of the American Federation of Art or American Library Association, he poured out ideas and generalities with the same self-assurance that characterized his handling of nit-picking project details.

Before industrialization, Parker asserted, Americans shared and understood art. The pioneers possessed and appreciated a feeling for rhythm, design, and color; and during the transcendental era of the mid-nineteenth century the forefathers praised values that had no relation to material things. When America shortly began amazing the world with its inventive and business genius, the values of art were lost in the midst of national pride in physical achievement. At the same time the novelty of machinemade goods weakened the desire for good form. Industrial power prostituted and patronized some toadying artists, but most

native talent languished. "We had not lost our culture; we had merely forgotten it," affirmed assistant director Parker. The FAP then "realized its responsibilities in helping to integrate a culture that is potentially strong and healthy, but which has been subjected to too many diverting influences." His culminating point was that the FAP had devoted itself "to returning art to the people—to all the people." FAP art centers would correct the unequal distribution of cultural advantage, and through its workshops, exhibitions, and other activities correct the condition which had left "art a stranger in thousands of communities."[32]

Although Parker declined to mention it within hearing of artists, the FAP's obligation to employ artists on relief, and its judgment that most in the far hinterlands were incapable of unsupervised creative work—though competent to direct educational and recreational work—also dictated creation of Community Art Centers. With other audiences FAP administrators took the approach that the tools and techniques of industrialism had thinned and impoverished community life. They invoked the findings of unnamed "leaders of social thinking" that America's greatest need was "awakened social consciousness and a method of bridging the gap between doing and thinking, between theory and practice, in education and creative activity." Popularizing the community center idea was one step toward filling the need, and it seemed a "logical and appropriate" project for WPA.[33]

The art centers provided frequent exhibitions of local and national art, free lectures and films, free classes, free workshops, free meetingrooms for clubs, political rallies, and cultural events. Most important, said champions of the centers, they offered a new "opportunity to share in the experience of art." The centers' most optimistic friends believed they could teach the entire community to discriminate between the shoddy and the authentic and, in time, become as indispensable as the public library. And by placing most of the centers in the South and West, areas with a paucity of art experience, the FAP hoped to take its message of art in daily life "to millions instead of mere thousands in our ten or twelve largest cities."[34]

From the opening of the first center in Raleigh in December 1935, the FAP assumed that it was helping communities start permanent institutions of their own. "We are starting a civic proj-

68 Costume design class at the Walker Art Center, Minneapolis, operated by the FAP

ect with federal aid, we are not starting a federal project with civic aid," Parker reminded center organizers. WPA supplied the staff, the traveling exhibitions, and some of the equipment. A sponsoring group in the community donated the building or paid the rent and utilities and helped plan the program. The FAP refused to accept city governments as the sole local collaborator. For if it did, the FAP feared it might find itself pleading for funds before the city councils, and residents would see the centers as one more WPA project imposed upon them. Working through civic committees with a financial stake in the enterprise assured interest. Civic committees could also be expected to handle the publicity and, in case of any trouble, share in the responsibility. However, if the centers were to enjoy stability and perhaps become permanent, they needed some commitment from city government. Most sponsoring committees appealed for local

tax funds—with noteworthy success considering the depression strains on city coffers and the city councils' inability to control the way the centers spent the money. Raleigh wrote $50 a month into the city budget for its center; Jacksonville appropriated $2,000 in the first two years; Miami, whose mayor told Cahill he was tired of bathing beauties and gambling and wanted something more for the city, found $500 to equip a new gallery; Laramie, Price (Utah), Gold Beach (Oregon), and practically every town with an art center cared enough or felt sufficient pressure to contribute something.[35]

Getting and keeping a community's attention was as important as getting some of its money. The FAP asked each community to find an unimposing building in the central downtown. The center needed quarters that were easily accessible, inviting to working people, and conducive to informality. The center needed to stay open until at least 9:00 p.m. to insure maximum use. Parker warned art center directors against turning the centers into dry lecture halls and devoting too much attention to past masters, since such activity frequently resulted in "a rather deprecatory attitude toward contemporary art and possibly a drying-up of creative resources rather than a stimulation of them." In each center the director's job, as Washington administrators saw it, was to adapt himself to the community's needs, not to impose art standards on the community. A director in Montana, who was accurate but singularly lacking in cleverness, recalled: "We were there to hang the picture; if the public wanted to hang the painter that was up to the public."[36]

Twenty-five southern and western towns and cities had art centers within a year after the first center opened in Raleigh. Two years after the beginning, 47 communities supported art centers. Bringing together sponsoring committees with money and "a very difficult time finding the right kind of people for the community centers" explained this "rather slow" progress, Cahill wrote. Though two or three good people could make the project and the rest could be trained, some states where the centers were most numerous had never had a gallery where continuous exhibitions were shown, and they did not have two or three good people. FAP looked to the concentration of artists and teachers

69 Art Center, Melrose, New Mexico

in New York City to augment center staffs and to improve technical standards. In 1938 and 1939 the New York City FAP permitted 50 or more artists to leave the city for work in distant centers. The Chicago project released about half a dozen for the work. Transfer of each artist usually required piles of paper and hours of argument because state WPA chiefs chafed at putting another state's reliefer on their rolls. Not many artists wanted to leave the community of like spirits and higher WPA rates for the South and Great Plains. And not all artists who agreed to go were happier for the experience. Several were ordered back to the city. The FAP director in Oklahoma City considered the Manhattan artist sent to the local center "both ignorant and rude." The Negro artist sent to the extension gallery in Greensboro, North Carolina, said the state officials, "found it impossible to adjust himself to the manners and customs of the Southern Negro." Another Negro artist, sent to Raleigh, North Carolina, returned to

New York because of her "unsympathetic spirit toward the South and her unwillingness to mingle with the proper people in the Negro community." Facing the remoteness and provincialism of Melrose, New Mexico, one loan artist refused to fill out daily activity sheets and "regaled the director with profanity" when the latter objected. At the Salem, Oregon, art center the director ordered two New Yorkers back across the continent because of their "very marked lack of cooperation." Whatever the difficulties, the transfers did help the program by enhancing the reputation of existing centers. Most loan artists did commendable work; some were offered directorships of the art centers, and a few made permanent homes in the new locale. Hoping to spread the art center idea along the east coast, a former Guggenheim scholar and other top project artists wheeled exhibition units on trucks through the smaller communities of New York, New Jersey, and Pennsylvania. Then Congress, in the appropriations act of 1939, furloughed all reliefers on the rolls over 18 months, ended federal sponsorship, and returned the loan artists home. Thirty of the 66 art centers temporarily or permanently closed.[37]

The shift of emphasis brought by state administration of the art programs from creative production to service and recreation soon revived the art center movement. Most of the key people returned after their forced leaves as soon as the law allowed, placated the local sponsors and WPA officials, and reopened the centers. WPA workers grew from 400 in 1939 to 725 in 1940, and art centers increased to 82 in June 1940 and finally to 103 in 1941. By that date, communities had contributed over $850,000 in cash and kind and, by WPA count, over 8,000,000 people had visited art centers.[38]

Behind the statistics lay vast differences in local reception, size, and programs. When four art centers opened in New York City in 1937, residents seemed to take the additions in stride. Farther west the possibility of a community center frequently awakened unusual civic spirit and ingenuity. Sponsors of the Sioux City center found a downtown fur merchant willing to donate some basement rooms, convinced electricians, carpenters, and plumbers to join Junior Leaguers and businessmen in remodeling, and with 150 volunteer workers saved $2,000 of the $3,000 in their renovation budget. Volunteers in Salt Lake City fixed up the old Elks Club building with paint and soap and employed expedients learned in Sioux City, such as making the ceilings from bed sheets stitched together and stretched tight to save the price of frosted glass. Utah workers built each of the centers' benches and chairs from about 50 cents worth of scrap lumber and leatherette, and shaded their floor lamps with 18-cent dishpans. The night Governor and Mrs. Henry Blood of Utah led the opening tour, the gallery, said the local newspaper, looked "smart as a new ladies ready-to-wear shop."[39]

In Skiatook, Sapula, and Okmulgee, Oklahoma and Rawlins, Torrington, and Lander, Wyoming and Melrose, Roswell, and Gallup, New Mexico and two score more small cities, modest centers opened with less drama. If they were "average," they devoted 60 to 70 percent of the instruction time to painting, drawing, and pottery and 30 to 40 percent to handicrafts. Small-town directors reported that public interest declined after first enthusiasm, and they discovered that small-town intimacy precipitated an occasional conflict between WPA appointees from out of town and local sponsors. In conservative areas the fact that WPA had anything to do with the centers alienated some potential supporters. Still, the smallest centers seemed closest to the people. About 1/2 percent of the people in cities of 100,000 enrolled in art center courses; 2 percent of the people in cities of 20,000 signed the rosters each month; and the percentage was larger for cities of less than 10,000.[40] Monthly head counts in the smallest communities often exceeded the local population.

Many of the centers had little in common. Between art classes and exhibitions the Miami center scheduled fencing nights, radio nights, sessions to learn mask, marionette, and airplane making, receptions and club meetings, music project rehearsals, and concerts. Some of the more remote centers, in contrast, did little more than exhibit local art and that circulated by the FAP. However, the size of the community or the project did not necessarily measure the richness of the program. The art center in Gold Beach, Oregon, offered the community's 500 citizens an exceptional range of activities. There, enterprising leaders added a

70 The student and his work, Negro extension art center, Jacksonville, Florida

music teacher to the staff from the state's WPA music project. In contrast, the 60 to 70 WPA workers who staffed the large Walker Art Center in Minneapolis restricted their work to traditional exhibitions and classes. And some Southwestern centers mirrored the interest of their archeological society sponsors.[41]

Then there were the Negro art centers. The FAP, like most New Deal agencies, honored local customs on segregation of races. Cahill, having spent his youth in the Indian country of the upper Plains, understood white separatist feelings and never objected. He was grateful that "the best people in the community, very forward-looking and good people" sponsored the Negro centers. The facilities for these centers ranged from the baseball magnate Charles Comiskey's old Victorian house on Chicago's South Side, where 3,000 people followed Mrs. Roosevelt on the first tour through the bright workrooms and galleries, to the one-room, second-class "extension galleries" in North Carolina and Florida. Negro leader A. Philip Randolph watched housewives busy at looms and men laboring over lithograph stones in the Harlem center and wondered if the experiment might not be "the cultural harbinger of a true and brilliant renaissance of the spirit of the Negro people of America." The state director of the Florida FAP approved of the Negro centers too, but as "a behavior corrective, as an instrument of experimental therapeutics."[42]

In 1938 the art editor of *Time* magazine echoed the feeling of most critics in his statement that there was "no fresher news in the world of art than the mushrooming of these Community Art Centers."[43] Friends of art applauded them because they belonged not to the federal government but to the communities they served and because they were designed to be and promised to be permanent. Some did last. When WPA phased out in Minneapolis the reviving income of the predepression benefactor enabled it to again assume responsibility for operating the Walker Art Center. Twenty-five years later this center was internationally renowned for its exhibitions and acquisitions. Sioux City survived the basement rooms with bed sheet ceilings to build, through subscriptions and taxes, an art center which welcomed over 20,000 annual visitors to its three-and-a-half story building. A citizens' committee in Greenville, North Carolina, went before the city council for money when WPA dissolved. The forthcoming appropriations and local contributions kept the center open. Art collections once under WPA center care formed the nucleus of the Mobile Museum, an institution provided for after 1942 by the city, Junior League, and local art and historical societies. The Roswell, New Mexico, Museum and Art Center limped through the war years and blossomed thereafter into a source of community pride with its concert series, Robert Goddard rocket collection, and works of famed nineteenth and twentieth century painters. Sponsors of the Salem, Oregon, center reorganized, bought a mansion in what later became a 100-acre city park, obtained small grants from the city, and perpetuated art in Salem.

In some communities where WPA left no linear descendants lingering interest later spawned public art events. In perhaps the most striking example, the art-conscious citizens of Key West rallied in 1960 to save the condemned, nineteenth century grocery store near the waterfront that had housed the WPA center. At the same time they persuaded the city fathers to sponsor the "rebirth" of the Key West Art Center. Successful merchant-sponsored art exhibits and sales dotted the Great Plains after World War II, a former art center patron reflected, "because the early [WPA] exhibits paved the way for the later activities and helped to make them a part of the whole community's way of life."[44]

Most of the centers dissolved during the war. The 8 centers in Wyoming left no organizational legacy. Nor did the 11 in Oklahoma, nor 13 of the 14 in Florida, nor 4 in Tennessee and Utah. Learning of his community's cultural resources in the depression a quarter century later, a city administrator in the Plains pronounced the sad benediction to the WPA ideal. "I see no evidence," he said surveying the former center site and his community, "of the project ever having been here."[45]

The art centers and other practical art projects realized only partially fulfilled expectations. They did preserve skills that might otherwise have been lost, and they did protect the quality of WPA's creative art projects by providing alternative kinds of work. Whether the art centers, Index of American Design, teaching programs, and smaller projects did much to integrate art with the daily life of the average citizen during the 1930s, and whether they generated forces which affected American life after WPA ended, is perhaps impossible to assess. Successes, if any, are not obvious. Indeed, had these projects not succeeded in maintaining and developing the skills of so many workers, one might question whether they justified the expense. That is, if one were also willing to ignore the mountain boy who walked 14 miles to winter classes in a North Carolina art center, the WPA pick and shovel worker who began a promising art career when he was assigned to the Index of American design project, the housewives and workmen who came to the art centers for "self-improvement," and the unspoken pleasures of countless children upon completing their first painting.

[1] "The WPA Art Program, June 30, 1939-June 12, 1940," typescript, RG69/211.53.

[2] Clippings from *New York World Telegram*, June 8, 1936, *New York Herald Tribune*, July 24, 1936, RG69/DI; State Final Reports: New York.

[3] Benson, "Accomplishments of the WPA Federal Art Project"; *New York Times*, Aug. 14, 1938, Jan. 26, 1941; clipping from *New York Herald Tribune*, March 23, 1936, RG69/DI; speech "The Artist Teaches," na, nd, Cahill Papers.

[4] "The WPA Art Program, June 30, 1939-June 12, 1940"; Progress Report . . . City of New York, Jan. 15, 1936, Supplement C, RG69/FAP; Public Use of Art Committee, "Report of Class Room Experiment," mimeographed, nd, RG69/216.212; New York City WPA Public Information Section Press Release, Nov. 1, 1939, RG69/DI; Mrs. Frances M. Pollak to McMahon, Nov. 20, 1936, Cahill Papers; *New York Times*, Jan. 26, 1941; O'Connor, *Federal Support for the Visual Arts*, 46.

[5] Gilbert Rohde, "The Design Laboratory," *American Magazine of Art*, XXIX (Oct. 1936), 638-43, 686; *New York Times*, Oct. 25, 1936; New York City WPA Department of Information News Release, July 2, 1937, RG69/FAP.

[6] Josiah P. Marvel to Hopkins, Dec. 4, 1936, McMahon to Cahill, Dec. 12, 1936, Marvel to McMahon, Dec. 6, 1936, McMahon to Parker, Dec. 15, 1936, Cahill to Ralph M. Pearson, Jan. 15, 1938, RG69/211.5; William Friedman to McMahon, June 24, 1937, RG69/FAP.

[7] Benson, "Accomplishments of the WPA Federal Art Project"; New York City WPA Public Information Section Press Release, Nov. 1, 1939, RG69/DI; Cahill to Regional Advisers, Jan. 18, 1936, RG69/211.5; Kerr to Earl V. Minderman, Dec. 7, 1940, Cahill Papers.

[8] *Art Front*, II (March 1936), 3; McMahon to Parker, Aug. 18, 1937, RG69/211.5; Benson, "Accomplishments of the WPA Federal Aid Project"; O'Connor, *Federal Support for the Visual Arts*, 46.

[9] Progress Report . . . City of New York, May 1, 1936, RG69/FAP.

[10] Artists of Costume Design unit to Cahill, June 30, 1937, "Costume Illustration and Design Unit of the Federal Art Project," mimeographed, na, 1937, RG69/FAP, petition filed in RG69/651.317.

[11] "The WPA Federal Art Project: A Summary of Activities and Accomplishments," mimeographed, na, nd, RG69/651.3115; Federal Project Number One, New York City, "Quarterly Report . . . March 31, 1937," New York City WPA Federal Art Project Press Release, Oct. 29, 1937, RG69/FAP. In addition the New York City unit prepared and distributed an extensive series of mimeographed booklets, mostly under the heading "Technical Problems of the Artist." In the first 2 years they distributed 24,500 copies of 51 titles.

[12] Progress Report . . . City of New York, July 1, 1936, Parker to Samuel H. Friedman, May 19, 1937, RG69/FAP; WPA in Ohio Press Release, June 17, 1941 in RG69/DI; George G. Thorp to Kerr, May 29, 1940, RG69/651.313; State Final Report: Iowa, Louisiana, Massachusetts, Oregon; Rubenstein, "The Tax Payers' Murals," 60, 61; clippings from *New York World Telegram*, Dec. 26, 1936, *Milwaukee Journal*, Sept. 6, 1936, *Boston Globe*, April 27, 1938, RG69/DI; Federal Art Project, *Federal Art in New England*, 14, 15; Kerr to Earl V. Minderman, Dec. 7, 1940, Cahill Papers.

13 Memorandum, Crafts Function and Criteria, June 25, 1940, Cahill Papers.

14 Holger Cahill, "Introduction," in Erwin O. Christensen, *The Index of American Design* (New York, 1950), ix-xvii; "Typical ten-minute speech for Index of American Design," typescript, na, nd, RG69/211.55.

15 Cahill, "Introduction," in Christensen, *Index of American Design*, ix-xii; "Cahill Reminiscences," 259-61.

16 Cahill to Philip Newell Yountz, March 9, 1936, RG69/211.5; *Index of American Design Manual* (Washington, 1938), mimeographed; typed press release, nd, Benson Papers.

17 Parker to McMahon, Dec. 24, 1936, Jan. 5, 1937, Richard C. Morrison to Parker, Aug. 12, 1938, RG69/211.5; C. Adolph Glassgold to Parker (draft memorandum) nd, Cahill Papers.

18 Cahill, "Introduction," in Christensen, *Index of American Design*, xiv; "Typical ten-minute speech for Index of American Design."

19 Cahill, "Introduction," in Christensen, *Index of American Design*, xii, xiv; Federal Art Project, *Federal Art in New England*, 12; Glassgold to Mrs. Eve Alsman Fuller, Dec. 28, 1936, Cahill Papers.

20 Cahill, "Introduction," in Christensen, *Index of American Design*, xiii; Field Trip Report by Richard C. Morrison, Nov. 1938, RG69/211.5.

21 Field Trip Report by Benjamin Knotts, Aug. 3, 1941, RG69/211.5; Prospectus for the Publication of the Index of American Design of the WPA Art Program, typescript, in RG69/211.55. Before Index policy was well-established, artists in New York City compiled a record of city dwellings and other buildings from 1760 to 1835. When in 1938 the architectural renderings, drawings, and photographs went to Columbia University on permanent loan, the librarian of the architectural library called the collection "the most complete and accurate record . . . of that period in existence." See WPA Department of Information Press Release, Aug. 22, 1938, RG69/DI.

22 Cahill to Woodward, Dec. 17, 1938, Cahill to M. Roane, Jan. 11, 1941, C. Adolph Glassgold to Samuel J. Wallace, Aug. 25, 1939, RG69/211.55; "Cahill Reminiscences," 370.

23 Lawrence Morris to Kerr, April 24, 1939, Cahill to Archibald MacLeish, Oct. 31, 1940, RG69/211.55.

24 MacLeish to Kerr, Dec. 20, 1940, RG69/211.55.

25 Draft of confidential memorandum, Cahill to Paul Edwards, Nov. 13, 1940, Cahill Papers.

26 Cahill and Paul Edwards to Kerr, Jan. 22, 1941, MacLeish to Kerr, Feb. 5, 1941, RG69/211.55.

27 Kerr to Howard O. Hunter, June 4, 1941, RG69/211.5.

28 Walter M. Kiplinger to Kerr, Sept. 24, 1941, Kerr to Mrs. Franklin D. Roosevelt, Oct. 4, 1941, Prospectus for the Publication of the *Index of American Design* of the WPA Art Program, RG69/211.55.

29 Roosevelt to Kerr, Nov. 22, 1941, RG69/211.55; Roosevelt to Harold D. Smith, Nov. 22, 1941, Smith to Roosevelt, April 24, 1942, AAA Reel NDA/HP4.

30 Luther H. Evans to Kerr, Feb. 10, 1942, RG69/211.155; Horace H. F. Jayne to Cahill, March 13, 1942, Jayne to Kerr, March 23, 1942, Cahill to Mildred T. Law, April 6, 1943, RG69/211.154.

31 MacLeish to Philip B. Fleming, April 23, 1943, Fleming to Trustees of National Gallery of Art, May 13, 1943, transcript of telephone conversation between David Finley and Fleming, Sept. 13, 1943, RG69/211.155; "Cahill Reminiscences," 526.

32 "Development of Community Art Centers," speech by Parker before 30th Annual Convention of the American Federation of Art, May 19, 1939, copy in RG69/211.5; typed speech by Parker, nd, Benson Papers.

33 "Concerning the Development of Community Art Centers," speech by Parker before convention of American Library Association, June 14, 1938, Cahill Papers.

34 "Federal Sponsored Community Art Centers" (Washington, 1937), mimeographed.

35 Parker to Nelson H. Partridge, May 12, 1937, RG69/651.315; Parker to Woodward, Sept. 2, 1937, RG69/211.5.

36 Cahill, *New Horizons in American Art*, 21-22; State Final Report: Montana; Parker to Morrison, Oct. 22, 1937, RG69/211.5.

37 "A Brief Summary of the Federal Art Project: State of Wyoming," mimeographed. Also see notebook on loan artists, Cahill Papers; Cahill to Pearson, Jan. 15, 1938, Parker to Robert Armstrong Andrews, April 4, 1939, RG69/311.5; Woodward to Edwards, April 9, 1938, RG69/FAP; "The WPA Art Program, June 30, 1939-June 12, 1940"; clipping from *Philadelphia Record*, May 21, 1939, RG69/DI; *New York Times*, Sept. 14, 1938.

38 "The WPA Art Program, June 30, 1939-June 12, 1940"; Cahill, "Record of Program Operation and Accomplishment," 10; *American Art Annual*, xxxv (1941), 16 (list of art centers, pp. 753-54). The $850,000 contributed by communities was not all cash. Much of it was in the form of quarters and services donated to the centers.

39 Jean B. Kern, "WPA Project Ten Years Later," *Palimpsest*, xxx (Jan. 1949), 16-17; clippings from *Sioux City Journal*, Feb. 20, 1938, Salt Lake City *Deseret News*, Nov. 26, 1938, *Salt Lake City Tribune*, Nov. 26, 1938, RG69/DI.

40 See State Final Report: West Virginia; Daniel S. Defenbacher to George G. Thorpe, Jan. 4, 1939, RG69/651.315.

41 Defenbacher to Parker, Oct. 25, 1938, Field Trip Report by Julius Davidson, Dec. 19, 1939, RG69/FAP; clippings from *Miami Herald*, April 25, 1937, RG69/DI. Offerings of most of the centers are listed in the "Art Schools" section of the *American Art Annual*, vols. xxxii-xxxv.

42 "Cahill Reminiscences," 377; Field Trip Report by Cahill, May 13, 1941, RG69/211.5; William H. Brumett to Anna L. Week, May 21, 1940, RG69/651.3159; State Final Report: Florida; *Newsweek*, xvii (May 19, 1941), 67; clipping from *New York Herald Tribune*, Dec. 21, 1937, RG69/DI.

43 *Time*, xxxii (Sept. 5, 1938), 35.

44 Noel Kaho (Claremore, Okla.) to author, June 1967.

45 Jack Bradshaw (Skiatook, Okla.) to author, June 1967.

9

Relief Art on the Defense, 1938 — 1943

Between 1938 and the demise of the WPA art project in 1943 a series of events threatened project morale and stability, weakened Cahill's control, and undermined much of the public support for federal subsidies. Most of these destructive events resulted not from the FAP's actions, but from its associations. Beginning with the defection of Harry Hopkins and takeover of the cultural projects by more cautious officials, FAP fortunes began to decline. Those who demanded long-range government support to the arts urged upon Congress an ill-timed plan to make Federal One permanent. Congress rejected the scheme overwhelmingly and in the process demeaned Federal One, making WPA officials more skittish. Then the House Committee on Un-American Activities focused on radicalism in two of the components of Federal One, the theater and writers projects. While the Committee found little that was "un-American" in the FAP, Congress and the public inclined to the belief that all the parts of Federal One were guilty almost equally. This mood carried over to the House Committee on Appropriations. Testy anti-New Deal congressmen again publicized the alleged sins of federal actors and writers, then abolished the theater project and severely weakened federal control over the other cultural programs. Artists on relief after 1939 fared in accordance with the competence of the state officials who fell heir to control of the projects. When the United States soon began to prepare for the possibility of war,

71 Jack Markow, cartoon (from *12 Cartoons Defending WPA by Members of the American Artists Congress*, New York, 1939)

already abbreviated programs for the creative arts gave way to service to defense agencies. By the time WPA ended in 1943 the art project as conceived in 1935 had ceased to exist.

By 1938 Harry Hopkins had changed. The relief administrator who had come to Washington in 1933 as the stereotype of the New Deal idealist and crusading social worker nurtured presidential ambitions of his own. In addition, personal reverses dampened his enthusiasm for WPA. The death of his wife and his own illness kept him away from Washington during the first months of 1938. Between his return to the capital in April and his resignation from WPA in December, he devoted his energies to the off-year elections and the President's attempt to purge Congress of obstructionists. Hopkins's political activities, whether for his own or Roosevelt's greater glory, increased congressional hostility toward the WPA. A special Senate committee chaired by Senator Morris Sheppard of Texas concluded that there had been in several states, and in many forms, unjustifiable political activity in the WPA program. Senator Josiah W. Bailey of North Carolina was more emphatic. "They propose to use the money which we appropriate for the purpose of eliminating us," Bailey ranted at his Senate colleagues. "The idea of my state having to go to Harry Hopkins and ask him for money! The idea of my voting money for him and the other conspirators!"[1] What legislator who felt WPA imperiled his career would not delight in spotlighting WPA inefficiencies, malpractices, and activities which many voters would consider a waste of money and energy?

The more Hopkins practiced politics the more he lost interest in the details of the relief program. In November, Roosevelt upbraided him for neglecting the important detail of the rate of WPA spending. The President in October had told Hopkins's assistant, Aubrey Williams, to adjust WPA employment to available funds. Williams, Roosevelt charged, "went right ahead and kept on adding to his rolls." Dreading the prospect of declaring another emergency and asking for another deficiency appropriation from Congress, Roosevelt wrote sharply to Hopkins: "the money must last. . . . That is that!" The embarrassment of employing more people than could be paid, Roosevelt told his assistant Marvin McIntyre, was "Williams' fault and indirectly

Harry's because he should have checked."[2] Hopkins's failure to check—or lead or defend individual projects—meant increased responsibility for the more cautious assistant WPA administrators. At the same time his political activities provoked unprecedented criticism of the entire work program.

At that moment, ironically when the cultural projects were vulnerable as never before, cultural workers and friends of the arts attempted to make them permanent. Representative William I. Sirovich of New York was first to hold hearings on the question of creating a cabinet level Department of Science, Art, and Literature. Sirovich, chairman of the House Committee on Patents, proposed to bring into the department the Patent Office, the Copyright Office, the Bureau of Standards, the Commission of Fine Arts, the Office of Education, the Bureau of Mines, and the Weather Bureau, and to assign to the Department the cultural objectives of Federal One. Sirovich was slow and vague in working out the mechanics for permanent patronage. Nonetheless, his idea was met with enthusiasm from younger, lesser known, and politically liberal members of the artistic community, tolerance from the White House, and opposition from cultural elitists. Hearings before the Committee on Patents in 1935 had proved inconclusive and attracted little public notice. However, when Sirovich held further hearings in February 1938, Congress and the public showed more interest.[3]

Sirovich's plan received consideration by virtue of its constant comparison with the controversial legislation introduced by Representative John M. Coffee of Washington and Senator Claude Pepper of Florida in January 1938. The Coffee-Pepper bill (a title quickly noted by media pundits) proposed an independent Bureau of Fine Arts to assume "all functions, powers, and duties exercised by the WPA" in the arts. The legislation called for transfer of all "competent" WPA cultural workers to the new agency without interruption of time or salary and employment of such additional artists—regardless of relief status and at trade union wages—as funds permitted. In short, Federal One would become the nucleus of the Bureau of Fine Arts. The bill called for the largest organizations in each of the arts to submit names from which the President would choose a commissioner. From other names submitted by the arts workers' organizations the commissioner would choose regional committees to determine eligibility, competence, and assignments. The plan gave arts trade unions, since they had the largest memberships, clear advantage if not control over the Bureau.[4]

The congressmen who introduced the bills proceeded from the assumption that cultural enlightenment was a primary function of democratic government and that the WPA effort, because of its temporary nature, was "too feeble, and quasi-impotent." Coffee saw a parallel between the tasks of eradication of illiteracy and that of bringing culture to the people in terms understandable to the people, and for him the campaign for a permanent art program was comparable in almost exact degree to the free public school movement of the previous century. Sirovich argued that America had come of age culturally largely through WPA efforts and that American culture had to be protected by the national government. Failure to do so, he said, would "make the creative genius the stepchild of the nation." Pepper, championing the right of Americans to leisure and recreation, saw inequity in the loneliness and limited opportunities for recreation in rural communities. The Bureau of Fine Arts, he told his constituents, would give people who otherwise could not afford it every possible opportunity to enjoy art, music, and cultural advantages which presently only the rich or those living in cities were able to enjoy.[5]

These sympathetic congressmen did not anticipate the passions that their proposals generated. They had the full support of the unions in drafting the legislation and the endorsement of most of the stars of the arts. They could read Holger Cahill's public statement that, without government projects, art in the United States virtually had no place to go. They knew about Hopkins's belief that government was "in the subsidy of arts once and for all time."[6] But when testimony on the bills began, politicians and a small-but-vociferous segment of the public violently objected to the proposed mechanism for diffusing culture among the people.

The issue to artists and professional critics was not so much the desirability of a department or bureau for the arts. To them the important questions were the aesthetic creed, the attitude to-

151

ward "unionism," and the quality standards the new agency might adopt. The supporters of the bill seemed to envision awakening and stimulating latent folk arts when they spoke of cultural development. So-called great works, they argued in terms long used by WPA, would emerge from the mass of useful production. Jerome Klein, art editor for the *New York Post*, spoke for Coffee-Pepper bill supporters in his column. Klein insisted the WPA cultural projects were "the most positive creative force on the American art horizon." It made sense that permanence, which would enable long-range planning, better geographic distribution, and raise morale, could only improve them. Burgess Meredith, president of Actors Equity, denied that the Coffee-Pepper bill was an attempt by labor unions to control art. If, because of their larger membership, unions submitted the names from which administrators were chosen, it meant only that more artists would be consulted. Other supporters argued that art was better served by organizations representing artists' views than by the alternative of a Washington autocrat or a society woman who prided herself on being a patron of the arts.[7]

Opponents of the bill predicted that the songs, pictures, and plays produced by the new agency would be so inferior as to degrade the arts. The composer and conductor Walter Damrosch, who led the opposition, declared that he would "fight to the death" against the Coffee-Pepper idea because art was "something so sacred." The views of Damrosch and his allies were too aristocratic to ever permit them to endorse broad production, stimulation of folk talents, and ultimate judgment of quality by posterity. They were certain of their ability to distinguish good art from bad, and certain in their belief that the association of unions and WPA workers with the proposed bureau would result in cultivation of the arts by those least competent to do the cultivating. Using the American Federation of Musicians as a case in point, Damrosch judged that only 2,000 of the 15,000 members were really good musicians. Forbes Watson, in the Treasury's Section of Fine Arts, supported Damrosch with the statement that the largest organizations of artists had always been those which encouraged and bowed to the will of the greatest number of mediocrities. Union influence, he and other elitists insisted,

would put creative art on the basis of a trade product, and employment of WPA workers would put the emphasis on relief rather than furthering art in its highest forms. The Fine Arts Federation of New York, the affiliation of organizations which opposed the PWAP in 1933, released a brief in support of Damrosch's position charging that the Coffee-Pepper bill, short of creating a true Bureau of Fine Arts, attempted to legislate a "Bureau of Labor in the Arts and for Permanent Relief to Artists."[8]

The hearings conducted by Pepper and Sirovich in February and March 1938 intensified the wrangling over method if not principle. Damrosch began writing his own version of a fine arts bill, one which put control in the hands of 11 trustees—unpaid and presidentially appointed—in the manner of museum and orchestra boards. Other elitists inveighed against the American "obsession of quantity" which they saw in the WPA philosophy and called for high quality standards. Upset over the lack of a rigid standard of craftsmanship in the proposal, Edward Bruce wrote Secretary of the Treasury Morgenthau: "I hope the Treasury is taking the necessary steps to make sure that the Coffee-Pepper bill won't go through." At the same time Hopkins told reporters at his Florida retreat that "we can develop greater things with—call it a government subsidy if you like—than have ever been done before." Roosevelt, more reserved, sent word that he was conscious of the pressing nature of the problem of the arts in America but that he did not wish to comment on specific proposals. Reflecting the timidity in top WPA ranks, Ellen Woodward lectured the directors of Federal One on loyalty, cooperation, and standing together before parading them before the Sirovich and Pepper committees. They took the safe position that "as executives of a government department it would be unwise . . . to discuss pending legislation."[9]

The project administrators confined themselves to discussing WPA achievements at a time when Federal One needed to lay bare its problems and to assess its potential should it become permanent and no longer have to accept employment of reliefers as its first purpose. Cahill's personal view was that the proceedings were "most foolish and annoying." He resented the time-consuming chore of preparing testimony and regretted that Hopkins was out of town and did not keep WPA completely out of the hearings. Cahill and the other directors, nonetheless, adhered to the WPA line of strict neutrality. The absence of a WPA "position" and the strong stands taken by the unions produced a mixed public reaction, as illustrated by balloting at a mass meeting of artists at the Cleveland School of Art. The artists favored a Board of Fine Arts by 13 to 1, but opposed using the WPA arts projects as its basis by 2 to 1. They voted 10 to 1 in favor of giving practicing artists the right to nominate officers for the bureau, but rejected the Coffee-Pepper mechanics for doing it by 9 to 1.[10]

Electioneering and bickering over form threatened to kill any chance of congressional action. Pepper ended hearings on March 2 with the publicity rich appearance of screen star Lillian Gish and was in Pensacola making his first speech of the 1938 campaign on March 10. Since the House did not hold hearings on the Coffee-Pepper bill, strategists planned to have the Senate act and then lay the matter before the House. The scheme failed because Pepper was too infrequently in Washington to guide the bill through committee and onto the floor.

Sirovich, whose idea of a Department of Art, Science, and Literature was too nebulous to attract the support of arts lobbyists, now worked out a third scheme with Coffee and Pepper and supporting organizations. It would create a permanent Bureau of Fine Arts in the Interior Department managed by a presidentially appointed director and five presidentially appointed assistant directors, all supervised by the Secretary of the Interior and confirmed by the Senate. At his discretion the President might transfer WPA activities to the Bureau, but WPA artists thus transferred would be "subject to the approval of the Director of the Bureau as to their qualifications."[11] The revision allayed the fears of many former opponents, retained the enthusiastic support of the unions, and reconciled the supporters who had divided over the question of whether the amorphous Sirovich plan or more developed Coffee-Pepper bill offered the best chance of approval. The Committee on Patents hurriedly reported the bill and Sirovich managed to get it on the House calendar for June 15, the day before Congress adjourned for the summer. It was too late.

Newspaper criticism of the arts bills, especially the Coffee-Pepper bill, had begun in the art columns in early February and quickly spread to the editorial pages. Editors who barely tolerated or opposed the New Deal version of the welfare state regarded the WPA in general and the arts projects in particular as boondoggling. If the most nonutilitarian part of an inefficient program became permanent, what after that? Perpetuating Federal One through a Bureau of Fine Arts demonstrated, to those who wanted to believe the axiom, that bureaus never die. As the hearings progressed editors across the country began to assess the worth of Federal One—usually in keeping with their political convictions.

Such diverse and scattered papers as the *Miami Herald*, the *Baltimore Morning Sun*, the *Chicago Tribune* and the *Kansas City Star* conceded that the emergency might justify temporary WPA activity in the arts, but none of them wanted permanent cultural projects. The *Baltimore Morning Sun* saw the scheme as too different from predepression precedents. The *Miami Herald* failed to see how the "untrammeled and inquiring spirit which alone makes art vital in a democracy" could come from "so-called artists" of the WPA "who have outlived their usefulness." The *Kansas City Star* envisioned political interference and resulting paralysis in the arts. The *Chicago Tribune* believed the worst artists had the most political influence and would inflict injury on public taste while "real artists" struggled against the advantages of "the subsidized unfit."[12]

Editors of other papers suddenly discovered WPA's inferior quality and inherent political entanglements. The editor of the *Portland Oregonian* opposed a bureau based on WPA projects whose "whole output could be destroyed without irreparable loss." And the editor of the *Manchester* (New Hampshire) *Union* declined to support any attempt to renew appropriations for art from which the public received, in the graphic arts, "square miles of uninspired canvases and acres of walls that would look better without 'mural' adornment." Editors who shared Booth Tarkington's view that the "least possible amount of government is the happiest and most progressive" widely publicized the Hoosier writer's quip that government patronage meant simply that "somebody's cousin gets to do the murals in the courthouse." The whole arts proposition, the *Indianapolis Star* neatly summed up, was an "attempted Treasury raid," by people who would "put the cultural arts in a strait jacket." Such an attitude dominated Congress on the day the arts bill came up for consideration.[13]

A combination of forces molded the congressional reception. Conceding that some members of Congress formed opinions on the merits of the bill, others undoubtedly voted under influence of the editorial opposition, the increasing militancy of the conservative coalition toward New Deal creations, a modicum of congressional anti-intellectualism, the biennial cut-out-the-frills syndrome of House candidates for reelection, and the aftertaste of a recent clash between some conservative senators and the Federal Theatre Project. The latter event resulted from the theater project's play *One Third of A Nation*, an indictment of slum life in a well-received example of the project's attempt to make theater relevant to contemporary life. Actors who played Senators Harry Byrd, Millard Tydings, and Charles O. Andrews took their lines directly from the *Congressional Record*, but the real Senators felt held up to "opprobrium" when their reserved statements on a federal housing bill came after scenes of slum misery. Exuding sarcasm and ridicule Senator Bailey explained in the Senate chamber that WPA would confer immortality on the assembly because "down yonder at the WPA there are some playwrights who are putting us down in books . . . to become part of the permanent literature of the ages." Then in another tone he asked: "Whoever thought of the Federal Government getting into anything like that?" Georgia's conservative Democrat, Senator Richard B. Russell, echoed this question in the Appropriations Committee. He lectured Aubrey Williams that using Treasury money to exalt or minimize public figures set a very dangerous precedent. Republican Senator John G. Townsend of Delaware added that plays produced with tax funds ought to be "very carefully censored" to avoid ridiculing anyone. No one could possibly reconcile that view with theater project director Hallie Flanagan's idea of "relevant theatre," which included giving "apoplexy to people who consider it radical for a government-sponsored theatre to produce plays on subjects vitally concerning the governed."[14]

Sirovich took the floor of the House unprepared for the opposition he encountered. He asked his colleagues to join with "every civilized nation" in officially cultivating the arts, to remember that the glory of Greece was art not industry and to rest assured the bureau would give new importance to "all the beautiful things that go to ennoble mankind." He began to explain that the arts could never be regimented since art symbolized man's soul, which is inviolable. Then, before he could continue, a red-faced critic in the gallery shouted down, "Why can't they be regimented?"

The breech of House decorum signaled a new level of discussion. Noting the list of occupations the Bureau might subsidize, Representative Allen T. Treadway demanded to know "just what 'puppeteers' may be." "A man who raises puppies," shot back Representative Harold Knutson. The latter, demonstrating his skill with the double entendre, wondered why provision had not been made for New Deal acrobats. Representative Noah M. Mason, demonstrating his also, wanted to know "why they left out milkers." These amateur wits sat back when Representative Dewey Short, a former preacher from the Missouri Ozarks, took the floor. After testing the mood of the House with sarcastic remarks about not overburdening "Honest Harold" Ickes with more bureaus, Short assured his colleagues that if offered one of the Bureau's $7,000-a-year administrative jobs, "I would tender my resignation from this House today in order to take over the particular division that deals with dances and the allied arts." As the congressman finished the sentence, he began burlesquing a toe dance in the aisle. Amid howls of laughter he drove home his point—the proposal was frivolous in the face of the material needs of 12,000,000 unemployed. To emphasize its frivolity and inappropriateness, Short punctuated his speech with rises on his toes, arms spread in mimicry of a ballet dancer's gestures. Every grade school graduate knew, he continued, that good art emerged from suffering artists, while "subsidized art is no art at all." More important, the Missourian failed to see how anybody could "feel comfortable or enjoy listening to the strains of Mendelssohn with the seat of his pants out." Now the House applauded while it laughed. Two or three other congressmen tried to sustain the hilarity with less success, and shortly someone suggested they give the bill "at least a decent burial." Sirovich, white-faced, perspiring, and so confused that he voted both for and against the tabling of his measure, managed to express his regret that the "Nation has been ridiculed today" before the House set aside the bill by a vote of 195 to 35.[15] The congressional sponsors of the legislation and the WPA had been humiliated, and WPA, understandably enough, was pleased that no similar legislation again reached the floor of Congress.

Leaders of the arts projects gasped incredulously when the next month charges by Representative J. Parnell Thomas presaged a second blow from Congress—this time through the legislature's investigatory powers. Thomas branded the theater project and the writers project "a hotbed for Communists" and "one more link in the vast and unparalleled New Deal propaganda machine." The New Jersey Republican, a member of the newly created House Committee on Un-American Activities, promised to haul up the subversives for full exposure.[16] Thus began a new ordeal for all the components of Federal One.

Thomas's idea appealed to the committee chairman, Texas Democrat Martin Dies. A smooth-featured, boyish, cigar-smoking populist from Orange County, Texas, Dies had sounded the tocsin to his congressional career the day after he took his seat in 1931 by introducing a bill to suspend immigration to the United States for five years. He represented a district that was 90 percent Anglo-Saxon, "100 per cent American," and he embodied his constituents' suspicion of big cities, big labor, big capital, foreigners, and "foreign ideology." With conservative Republicans and southern Democrats Dies shared a fear of the New Deal's leftward skid and the growth of militant groups demanding even greater change. When the patronage of Vice-President John Garner and House Majority Leader Sam Rayburn and sympathy of House Speaker William B. Bankhead netted him the chairmanship of the Un-American Activities committee, Dies saw an opportunity to stay the liberal-radical tide.[17]

Dies began his work with an intuitive idea of what was un-American and a propensity to identify much of it with the New Deal. Since he had little money to hire investigators, he opened

72 William Gropper, cartoon (from *12 Cartoons Defending WPA by Members of the American Artists Congress*, New York, 1939)

155

hearings to which he subpoenaed known fascists and communists and invited almost anyone who claimed to possess information on subversive activities. One student of the Dies Committee later observed that the best people in the depression decade did not offer themselves as volunteer witnesses and that "the volunteers of 1938 turned out to be a gamy bunch."[18]

From the first, the Dies Committee captured headlines. On its second day of operation, August 13, the American Federation of Labor officer John P. Frey called national attention to the committee by charging that communists controlled the rival union, the Congress of Industrial Organizations. Dies kept the issue alive by releasing his investigator's report that "an outstanding official" in the Department of Labor shielded West Coast CIO chief Harry Bridges, a man with an unquestioned affinity for communist causes.

The fifth day of testimony the volunteer witness Walter Steele, editor of the conservative *National Republic* and representative of 114 patriotic organizations with membership of 20,000,000 people, opened the topic of the federal arts projects. After filling the record and newspapers with hundreds of names of alleged communists and infested organizations—from the American Civil Liberties Union to the Camp Fire Girls—he read into the record a long statement on communist cultural activities. His list of "revolutionary" actors and musicians included the best on Federal One. He advocated destruction of the art "smeared upon walls . . . by Communists on the Federal relief." He wanted the committee to know that Federal Music Project director Sokoloff was born in Russia, that communist publications favorably referred to theater project director Flanagan, and that the writers project director Alsberg "procured relief funds for Russians in 1922."[19] No one questioned Frey or Steele closely, demanded supporting evidence, or disallowed their insinuations. They had set the tone for the Dies Committee.

By the end of the first week the Dies committee had struck the New Deal in a vulnerable spot, Federal One. Since there was no law against it, communists did work on the projects, and in larger percentage than on WPA in general. In summer 1938 WPA chiefs were reluctant to defend them in light of the recent de-bacle over the arts bureau. Now the Dies committee welcomed a long line of witnesses from New York City to Washington's August heat and the raucous hearings.

Ex-workers and investigators of New York City's theater project testified that the Workers Alliance, a relief workers union, practically ran the project and that the Communist Party controlled the Workers Alliance. Some witnesses talked of director Flanagan's "communist sympathies" and of her production of blatantly communist plays and others which implied contempt for the government. Witnesses swore that theater project leaders squelched documented reports of communist influence and contributed to the "un-American atmosphere" communists had created on the project. Pretty Sallie Saunders, a federal actress, volunteered that the communist program "for social equality and race merging" produced most indiscriminate associations in federal theater. It was the kind of testimony guaranteed to raise public attention for the committee and embarrass the administration. There seemed little discrimination in the minds of the public, the press, and the committee between the theater project and the other cultural programs.[20]

Dies next sent invitations and subpoenas to critics of the writers project. An elderly writers project librarian, Edwin P. Banta, pointed out that more than 100 of his colleagues were communists. He displayed a copy of the communist chief Earl Browder's book, *The People's Front*, autographed by his project comrades. Other witnesses swore that a third of the New York City writers project carried communist party cards. In closed session Mrs. Louise Lazelle, a watchdog hired earlier by Mrs. Woodward, informed the committee that the writers project seemed to have no qualms about "editorializing; that is, giving a point of view for or against." She saw many "flammatory statements" which "constituted appeals to class hatred."[21]

Throughout the presentation of these bits of factual information, unchallenged truth, half-truths, and outright falsehoods, the WPA muzzled the project officials. Neither Dies nor Thomas remained silent. To the radio and press they offered a stream of sermonettes against the national disgrace and danger. Shortly after the 1938 election a decision materialized somewhere in the upper reaches of WPA to allow representatives to appear before Dies. Both Flanagan and Alsberg asked to testify but Mrs. Woodward, for reasons best known to her, insisted on her right to speak, "as the responsible official."

Mrs. Woodward did not lack sympathy for the experiments of the cultural projects. She had condemned as "unbelievably medieval" the conservative admonition that they should avoid bringing social and political matters to the public attention. When Mrs. Roosevelt told a reporter, "I don't believe in censoring anything," Mrs. Woodward had been quick to quote her. She told Hopkins that among cultural project workers silence on social and political themes "could only be imposed by a censorship as vicious and depraving to the spirit" as that recently forced upon the German people by Adolf Hitler. For all that, Ellen Woodward's testimony before the Dies committee was a mistake. She simply did not have the facts or the firsthand knowledge to answer the specific questions of the committee. They persistently interrupted the graying Mississippian as she drawled her prepared statement into the record. She became testy, argued with the committeemen—alternately hedging, generalizing, and overstating—and ended with embarrassing retractions or admissions of ignorance. Her main point seemed to be that the projects were far better than the accounts rendered by incompetent witnesses and that the Dies committee had handled the charges in a "very un-American way."[22] Having aroused the committee, Mrs. Woodward finally asked to step down in favor of project directors Flanagan and Alsberg.

The strong-minded redhead who headed the Federal Theatre Project made a strong defense of herself and her project. Mrs. Flanagan never saw communist or other political activity in her project. She had issued orders forbidding it and would fire any violators. She admitted that some of federal theater's plays might be propaganda for democracy, better housing, or more jobs. Propaganda she pointedly told committeeman Joe Starnes, "after all, is education." To make theater relevant she thought it imperative that some plays deal with social and economic themes. When Starnes persistently referred to an article she had written on the Russian theater, one passage of which casually referred

to Christopher Marlowe, Hallie Flanagan took the opportunity to embarrass the committee. Who was this Marlowe, Starnes demanded, "Is he a Communist?" Joe Starnes, University of Alabama Class of '21 and a former schoolteacher in Guntersville, sputtered as Mrs. Flanagan turned to the clerk: "Put in the record that he was the greatest dramatist . . . immediately preceding Shakespeare." From the beginning Mrs. Flanagan and the committee had failed to speak the same language. Dies dismissed her, her statement unfinished, with a promise to include her refutations to specific charges in the record.[23] He never did.

Henry Alsberg took more care than Mrs. Flanagan to explain away his past radical affiliations and portray himself as a hardworking, good-intentioned bureaucrat. He admitted that much writers project copy came to his office in unsatisfactory form, but he said he "attempted consistently to tone it down." He admitted a "ball-up" in New York City, but enumerated the transfers and demotions he had ordered when he discovered it. He admitted that some part of the 500 project writers in New York City were trouble-making communists. Alsberg left the impression that he acknowledged the irregularities, that he deplored them as much as the committee, and wanted the committee's faith that he would correct matters. Dies commended him for his frankness and, in a slap at Mrs. Woodward and Mrs. Flanagan, for his nonantagonistic attitude.[24]

Cahill and Sokoloff did not testify. Although committee investigators could have found a few willing witnesses to air real and alleged sins of the art and music projects, the witnesses would have been less spectacular than those who had already appeared. Probably because the indictment of the theater and writers projects was having the desired effect, the committee did not invite testimony on the other projects. Cahill, however, always believed that "a very curious happening" had saved him from an uncomfortable questioning by chairman Dies. During the early days of the investigation, the popular journalist Ernie Pyle had written three articles about the federal art centers in Oregon, singling out their director, Val Clear, for praise. A few days later Cahill received a telephone call from an unidentified woman who demanded to know if he shared Pyle's high assessment of Clear.

After Cahill unqualifiedly endorsed the Oregon director, the caller identified herself as his sister. Later in a bar a fellow administrator pointed out the sister as "the spy in this administration for the Dies Committee."[25]

The Dies committee worked irreparable harm on all the components of Federal One, on federal art and music as well as the theater and writers projects. The press had seized upon the daily charges. The *New York Times* gave Dies some 500 column-inches during the first month and a half and other papers were more generous. It mattered little that only 2 of the 18 reporters regularly covering the hearings thought them fair. The reporter who pointed out the scarcity of hard evidence would be guilty of editorializing. It mattered little that WPA eventually refuted most of the charges. The refutations came late, lacked front-page appeal, and were buried on back pages with the obituaries.[26]

The WPA cultural program, its vitality sapped by two encounters with Congress, reeled from the Dies committee into a fatal blow delivered by the House Committee on Appropriations. Again the FAP contributed little of the damning evidence, but Congress still inclined to think of Federal One as a unit, not an affiliation of four autonomous projects.

When Roosevelt had to ask Congress for more relief money in January 1939, he had to expose his program to an opposition girded, preening, and spoiling to test its strength after the November election. Not only had Roosevelt's attempted purge failed, but Republicans gained 81 House and 8 Senate seats. At the same time conservative southern Democrats began to hope of capturing control of their party before the presidential nomination in 1940. Perhaps with the idea of pacifying Congress, Roosevelt recently had appointed Colonel Francis C. Harrington, an Army engineer assigned to WPA, as the new WPA administrator. Harrington, who had never voted, was immune from charges of playing politics, and his appointment pleased many who believed Army administration meant honesty, freedom from politics and efficiency—those who believed with the editor of the *Hartford* (Connecticut) *Times*: "The army gets things done." With the resignation of Hopkins, Ellen Woodward gave up her

jurisdiction over the 540,000 reliefers in the Women's and Professional Division and joined the more orderly and less strenuous effort of the Social Security Administration. Roosevelt appointed Mrs. Florence Kerr, a Grinnell College classmate of Hopkins, to replace her. The white-haired wife of the assistant to Grinnell's president, Florence Kerr brought experience as regional director of the Women's and Professional Division in 13 Midwestern states to her new job. Before the depression she had written some magazine articles, taught school for several years, directed Red Cross activities in Louisiana, and had "met a payroll" in connection with the operation of two farms.[27] Congressional committees would duly note and appreciate the latter qualification. They also would find to their liking the easy manner and sense of humor of the $9,500-a-year assistant. The new appointments had less effect on Congress in January 1939, however, than the Senate report confirming improper political activity by WPA in the recent election and the report of the Dies committee revealing what was un-American about the work program.

In the House Subcommittee on Appropriations which considered the relief bills, Clifton Woodrum, a conservative Democrat from Virginia, and John Taber, Republican from New York, formed in microcosm the greatly strengthened Republican-Conservative Democratic coalition. Woodrum and Taber now moved vigorously to dismantle the New Deal. Four times between January and June, WPA administrators faced the appropriations subcommittee. They came in January, March, and May to justify their requests for money. In April, when Congress handed the subcommittee a mandate to investigate all WPA preparatory to drawing up a new relief bill, administrators came to justify their existence. The subcommittee picked up the theme of the Dies committee that Federal One was fraught with subversives, especially the theater and writers projects and especially in New York City. The subcommittee also probed the costs, distribution, and local support of Federal One. And they found the new WPA administrator and Mrs. Florence Kerr unenthusiastic in their defense of the cultural projects, particularly when the publicity became more uncomplimentary and the entire WPA fell under stronger criticism. After six months the Taber-Woodrum forces could take credit for the death of federal theater and the crippling of the art, writers, and music projects.

Immediately the Woodrum-Taber alliance challenged the assumption that advancement of the traditional cultural arts was a proper function of government. The conservatives on the subcommittee did not deny that the arts could not, then or in the future, rely on subsidies from most predepression patrons. While liberals used that undisputed fact to argue the necessity for government patronage, the committeemen used it to argue that if there were too few patrons for the number of artists, there ought to be fewer artists. Recent improvements in the technology of "canned music," the motion picture, and color press reproduction, Woodrum added, meant that fewer artists would reach more people even when prosperity returned. "What industry or what situation," he demanded to know, "is going to arise that will relieve us of these public charges?" Neither Harrington nor Mrs. Kerr could answer, and clearly neither desired permanent government support. In place of Hopkins's assertions that Federal One enlightened while it provided relief and that official patronage should continue, Harrington volunteered that "the Government should go slowly in providing employment in a certain profession for people who can never get a job in that profession." Harrington explained that he had moved immediately to deal with the problem by cutting the number of Federal One workers from 40,000 to 33,500. And when asked if WPA cultural workers ought to learn to do some other work, Harrington responded: "If possible."[28]

Believing that Federal One perpetuated largely anachronistic skills, the subcommittee turned its attention to the projects' further sin on harboring radicals. An administration Democrat and member of the subcommittee, Clarence Cannon, charged that the attempt of the Woodrum-Taber forces to prove that WPA was subservient to subversive elements was a scarlet thread which ran throughout the hearings. Cannon probably came close to truth when he charged that the opposition coalition wanted to leave the public impressed with communist influence and the no-

73 Hugo Gellert, *Representative Woodrum's committee "investigating" WPA* (from *12 Cartoons Defending WPA by Members of the American Artists Congress*, New York, 1939)

tion that "the Roosevelt administration was responsible for it and must answer in the 1940 election."[29]

Cannon listened to the figures of Communist Party and Workers Alliance membership used by former Dies committee witnesses to embellish their repeated testimony, watched the record fill with exhibits including photographs of the title page of Earl Browder's book signed by writers project workers, and finally exploded: "Now, it is incredible that evidence, that ridiculous evidence like this should be submitted to the committee." No law, no WPA regulation prevented WPA workers from joining any party or any organization, labor, social, or otherwise. The fact that a man belonged to a party, Democratic, Republican, or Communist, that he wrote for journals in his spare time or signed a book, Cannon insisted, had nothing to do with the investigation. Cannon's argument seemed too narrowly legalistic to Woodrum, and the Virginian pressed the attack on grounds that "some people . . . make a distinction between what the Democratic Party and Republican Party stand for and the Communist Party." With Cannon insisting that WPA employment could not be denied because of an individual's beliefs, chairman Edward T. Taylor turned with interest to committee investigator H. Ralph Burton's "approximate estimate" that $6,282.46 a month in taxpayers' money went to communists on the New York City writers project.[30]

The committee regarded waste and inefficiency on Federal One as important as communism. One volunteer witness ventured that only 25 percent of the workers on the New York writers project were competent. Another compared 80 percent to fish peddlers and dishwashers and computed the cost of a thousand words of project copy at $51.09, an unthinkable cost for a private publisher. For all that, the charge of waste and inefficiency fell heaviest on the New York theater project. A rental contract between the project and a private theater owner or a supply contract was something a lawyer-legislator could understand. In New York City, it evolved, the theater project rented the New Yorker Theatre for $41,500 a year, the Maxine Elliott and Adelphi theaters each for over $2,200 a month and the Ritz for $375 to $450 a week. How was it that for the week beginning April 1,

the performances of *Androcles and the Lion* played to 383 people and 6,657 empty seats? And at such rentals why did rehearsals take so long—nine months for *Sing for Your Supper*. Then there was the matter of the *Swing Mikado*, a play with an all-Negro cast that took Chicago by storm. Why did the Federal Theatre Project bring the play to New York to compete with private enterprise on Broadway? Did the theater project spend $40,000 on make-up cream and beauty greases? And what irregularities made lighting equipment, idle most of the time, cost so much?[31]

The New York City music project escaped and the art project almost escaped the indignities endured by the theater and writers projects. American "common sense" told legislators what constituted a "class angle" in a book or play but that unlearned quality helped little in assessing a musical composition or painting. Some witnesses did swear that communism dominated all the city's Federal One projects and had harsh words for the artists who had instigated the first of New York's sit-down strikes.

About the only sensational items the committee's investigator could find were New York's female model books. The New York art project included a models division which assigned professional models on relief to project artists. The models, in the accepted practice of their trade, contributed photographs of themselves to their employer who filed them in a loose-leaf book for use in making assignments. Committee investigator Burton discovered the books and requisitioned them as exhibits. Woodrum labored to create the picture: photographs of women, women on relief, "with no draperies or any clothing of any kind," photographs "taken in different poses, with . . . the age and the height, with the names of the so-called models, some white and some black." Several people on the project saw the books, Burton testified, and Representative J. William Ditter helped Woodrum complete his image of lascivious behavior on the art project by suggesting that the books were "passed around generally for the benefit and appreciation of everybody."[32] Still, harboring an undetermined number of radicals and accumulating pictures of nude models seemed to damn the art project in New York City less than the fact that it held equal rank in Federal One with the theater and writers projects.

Harrington appeared before the committee to answer the charges and clarify the facts. "I wish to make a plea for all these Federal Arts Projects," the administrator began. He was quite prepared to admit past mistakes, and he believed he could meet committee objections by forcing the national project directors to spend less time in New York and more time in Washington under tighter WPA control. He proposed to get local sponsorship wherever possible, completely reorganize the theater project and bring efficiency through changes in personnel. Probably the administrator was thinking of a recent report of a special planning committee working under Mrs. Kerr. The committee had recommended "that all Professional and Service projects, and more particularly the arts projects, orient their activities toward the realization of community-centers—centers not of WPA projects but of *community participation*." Harrington read nearly 40 pages into the record and submitted written rebuttals to specific charges consuming, even in the Government Printing Office's smallest type, 70 pages more, after which Woodrum dismissed the administrator without questions. Much of the small print explained the philosophy and procedure of the New York arts projects.[33] The rebuttals made less interesting news copy than the sensational charges of subcommitteemen and witnesses. Perhaps strong denials and exposure of the committee's bias by national directors would have brought more equal press coverage and national attention. Whatever might have been, the earlier policy of muzzling the national directors to prevent escalation of the arguments obviously had not changed.

By the end of the appropriations subcommittee's investigation, the Woodrum-Taber forces, and an increasing public with them, believed that inefficiency and radicalism characterized Federal One in New York City and the theater project across the country. In addition the conservatives clearly resented the urban concentration of the cultural effort. Woodrum's Virginia manner lapsed when he interrupted: "Where are they concentrated, mostly in New York City?" Taber badgered project officials until Federal One statistics went into the record in the form he desired. Not content with a statement that 21 theater projects employed 8,145, the New York Republican carefully noted for the record that one theater project (New York City) employed over 3,500 and 20 others divided the remaining 4,600. Representative George W. Johnson of West Virginia tipped the anti-urban prejudice of the subcommittee. Johnson could not understand why New Yorkers refused to leave the city and move to the countryside where fewer people were on relief. "What are you going to do with the folks in the cities?" he asked a planning board expert, and then answered for the witness, "The answer is that we continue on with this relief business and permit people to go to the cities and live there."[34]

The appropriations subcommittee saw in urban America's financial plight a way to stop subsidizing the drift to the cities and at the same time cripple Federal One. Only the theater project, whose sins transcended locale, required specific demolition. Mayor Fiorello LaGuardia of New York City spoke to the subcommittee in January to admit the desperate financial condition of the larger cities and appeal for more federal relief money. Providing for cases not covered by federal grants, he said, had drained the New York City treasury. "I tell you frankly I cannot keep the pace at which New York City is going now," the mayor testified. More than provide for cases not covered by federal programs, New York City had to contribute a portion of WPA costs. And New York City's contribution was the lowest in the nation. Sponsoring agencies in the metropolis contributed but 8.2 percent of the WPA funds spent in the city from the beginning through December 1938. Yet rural states like Nevada, Wyoming, Iowa, and North Carolina managed to pay 30.3 percent, 29.3 percent, 24.7 percent, and 23.5 percent, respectively.[35] If the new relief act required a state agency to sponsor Federal One in each state and if the new relief act required the sponsoring agency to contribute 25 percent of each project's cost, the cultural projects in New York City would wither or die because New York City could not support them. If the 25 percent contribution applied to all WPA projects, widespread inability to raise the money would decrease federal outlays. Still, the disruption for rural America would be less than for urban centers.

The investigation and hearings provided other information about urban relief that enabled the rural-oriented appropriations

74 Victor Candell, *That's my meat!* (from *12 Cartoons Defending WPA by Members of the American Artists Congress*, New York, 1939)

subcommittee to curtail the number of city workers in general and cultural workers especially. The "average" WPA worker, the subcommittee discovered, remained with WPA slightly over a year. The figure owed to the vast number of the construction workers, only 15 percent of whom remained on WPA as long as three years. The more skilled and more urban projects had less turnover. Some 20.6 percent of the women on sewing projects gained three years seniority as did 22.2 percent of all white-collar project workers. Federal One workers had the greatest longevity; 33.2 percent of them drew WPA wages continuously for at least three years. Clearly, a provision in the new bill dismissing all workers with over 18 months seniority would not affect the "average" worker, but would curtail urban white-collar work and decimate Federal One rolls.[36]

The relief bill for the fiscal year 1940 emerged from the House committee on June 14. Taber's rationale for restrictions on Federal One was that Congress never intended relief money to be used for other than relief purposes. Adherence to the intent of Congress meant an end to renting theaters with relief money and an end to national offices dedicated to developing and spreading the arts. On the floor of the House, Woodrum noted the "domination" of the cultural projects by the Workers Alliance and showed photographs and newspapers purporting to prove that in New York City the Alliance and the Communist Party were "one and the same." He demanded a relief administration that would "stand up and throw down the gage of battle to these subversive elements." Taber and Woodrum had dealt with those problems by offering a relief bill which forbade the theater project to continue. If states wanted the remaining cultural projects, they would have to pay more for them—that is, "sponsor" them by paying 25 percent of the cost—and assume both technical and administrative control. Local responsibility, Woodrum believed, would bring localities to "try to clean them up." The bill furloughed all workers on WPA over 18 months. Woodrum, who surely understood the effect of the rule on project work, said it gave other workers who were eligible for work relief a chance to get on projects. Moreover, the bill eliminated employment at the prevailing wage and required 130 hours a month from all workers. Another provision sought to eliminate "subversives" by requiring a loyalty oath.

Before the bill passed the House on June 17, Clarence Cannon and Vito Marcantonio, the latter of whom probably was the only bona fide radical in Congress, tried to rally support for an amendment to reinstate the theater project offered by New Jersey's Mary Norton. The vote against it was 192 to 56.[37] The debate on the theater project probably diverted attention from the other projects and saved them from even greater vilification on the floor of the House.

The Senate changed the bill. Pepper brought a group of theatrical headliners before the Senate Committee on Appropriations to plead for the theater project. After Tallulah Bankhead, Blanche Yurka, and Hallie Flanagan, among others, had their say, the committee directed Harrington to draw up an amendment reinstating the theater project for communities who would pay all theater rentals and other nonlabor costs. When the bill came up, Senators Pepper, Robert Wagner, and Sheridan Downey introduced an amendment to finance all the cultural projects with an allocation of up to 1 percent of WPA funds.[38] If it passed, Federal One, although with less money, would survive and, as before, employ talented reliefers without consideration to any locality's ability to pay part of the costs.

In the debate that followed Robert R. Reynolds, a self-styled superpatriot from the North Carolina mountains, entreated Congress not to perpetuate the federal theater's "unsavory collection of communistic, un-American doctrines, its assortment of insidious and vicious ideologies" and its "putrid plays." Reynolds, described later by a scholar as an erratic and irrelevant clown, eventually exhausted himself. The Senate reduced the figure in the amendment to 3/4 percent and passed it.[39]

The House and Senate versions of the relief bill for 1940 differed on many points other than the disposition of Federal One. When the Senate bill passed late on the night of June 28, two days before the end of the fiscal year and exhaustion of WPA funds, Harrington urged Congress to pass a joint resolution permitting WPA to operate at the current level until Congress should reconvene and be able to deliberate without the pressure of time. Congressional leaders rejected the idea, and the conference committee met the next day to try to agree on a final version. The bill would either pass as the conferees wrote it or not pass at all, since there was no time for both houses to make changes and send it back to conference. When the subject of the arts projects came up, Clifton Woodrum was ready. He had brought the art project model books and evidences of communism into the conference chamber. Quickly the compromises fell into place, and on the arts projects, the original House language was restored. When the two houses of Congress received the bill the Federal Theater Project was eliminated. Individual states were required to assume full supervision and to contribute 25 percent of the cost of the other cultural projects. The bill furloughed workers with more than 18 months seniority, cut administrative funds, and required a loyalty oath of WPA employees. New York representatives Emanuel Celler, Sirovich, and Marcantonio protested the discrimination against large cities where there would be new "penury and want and distress" among creative professionals. Woodrum cut them off with the blunt assertion: "I want the Federal Government to get out of the theater business." The House applauded. In less than an hour the bill had passed, 321 to 23. No group in the Senate had power to stop the will of the new coalition. Two hours before the end of the fiscal year the bill went to the White House. Roosevelt had no choice but to sign since failure to do so would stop the entire WPA.[40]

While official Washington anxiously assessed the meaning of the conservatives' victories in the relief bill and the recently passed farm, tax, and neutrality bills, dazed Federal One administrators closed staff offices and tried to determine what part, if any, they might play in the new setup. Writers project director Alsberg and music project director Sokoloff shortly resigned. Holger Cahill stayed on with the art project to organize state projects and salvage some federal influence. Cahill's was no easy task.

Harrington and Mrs. Kerr discussed the future of the remaining cultural projects with state Works Progress administrators in mid-July. Harrington referred to the remnants of the federal staff as technical "consultants" who would be of no use whatever if they could not exert guidance and some degree of control over the operation of state cultural projects. At the same time he told state chieftains that the cultural "projects are yours and your responsibility from the first of September on." In case any state administrator failed to perceive the lesson of recent congressional action, Mrs. Kerr reminded them that "we can't go counter to what people want." She believed there "must have been something wrong with the theater project or what happened to it would not have happened."[41] She made it clear that WPA headquarters wanted the cultural projects continued, but wanted them to be "safe."

Much about the new system for operating arts projects distressed Cahill. To maintain high standards and high employment he needed to find a sponsor in each state who recognized that vitality depended upon national leadership and who had money to pay 25 percent of the projects' cost. In most cases he failed. He complained that too many public agencies merely wanted to supplement their regular activities with WPA labor and if it could be used at the clerical, custodial, and janitorial level, so much the better. Federal emphasis on creative production, skill maintenance, and rehabilitation gave way, under state direction, to "service" to sponsors. Moreover, most state sponsors—boards of education, state universities, state planning boards, or municipalities—accepted responsibility contingent upon freedom from financial obligation. Art projects had to exist on whatever money in excess of 25 percent sponsors contributed to other projects.[42] The arrangement made the art projects permanent suppliants for charity and hardly encouraged unconventional art. Most artists quickly learned that it was in their self interest (financially) to produce what sponsors wanted.

The worst shortcoming of the state projects, Cahill believed, was their independence from national guidance in technical matters and resulting deterioration of standards. New regulations required state Works Progress administrators to appoint the art project directors with the approval of the national WPA. That veto power, however, did not prove effective. The result was that state relief administrators, usually experts on construction but not art, often appointed supervisors for highly technical projects

without competent advice. Some of the new appointments occurred without Cahill's knowledge, even though in theory at least he was partly responsible for technical standards.

The art projects as reconstituted no longer enjoyed unique status among WPA projects. Shortly they found themselves restricted far more than they had been as "federal" projects by the gnarled web of WPA procedural directives and lines of command. Even competent state art directors frequently found obstacles to effective communication with their own project workers and the sponsor. By November 1940 WPA directives prohibited art directors who desired technical aid from Washington from writing directly for it. The art director had to convince a higher state official that a letter was necessary and then convince the higher official to sign it. Such letters, Cahill noted, lacked clarity because state bureaucrats wrote in such opaque official terminology. Such letters and Cahill's responses passed through many hands, suffering reinterpretation in each. Understandably, state directors soon stopped asking for technical advice. Regulations enabling nontechnical WPA officials to hire and fire on the art projects without consulting the state director, to make decisions affecting project operations and thus quality, to fragment authority and thereby leave the art director ill-informed about the project, all contributed to conditions which, Cahill lamely protested, "left much to be desired from the point of view of the standards set up by the Federal Art Project." In the end, the field trip proved the most effective device for influencing state projects. Cahill and his much-traveled staff sent blunt reports of their visits on the theory that a bad report from Washington would cause state Works Progress administrators to prod art directors to correct malpractices.[43] Still, federal influence declined while the local projects underwent major changes in operation and purpose.

The changes required by the law of 1939 had the effect of weakening the art project in metropolitan centers and of encouraging some state administrators in smaller states to expand their arts projects. The number of employees on arts projects, in fact, increased after reorganization, since art teachers and craft workers formerly with the Adult Education Project and state-operated craft projects now transferred to the art program. In states where local control encouraged expansion, new workers not funneled into some enterprise beloved by the sponsor often aided in operating new Community Art Centers. Classes and changing exhibitions in the art centers involved the community and required more competent teachers and adminstrators than creative artists, who were sparse in the hinterlands. Moreover, local groups rallied to raise the 25 percent contribution toward costs or donate an empty building, or pay rent, light, and heat bills.

New York City, the former recipient of 45 percent of FAP funds and source of the best art and worst disorders, suffered more than any project after the transfer to local control. Lieutenant Colonel Brehon B. Somervell, Colonel Harrington's friend who administered the WPA in the city, bore down mightily to purge the remnants of Federal One of the sins legislators attributed to it. Shrinking the art project presented no problem. The American Artists Union estimated that 85 percent of the New York City artists would lose their jobs under the new law because they had more than 18 months seniority. At the same time WPA officials estimated that between 2 and 5 percent of those dismissed would find private employment. The only decision for Somervell was how many to reemploy. From an employment of something over 2,200 in 1936, he now set a ceiling for artists at 1,000.[44]

The radical artists in New York City who somehow survived the reduction, felt the sting of Somervell's intolerance when Congress passed a bill the following year specifically excluding communists from WPA rolls. "Now, I don't want this thing turned into a witch hunt in the WPA and I mean that," Harrington told state administrators. That admonition notwithstanding, the New York administrator at last had power to rid his projects of the force he believed plagued them. Asked how he could find communists who falsely signed the loyalty oath, Somervell quoted Matthew 7:20: "Ye shall know them by their fruits." The city administrator promptly instructed Mrs. McMahon, who had stayed on after reorganization, to guard against the production of any thing in which the main idea was social content, rather than artis-

tic value, and to eliminate anything that might savor of propaganda, and to see that the project devoted itself to art and not politics.[45]

Shortly, Thomas Corwin, a Greenwich Village artist, and his WPA supervisor, Robert Godsoe, were fired. With Godsoe's approval Corwin had submitted a watercolor sketch for a huge window display at New York's WPA headquarters building. The sketch showed a pair of calipers crossed against a micrometer, an arrangement suggestive of the emblem of the Soviet Union. With Corwin protesting that he was not a communist and opposed communism for the United States, Somervell dismissed him for propagandizing and dismissed Godsoe as incompetent for approving the sketch.[46]

Somervell turned his attention to the artist August Henkel, a pacifist and once an admitted communist, and the murals he was installing at Brooklyn's Floyd Bennett Airport. Not only had Henkel failed to sign the proper oaths, but his four panels contained figures suspiciously like Lenin and a Soviet plane with a red star. In the furor that followed, Somervell admitted to a reporter, "As a painter, I'm a good bricklayer." He should have added, the artist Rockwell Kent told Harrington, "As a detective, I'm an ass." Henkel, backed by his CIO-affiliated union, explained that the figure in the mural was Franz Reichelt, an early parachutist, and they produced the photograph used as the model. The Soviet plane was an American-made Vultee; another photograph was shown as evidence. And the red star on white background was the error of an assistant who reversed the colors of the star emblem of the U.S. Naval Reserve. More important to Somervell were the facts that Henkel had not signed the oath and that the Flatbush Chamber of Commerce and the local American Legion had registered disapproval of the work. Somervell ordered Henkel fired, the panels taken down, and three of them burned. Mrs. McMahon had to comply.[47]

In an attempt to prevent further destructions Mrs. McMahon surveyed photographs of all murals recently completed. She found only two which invited further investigation. Abraham Lishinsky's "Major Influences on Civilization" at the Samuel J. Tilden High School showed a hammer and a sickle in one panel, and

165

75 August Henkel (FAP, NYC), one of four panels in mural installed at Floyd Bennett Airport, Brooklyn, and removed by official order

Arshile Gorky's "Aviation" at Newark Airport displayed a suspicious star. Visits to the sites relieved Mrs. McMahon's fears, but Colonel Somervell's lieutenant accused her of "superficial examination." Her superior noted that Lishinsky's work contained circular forms suggesting sickles, uncalled-for stars, and, if articles were removed from them, fists clenched in the Communist salute. Most damning, Lishinsky permitted shadows in one panel to form the numeral "441," an identification of New York's communist local. Gorky's cubistic work depicting the mood of flying rather than the fact contained a star not so obviously the trademark of the Texaco Oil Company to WPA officers as to Mrs. McMahon. The beleaguered art director commended both works and lectured her superiors that "all circular forms must not be banned because a sickle partakes thereof; that every hand that holds an object must necessarily be clenched if the object be re-

moved." She purchased a working gauntlet at random from a local Army-Navy store and sent it to her superiors to illustrate that the red star trademark existed widely and needed no explanation. She conceded that Lishinsky's dismissal had been justified on grounds that including the "441" shadow "put one over" on the art project, the Board of Education, and the New York Art Commission. The dispute over Gorky's murals, which early degenerated to such remarks as "They don't mean anything to the public and they irritate the aviators," wore on until the Army began operating the Newark Airport during World War II. Then the murals disappeared.[48] These events reminded New York artists and Washington administrators alike that the project now answered to Colonel Somervell. Less dramatically other state administrators made the same points.

State overlordship subordinated creative production to servic-

166

76 Arshile Gorky (FAP, NYC), study for mural in the administration building, Newark Airport, New Jersey, now on extended loan to the Museum of Modern Art, New York. The mural itself disappeared during World War II

ing sponsors and providing recreation. Cahill did the projects no harm—since they were changed already—when he proposed in June 1940 that the art projects enroll in the recently intensified defense effort. Although no evidence suggests that Cahill worked from other than patriotic motives and desire for greater efficiency, a national defense-aid program, if the War Department "sponsored" it, would free the projects from the states and restore the lost powers of direction to the national office. About the same time Harrington told state administrators to make WPA "a second line of defense," and put the relief organization "right out in front" in the defense effort.[49] Accordingly, art project workers began decorating service clubs, building training aids, and making posters for local military bases.

Not until January 1941 did the chief of the Operations and Training Section of the Army Corps of Engineers endorse Cahill's plan for a nationally coordinated or nationally administered defense art project. Most of the state projects—by that date reorganized and expanded to include volunteers, craft, art, museum, and visual aid workers—already concentrated on aid to local military facilities. But duplication and state regulations,

167

77 In 1942 Lee Krasner led a WPA team making window display units to advertise war-training courses in New York colleges. Abstract painters on the team, which included Jackson Pollock, William Eceron, and Ben Benn, exercised their art on the borders of the displays

78 FAP poster, New York City Poster Division, 1942

especially those requiring a contribution toward costs, prevented the best possible service. Bidding for higher quality and greater efficiency, Cahill recommended abolishing the means test and compulsory furlough after 18 months employment. The means test demoralized workers and deprived the projects of capable and needy-but-not-destitute artisans. Although she was unable to do anything about it, Mrs. Kerr even admitted that "the scarlet 'A' was nothing compared to WPA relief certification that seems to be stamped on the forehead of the workers." And the 18-month rule, Cahill protested, was "the sword of Damocles" over the project. Finally, Cahill enlisted Mrs. Roosevelt to write Secretary of War Henry L. Stimson "a word of support" for a national program. Nothing came of any of it because WPA chiefs would not ask Congress to modify the terms of WPA employment and Stimson preferred the supporting art work handled on a local basis.[50]

As the tempo of defense activity and art service increased during the spring and summer of 1941, Holger Cahill's influence over events decreased. WPA Community Art Centers began holding classes on camouflage for military officers and recreational craft instruction for enlisted men. Craft projects turned out recreation equipment, furniture, and draperies for service clubs and day-rooms. Visual aid workers constructed working models of aviation motors and tank engines, while museum workers undertook contour maps and models of trenches, tank traps, and mines. Artists now spent more time designing posters, murals, and useful items that less skilled workers could then complete. More frequently, now, project directors found ways to disperse art without substantial financial contributions from the receiver. New York presented the Navy's destroyer *Greer* with lithographs and etchings, and New Jersey enlivened Fort Dix with paintings left over from the project's more creative phase. In Oregon the art project took on housewives, carpenters, and foundry workers, used the artists on the project to train them and produced decorations and furnishings from ash trays to crap tables for the state's military installations. In Philadelphia the art project's painters, photographers, lithographers, and draftsmen silk-screened thousands of rear rifle-sights charts, posters, instruction sheets, and airport plans. Project headquarters, Philadelphia workers quipped, was now an "Artsenal for Defense." So in fact it was, and tens of project centers with it. The paintings and sculpture left on project building walls and in hallways from earlier days, one newspaper reporter observed, seemed somehow out of place amidst such activity.[51]

Creative art gave way almost entirely to the practical arts and production of training aids before Pearl Harbor. When the war broke out, WPA offered its entire manpower to the secretaries of War and Navy. In the reorganization that followed, former art, museum, and craft project workers came under the WPA War Services Subdivision. The metamorphosis was complete. "There are now no arts projects as such," Cahill announced. Most of the artists on the projects during the federal period and the first year of state control left to take jobs in defense plants or to join the military. A core of designers and craftsmen stayed to train the unskilled reliefers who joined the projects. And states where artist population was low but the number of military bases was largest now had the biggest projects.[52] Too, the old claims for special treatment disappeared when the cultural function of the WPA artists dissolved. Remaining artists, essentially production workers, resignedly shared the fate of the rest of the WPA workers.

Through 1942 Community Art Centers not close to military centers closed their doors, and projects unable to assist the war effort turned in their equipment and shipped their records to archives. In Georgia, Florida, New York, Illinois, California, and Massachusetts the work continued on posters, silhouettes of Messerschmitt, Fokker, and Nagoya aircraft, and training aids of a hundred varieties. Meantime the Senate Appropriations Committee evaluated the WPA war effort and recommended dissolving the relief program. Harrington's successor, General Philip Fleming, broached the subject of ending WPA with Roosevelt in November. Finally, with defense plants and the draft diminishing the manpower, Roosevelt ordered all projects phased out by mid-1943. WPA had served with distinction, he said, and had "earned its honorable discharge."[53]

[1] Special Committee to Investigate Campaign Expenditures and Use of Government Funds, *Investigation of Senatorial Campaign Expenditures and Use of Government Funds*, Senate Report No. 1, 76 Cong. 1 Sess. (1939); Robert E. Sherwood, *Roosevelt and Hopkins: An Intimate History* (New York, 1950), 77-122; Searle F. Charles, *Minister of Relief: Harry Hopkins and the Depression* (Syracuse, 1963), 206-19; *Congressional Record*, 75 Cong. 3 Sess. (1938), 7704.

[2] Daniel W. Bell to Roosevelt, Nov. 16, 1938, Roosevelt to Hopkins, Nov. 18, 1938, memorandum by Marvin H. McIntyre, Nov. 22, 1938, AAA Reel NDA/HP4.

[3] William I. Sirovich to Edward A. Jewell, Dec. 6, 1937, RG233/HR75-D27. See Hearings before the House Committee on Patents on H. J. Res. 220, *Providing for Establishment of an Executive Department to be Known as the Department of Science, Art, and Literature*, 74 Cong. 1 Sess. and the hearings on the same bill renumbered H. J. Res. 79, 75 Cong. 3 Sess.

[4] S.3296, H.R.9102, 75 Cong. 3 Sess. A number of organizations, artists, even congressmen, had earlier suggested various types of art bureaus. The artists unions seem clearly involved in writing S.3296 and H.R.9102. In 1935 a New York City union leader sent Edward Bruce a draft bill with the essential provisions of the Coffee-Pepper proposal. See Stuyvestant Van Veen to Bruce ("A Federal Art Bill"), c. Dec. 1935, RG121/122.

[5] *Congressional Record*, 75 Cong. 3 Sess. (1938), 818, 820, 2190; 1938 Campaign Speech file, Claude Pepper Papers (Federal Records Center, Suitland, Maryland).

[6] "Proceedings: Conference of State Administrators, WPA," mimeographed, Feb. 13, 1937, pp. 146-47, RG69/100; *New York Times*, Dec. 19, 1937.

[7] *Art Digest*, XXII (March 1, 1938), 3; clippings from *New York Post*, June 7, 1938, *New York Herald Tribune*, March 1, 1938, RG69/DI.

[8] *Art Digest*, XXII (Feb. 15, 1938), 12; Watson to Rowan, Feb. 1, 1938, RG121/124; *New York Times*, March 14, 1938; clippings from *Providence (R.I.) Journal*, March 7, 1938; *Washington Star*, Feb. 13, 1938; *New York Post*, April 11, 1938, RG69/DI.

[9] Bruce to Domenico Mortellito, March 18, 1938, Bruce to Morgenthau, March 11, 1938, RG121/124; Walter Damrosch, *Proposed Plan for a Bureau of Fine Arts* (New York, 1938); Hallie Flanagan, *Arena* (1940), 287-88; Roosevelt to Pepper, March 21, 1938, Pepper Papers; clippings from Jacksonville (Fla.) *Times Union*, Feb. 17, 1938, *Washington Post*, March 27, 1938, RG69/DI.

[10] "Cahill Reminiscences," 309; clipping from *Cleveland News*, March 16, 1938, RG69/DI.

[11] H. J. Res. 671 (reprinted in *Art Digest*, XXII [June 1, 1938], 10-11); *Congressional Record*, 75 Cong. 3 Sess. (1938), 818, *New York Times*, April 3, 1938; Hearings before a Subcommittee of the Committee on Education and Labor on S.3296, *A Bill to Provide for a Permanent Bureau of Fine Arts*, 75 Cong. 3 Sess. (1938).

[12] Clippings from *Chicago Tribune*, May 1, 1938, *Baltimore Morning Sun*, March 2, 1938, *Kansas City Star*, April 7, 1938, *Miami Herald*, Feb. 28, 1938, RG69/DI.

[13] Clippings from *Manchester* (N.H.) *Union*, April 30, 1938, *Portland Oregonian*, March 13, 1938, *Indianapolis Star*, March 11, April 17, 1938, RG69/DI.

[14] *Congressional Record*, 75 Cong. 3 Sess. (1938), 2304-08; Mathews, *The Federal Theatre*, 177.

[15] *Congressional Record*, 75 Cong. 3 Sess. (1938), 9491-99; clipping from *New York Herald Tribune*, June 16, 1938, RG69/DI.

[16] Quoted in Walter Goodman, *The Committee: The Extraordinary Career of the House Committee on Un-American Activities* (New York, 1968), 27.

[17] *Ibid.*, 16-17, 21-22.

[18] *Ibid.*, 36.

[19] Hearings before a Special Committee on Un-American Activities on H. Res. 282, *Investigation of Un-American Propaganda Activities in the United States*, 75 Cong. 3 Sess. (1938), I, 91ff., 538-55.

[20] *Ibid.*, I, 775-860.

[21] *Ibid.*, II, 981-1017, 1021-26; IV, 3109-39.

[22] *Ibid.*, IV, 2729-2830, 2837-38; Woodward to Hopkins, Dec. 8, 1936, Cahill Papers.

[23] Hearings before a Special Committee on Un-American Activities on H. Res. 282, *Investigation of Un-American Propaganda Activities in the United States*, 75 Cong. 3 Sess. (1938), IV, 2838-85.

[24] *Ibid.*, IV, 2886-2908.

[25] "Cahill Reminiscences," 311-12.

[26] See Goodman, *The Committee*, 28, 32; Mathews, *The Federal Theatre*, 205-09.

[27] Clippings from *Hartford* (Conn.) *Times*, Dec. 28, 1938, *Washington Daily News*, April 29, 1939, RG69/DI.

[28] Hearings before the Subcommittee of the Committee on Appropriations on H. J. Res. 209 and 246, *Further Additional Appropriations for Work Relief, Fiscal Year 1938*, 76 Cong. 1 Sess., 162 (hereafter, *Hearings on H. J. Res. 209 and 246*); Hearings before the Subcommittee of the Committee on Appropriations on H. J. Res. 83, *Additional Appropriations for Work Relief and Relief, Fiscal Year 1939*, 76 Cong. 1 Sess. (1939), 110 (hereafter, *Hearings on H. J. Res. 83*); *Congressional Record*, 76 Cong. 1 Sess. (1939), 7262.

[29] Hearings before the Subcommittee of the Committee on Appropriations on H. Res. 130, *Investigation and Study of the Works Progress Administration*, 76 Cong. 1 Sess. (1939), 1067 (hereafter, *Investigation of WPA*).

[30] *Ibid.*, 1128. (Eventually Congress explicitly barred Communist Party members, aliens, and those who sought to overthrow the government by any means, but only 317 workers in all WPA refused to sign loyalty affidavits—1/50 of 1 percent of the total. See Howard O. Hunter's statement before the House Committee on Appropriations, May 21, 1941, RG69/100.)

[31] *Ibid.*, 240-41, 264; *Hearings on H. J. Res. 209 and 246*, 228-31.

[32] *Investigation of WPA*, 276-78.

[33] Hearings before the House Subcommittee of the Committee on Appropriations, *Appropriation for Work Relief and Relief, Fiscal Year 1940*, 76 Cong. 1 Sess. (1939), 14 (hereafter, *Hearings on Appropriations for 1940*); *Investigation of WPA*, 1272, 1304ff.; [report of planning committee], typed, June 1, 1939, Cahill Papers.

[34] *Hearings on H. J. Res. 209 and 246*, 161; *Hearings on Appropriations for 1940*, 370-71; *Hearings on H. J. Res. 83*, 159.

[35] *Hearings on H. J. Res. 83*, 26-27, 183-84; *Investigation of WPA*, 1393-94.

[36] *Hearings on Appropriations for 1940*, 23.

[37] *Congressional Record*, 76 Cong. 1 Sess. (1939), 7166-70, 7370-74.

[38] *Ibid.*, 8084-89; Hearings before the Senate Committee on Appropriations on H. J. Res. 326, *Work Relief and Public Works Appropriations Act of 1939*, 76 Cong. 1 Sess. (1939).

[39] *Congressional Record*, 76 Cong. 1 Sess. (1939), 8089-8104; V. O. Key, Jr., *Southern Politics in State and Nation* (New York, 1949), 206.

[40] *Congressional Record*, 76 Cong. 1 Sess. (1939), 8452-59.

[41] "Proceedings: Works Projects Administrators National Meeting . . . July 12-13, 1939," mimeographed, 34, 43, RG69/100.

[42] Cahill, "Record of Program Operation and Accomplishment," 10-11, 17-18, 20.

[43] *Ibid.*, 11; Cahill to Kiplinger, March 10, 1941, RG69/100; Cahill to Triggs, Nov. 2, 1940, RG69/211.5. The decline of federal control was well illustrated in December 1939 when Parker asked the New York City project for 20 photographs. The New York City project refused on grounds that the national office had not made a 25 percent sponsor's contribution. See Parker to W.R.F. Stier, Dec. 21, 1939, RG69/651.315.

[44] Clippings from *Philadelphia Record*, July 9, 1939, *New York Mirror*, July 8, 1939; Somervell to Harrington, Aug. 22, 1939, RG69/651.315; summary of discussion . . . Ralph Hetzel, Harrington, Morris, RG69/211.59; Jay du Von to Kerr, Nov. 14, 1939, RG69/210.1.

[45] "Meeting of the State Administrators, National Directors, and Washington Staff of the Work Projects Administration," mimeographed, June 1940, RG69/100; *New York Times*, July 12, 1940; clipping from *New York Herald Tribune*, July 12, 1940, RG69/DI. Audrey McMahon intensely disliked Colonel Somervell. She believed he was driven by his "deep-seated belief that the projects were a hotbed of communism and that he had been appointed, not only to administer them (his cross) but to 'clean them up.'" He belonged to the school of critics, said Mrs. McMahon, "who felt that 'his little Mary could do as well' as shall we say, a distinguished painter like Ben Shahn . . .'" and never overcame his belief "that to create 'pictures' was not 'work.'" "I realize with a certain amount of joy," the FAP administrator wrote years later, "that I must have been as great a burden to him as he was to me." O'Connor, *Federal Support of the Visual Arts*, 47.

[46] *New York Times*, July 7, 1940; clipping from *New York World Telegram*, July 3, 1940, RG69/DI.

[47] United American Artists, "Statement on the Burning of the Floyd Bennett Mural," nd, Rockwell Kent to Harrington, July 13, 1940, Somervell to Harrington, July 19, 1940, RG69/651.315; *New York Times*, July 10, 1940.

[48] McMahon to Ernest P. Bergmann, July 30, 1940, RG69/651.315; *Newark (N.J.) Evening News*, Sept. 30, 1939. Somervell next appointed a large advisory committee of prominent artists to make "oral or written comments or criticism" which would "be a contributory factor in the efficiency record of the artists." Convinced that the committee would become "a firing squad" to rid the project of undesirables, Stuart Davis led the committee in a walkout. Somervell immediately replaced them with artists of much more conservative political and aesthetic tastes. The new committee served only a short time. See *New York Times*, Nov. 3, 1940; clipping from *New York World Telegram*, Nov. 2, 1940; Advisory Committee Report [Dec. 1940], RG69/651.3; State Final Report: New York City.

[49] Cahill to Triggs, June 20, 1940, RG69/211.5; "Meeting of State Administrators, National Directors and Washington Staff," mimeographed, June 1940, RG69/100.

[50] "Conference on the Arts Program of the Work Projects Administration, Oct. 8, 1941," mimeographed, Cahill Papers; Cahill to Kerr, Jan. 6, 1941, S. C. Godfrey to Kerr, Jan. 2, 1941, Cahill and Dornbush to Eleanor Roosevelt, March 25, 1941, Henry L. Stimson to Eleanor Roosevelt, April 24, 1941, RG69/211.5; Cahill to Kiplinger, March 10, 1941, RG69/100; "The Art Program and National Defense," typescript, na, Feb. 1, 1941, RG69/211.15.

[51] Clippings from *Philadelphia Record*, April 4, 1941, March 1, 1942, *Boston Globe*, April 1, 1941; *PM* (New York), Aug. 17, 1941, *Baltimore Sun*, Jan. 29, 1942, *Washington Daily News*, Feb. 13, 1942, RG69/DI; see also State Final Report files.

[52] Howard O. Hunter to Stimson and Frank Knox, Dec. 8, 1941, AAA Reel NDA/HP4; Cahill to Kiplinger, Sept. 8, 1942, RG69/211.5; "Arts Projects," typescript, na [May 1942], RG69/211.5; Agnes S. Cronin to Kerr, April 25, 1942, RG69/651.3. Many artists had been assigned to Museum, Education and Recreation, Library Assistance, and Visual Aids projects from their beginnings. Since all WPA projects were transforming themselves into defense aid projects in 1941, the consolidation of the art and museum projects had little effect on operations. The chief effect was to obscure the accounting of numbers of artists and amount of money spent for art. In March 1941, for example, "art and museums projects" employed nearly 12,000 workers. Financial and employment statistics did not differentiate between artists and carpenters or truck drivers. See reports of WPA Division of Research, Statistics, and Records in Holger Cahill Papers.

[53] Hopkins to Roosevelt, Nov. 19, 1942, Roosevelt to Fleming, Dec. 4, 1942, AAA Reel, NDA/HP4; Senate Committee on Appropriations. *Transfer of Employees, Conserving Office Space, Relief in Housing Conditions and Promotion of Economy and Efficiency*, Senate Report No. 1554, 77 Cong. 2 Sess. (1942).

10

A Masterpiece?

No presidential committee assessed the state of the arts in America at the end of the 1930s as one did at the end of the 1920s. Had one done so surely it would have asked the questions: Were the New Deal art programs a success? Why did they fade? Is government support of the arts, on the basis of this experience, a good idea?

An evaluation committee on the eve of World War II would have been hard put to demonstrate that many depression taxpayers felt differently about the art programs than they felt about the WPA and public building program in general. Individuals who approved of these relief and pump-priming programs frequently cited these art projects as examples of New Deal com-

passion for all depression-debilitated Americans and as examples of New Deal aspirations to bring, through art as well as fiscal measures, the more abundant life. Individuals who disagreed with Roosevelt's experiments for recovery often focused on the art projects for examples of frivolous spending the nation could ill afford. In short, 130,000,000 Americans reacted to Treasury and WPA art projects in close relation to their response to the larger programs of which the art programs were a part.

That more people in 1940 than 1930 spent their Sunday afternoons in art museums is no demonstration of success for the New Deal projects. There is no way to tell why more people turned out. The trend toward greater attention to the fine arts had be-

173

gun before the federal art programs. And most of the large museums which received the increased attendance featured traditional displays, not the contemporary American art stressed by the government projects. That is not to say that the federal projects had no part in expanding American art consciousness. Statistics on art museum attendance compiled by the American Federation of Art in 1941 indicated that "in ratio to population" the WPA art centers enjoyed "the biggest public response." Of the 77 new art museums between 1938 and 1941, 32 opened with the direct cooperation of the WPA art program. And the sale of art—never well recorded—seems to have benefited from the federal emphasis on contemporary artists. The *American Art Annual* reported that "in the field of art sales, the period 1938-41 was the most exciting since 1929."[1]

Success or failure of a project is determined, in part, by the opinions of professional critics and national leaders. It is not sufficient to say—although technically it would be true—that most critics in the 1930s applauded the federal art output. In the main, critics harbored and reflected the same loves and hatreds of the New Deal as the population at large. Critics with traditional or academic tastes most often associated with people who considered everything about the New Deal offensive. Those who preferred various types of realism tended to move in circles of Roosevelt backers. The seeker of professional judgment, then, could eliminate perhaps half the critics because political passions tinged their verdicts. Among the remainder, the problem was finding those who were aesthetically dispassionate. While Holger Cahill characterized the 1930s as a period of searching for new themes and means of expression, and responded sympathetically, many critics did not. They were more certain of the criteria of greatness and the appropriateness of subject and style. Lacking catholicity in taste, contemporary critics found large amounts of government art production unworthy. Some of it was incompetent, but how often did a critic take a position for or against government art based on the quantity and quality of work in the genre he championed? The *Washington Star* critic, Leila Mechlin, to mention but one example, never understood or approved social realism or the distorted forms used in its presentation.

79 Joseph Stella (FAP, NYC), *Factory Scene*

80 Edward Chavez (FAP, Colo.), *The Watering Tank*

When exhibitions of WPA or Section work contained pieces suggestive of that alternative of expression she wrote disparagingly of the government projects. When it did not reflect political bias, critical opinion, then, was as often a statement of the art establishment on a given point in the changing style of American art as it was of the competence of the artists on the projects.

The passing of a generation did little to unify opinion on the success and worthiness of the projects. Aesthetic and political prejudices still crept into some of the judgments. The art historian and longtime director of the Whitney Museum, Lloyd Goodrich, considered the Section and WPA program "the greatest single factor in our history for extending the influence of art throughout our people." The art critic and historian James Thrall Soby somewhat more cautiously offered the view that "the vast increase in American respect for the visual arts stems in good part" from the federal projects. *New Republic* critic Frank Getlein wrote that "a very large part of whatever interest, sympathy and understanding" of art and craft that existed among Americans could be traced to the depression projects "at one or two removes." Senator Jacob K. Javits, speaking in support of a new scheme to aid the arts in the early 1960s, invoked the WPA experiments, which, he said, "made a substantial contribution to the development" of the arts in America. In support of the liberal Republican, Democratic Senator Ralph Yarborough added that

175

"the program resulted in stimulation . . . such as this country probably never had before or since." Republican Senator Barry Goldwater, soon to be the presidential nominee of his party, objected: "I do not think the Government did anything to inspire artists during that period." As for the painting produced by the New Deal projects, the Arizona Senator testified: "I would not have one of them hanging in my backroom." Cultural historian Jacques Barzun represented a larger group that contended "all the WPA proves is that from a huge grouping of American artists a sizable amount of good work can be obtained."[2]

Whether artists considered the federal projects a success depended upon how individual artists understood their purpose and what they expected of them. Few artists on the relief rolls denied that WPA lived up to its purpose of "preserving skills," of keeping artists alive during the country's worst economic disaster. Material aid was inherent in the effort of the Section of Fine Arts to acquire the "best available American art." Obviously the projects enabled a good many artists to remain artists. Of 155 survivors of the FAP in New York contacted in 1968 by Professor Francis O'Connor, some 65 percent admitted that they could not have existed during the thirties without the FAP, 79 percent were able to continue careers in art after the project ended, and 36 percent believed that their work on the FAP helped them obtain work in the private sector. The federal census takers in 1930 found slightly more than 57,000 artists and art teachers in the country. In 1940 the Bureau of the Census identified some 66,000 artists and art teachers, about 12 percent more than in 1930, against a background of a little more than 7 percent total population growth.[3] Without the federal programs the trend toward a greater percentage of artists among Americans almost certainly would have been interrupted for lack of patrons.

The statistical record reflects only what the artists did, not what they felt. That project artists led the drive to make the New Deal cultural programs permanent speaks of their approval of the idea of federal patronage. That many others vigorously opposed the operating procedures of the Section of Fine Arts and the seemingly insensitive bureaucracy of the WPA speaks for their displeasure with the manner in which New Dealers applied the idea. If those actions betrayed those feelings, artists outside of New York City felt less strongly that government patronage should be permanent and that the administration of the programs required overhaul.

In the end, the question of the success of the federal experiments, for artists, is reduced to the effect of the patronage on each individual's esprit and his growth as an artist. A large number of artists, later successful, have testified to the positive effect of the government work on their careers. Artists Anton Refregier and Willem de Kooning, for example, had worked for an interior decorator who specialized in stylized murals for hotel lobbies and speakeasies in the early years of the depression. The FAP gave them a chance to turn from painting fake Bouchers, Fragonards, palm trees, nude girls, and goldfish and begin to "look at people's lives" through their painting and, according to Refregier, to "connect up with the great tradition" of mural art. Both de Kooning and Refregier credited the FAP with advancing them in their profession. Seymour Fogel, after he was prominent in art circles, admitted that the FAP "not only saved my life financially, but launched my career as an artist." Chaim Gross worked as a delivery boy and at odd jobs until he went on WPA. Shortly thereafter he won a $3,000 commission in one of the competitions of the Section of Fine Arts. "That was my beginning," he was pleased to admit. Texas artist Peter Hurd, in his mature years, called his commission by the Section of Fine Arts "the greatest thing that ever happened to me aside from meeting N. C. Wyeth."[4]

Other artists have contended that the projects inspired a "sense of community" which buoyed them up and had some effect on their development. Only 7 percent in O'Connor's sampling of opinion of New York artists failed to experience the community feeling. Printmaker Elizabeth Olds liked to recall that the FAP

81 Peter Hurd (Section of Fine Arts), mural in the post office of Big Spring, Texas

82 Chaim Gross (Section of Fine Arts), relief on the Federal Trade Commission building, Washington, D.C.

"freed the artists from the idea that another artist is a competitor ... and it made it possible for artists to work together." Art teacher and painter Edward Glannon wrote nostalgically in the late 1960s: "I knew hundreds of artists during those years. In the last twenty years I have known less than half a dozen." Various other artists recalled the FAP through the mists of time as "like one big family caring for each other's needs," and as giving them "a sense of belonging."[5]

Not all federal artists continued in the profession, and not all of those who continued believed government employment affected their careers or their work in a dynamic way. Maurice Glickman, who received $10,000 in WPA checks and produced $150,000 in art by 1968 prices for his work, did not think his FAP experience was either enriching or of any influence on his aesthetic or technical development. Lee Krasner, project muralist and later wife of Jackson Pollock, represented the views of many in her remark that the most important federal contribution was simply "continued painting." Printmaker Adolf Dehn considered the project "sad—for my own creativity." The project allotted him one lithography stone every six weeks. Dehn, who worked rapidly and compulsively, did work in two days the project wanted him to spread over six weeks, and then he had to make sketches until his next stone arrived. "Well, you know that's not right, it's frustrating," he said. Muralist Marion Greenwood did not believe that she or many of her colleagues developed "anything really significant," because "an artist must be proud of what he's doing, and not make excuses to people—that it's a relief project to help him survive."[6]

There is no way of knowing exactly how many artists were stimulated by federal efforts to aid them. The available evidence suggests that the number was high. Some 88 percent in O'Connor's small survey said their experience with WPA had been artistically "rich and satisfying." Artists supported the projects in far greater proportion than the public at large or government officials. Doubtless the effects would have been aired more freely by more artists if there had been no humiliating relief certifications, no harassment by timekeepers, no shortage of equipment,

83 Adolf Dehn (FAP, NYC), *Central Park*, lithograph now in the collection of the Newark Museum

and more job security. Still, letters in the files of art organizations and journals, government agencies, and congressional committees indicate that with few exceptions artists could endorse sculptor Ibram Lassaw's feeling that the depression program was "a providential thing."[7]

Had a commission investigated the state of American art at the end of the 1930s it could not have concluded, as President Hoover's did earlier, that for the overwhelming majority of Americans the fine arts of painting and sculpture did not exist. The nation had purchased thousands upon thousands of art objects at a fraction of their cost in the artificial private market. There were too many murals and easels and graphics in too many post offices and federal buildings, schools, and community halls; too many graduates of Community Art Centers and WPA classes in settlement houses and civic clubs; too many producing artists at work to contend that American art was stagnant. With the depression consuming the energies and attention of the people, with the government increasingly criticized and financially distressed, and with wrenching uncertainty and change characterizing American art, perhaps limited success was enough to expect.

The federal art projects faded because they were born of the need to sustain professionals through the depression and they failed to transcend their depression purpose. When the Second World War displaced the depression as the nation's foremost concern, the American people, the Congress, and the executive bureaucracy were unconvinced that continued patronage of artists served the national interest. It was not that the depression-born art agencies had not tried. Both had aspired to integrate art with daily life in America and thereby improve its quality. Both realized that the kind of reordering of values they sought—if ultimately obtainable—could not occur in a decade. Both, therefore, tried to embed themselves, or a linear descendant, into the structure of government as concern for the depression waned. The Section and WPA art program had convinced thousands of Americans and confirmed countless others of the principle of federal art patronage. Even so, desires for government frugality and more spectacular diversions still ranked far above thirst for the traditional arts with the average taxpayer. And among the "important public," the individuals with influence enough to make things happen, the art agencies failed to spark a movement large, loud, and zealous enough to survive World War II.

To endure, federal art programs needed more than well-wishers; they required legions of crusaders among artists, the public, and the government hierarchy. To enlist legions it was not enough to be competent and culturally justifiable; the art units needed to prove that they were in every way exemplary and uplifting. In that, they failed. They could not escape the stigma of make-work relief or the taint of Rooseveltian politics. Perhaps most important, the bureaucracy of the art agencies, by the end of the 1930s slow and hyper-cautious, displayed little in the way of innovative administration. Moreover, the bureaucracy failed to perceive that its cautious exercise of prerogatives, which were too limited to engender real enthusiasm in the first place, cost it support. In short, the Section of Fine Arts and the WPA art program were not exemplary and uplifting for enough people.

Edward Bruce's Section of Fine Arts touched well under 1,000 of the 57,000 artists and art teachers in the country, and many of those who took commissions lacked enthusiasm and inspiration after enduring the cautious Section's "suggestions" and delays. Artists who "painted Section"—however few and however they may have justified it to themselves—were not ambassadors of the system. Other artists objected to the Section's selectivity, its arbitrary "standards," its mysterious and eternally invoked jury system. To those artists with activist commitments, such intervention and self-proclaimed ability to judge recalled the elitism of an earlier age, and they saw Bruce, Forbes Watson, and Olin Dows as self-gratifying proprietors of an enterprise usurped from the public trust.

The 10,000 or so artists who were on the FAP rolls at various times and thousands of others who wanted to be on them were piqued on occasion by the impersonality and rigidity of the relief agency. They could not understand why they had to submit to the humiliation of the pauper's oath. The rural California artist who sent President Roosevelt a photograph of her nine children,

179

84 Lobby of the Cook County Hospital in Chicago, decorated by the
FAP, Illinois; murals by Edwin Boyd Johnson, sculpture by Charles
Umlauf

a pathetic account of their condition, a dime to help her President in his own troubles and the query: "Why wouldn't they put me on the Federal Art Project?" expected more than the "usual reply" that assistant administrator Parker penciled on the routing slip of her letter. So did the artist who did not have the required length of residence to qualify for relief in any state who was driven to exclaim to the President: "I *am* an American and by God I *can* paint;" and so did the artist who exhausted his resources, discovered his wife needed medical attention, borrowed the limit from friends and spent days tracking down relief officials, without effect. The "usual" form letter explained that since Washington had no control over hiring, the writer's letter would be forwarded "to the proper official in charge" in the state. The "unconditionally disapproved" request of artists to use project facilities after hours on grounds that it increased costs of light, power, and equipment, and also led "to a relaxing of discipline" hardly rallied artists to defense of the art units.[8]

Washington passed on rigid orders and procedure requirements to local project officers and carrying them out not only consumed their energies but often estranged them from the project workers. It took about a month from requisition to receipt of materials essential for project operations in New York City and three weeks to get postage stamps in Connecticut. The Treasury Department froze funds and forbade the purchase of some items that the projects deemed essential. After a month with the FAP one experienced administrator exclaimed: "I thought I knew what red tape was!" To circumvent it one California project chief asked the receivers of federal art to make their "co-sponsor contribution" checks to an account in a local art shop against which the project drew supplies. In another case a supervisor granted a worker a $35 a month raise with the understanding that $25 of it would be kicked back to buy a multilith press (forbidden by the Treasury Department on grounds that the Government Printing Office was the nation's authorized printer). Desire for personal gain prompted neither fraud. The harassed administrators only wanted to operate efficiently. After the WPA's Division of Investigation descended upon them, little innovative spirit remained. And if the administrators had any standing left among

artists after their exposure as violators of rules, what remained to them after they delivered the pink slips required by Washington-dictated quota cuts? The files bulged with letters complaining that an impregnable "inner circle" and "rotten politics" determined the course of unhappy lives. The local official who sided with the artists against a federal decision learned from Parker that it was his "responsibility as the representative of the Federal Director to carry out administrative orders and not to question them."[9]

Colonel Harrington and other administrators in the late 1930s always contended that the WPA cultural projects' difficulties resulted from too much independence from WPA. The opposite seems the better conclusion. The WPA, unpopular with tenured civil servants in the Bureau of the Budget and Comptroller's Office and often obstructed by them, was a morass of directives and procedures and checks and delays, an administrative tangle with its own internal make-work operations. The FAP did not enjoy enough freedom from WPA domination to establish the efficient program and support among project workers and the public that would perpetuate federal art patronage. Cahill warned his staff to "be vigilantly on guard against getting over-procedural or getting into a bureaucratic frame of mind." And Parker affirmed that "a creative fine arts project cannot be conducted by the distribution of impersonal rules and regulations." Yet in the end there was little choice; Cahill and Parker had to observe WPA regulations and had increasingly less power to make fundamental decisions on their own. All the national directors of Federal One saw need to give the projects wider geographic distribution and better promotional machinery, to mention but two sensible reforms. The technicalities of WPA prevented it. The national directors, at one point, had to send their own outgoing mail to a higher official for "review, approval, and release." And like their underlings in the states, national officers on occasion found it advantageous to present a distorted image of themselves and the state of the project. Derogatory reports to Washington from local projects were considered rather bad form, particularly when names of the art or WPA hierarchy were mentioned. The writer who steeled himself to differentiate between spades and bloody shovels was likely to receive an officious acknowledgment and the assurance from the Washington recipient that "in compiling these reports . . . I will see fit to omit such references." Thus the reports that were shuffled up and down the chain of command often bordered on the inane. The FAP Progress Report six months after the strikes of 1937, for example, which announced that project successes had "compelled the oppositionist press to cool its heels at the threshold of public opinion" was sheer flatulence. If FAP artists lacked proof of the disparities between appearances and realities and operations and intents of the WPA, they sensed them. And they hedged their strongest loyalties.[10]

The large following among the public which might have prevented the projects from fading never developed. A large part of the reason was that administrators were too rule bound and lacked imagination and flair for communicating in any other media than painting. Both the Section of Fine Arts and Federal Art Project perceived that they could increase enthusiasm and awareness if they could reach the influential magazine and book reading public. Both fumbled their attempts.

Edward Bruce and Forbes Watson in 1937 determined to write their own book, *Art in Federal Buildings*. They declined to work through a commercial publisher on the traditional terms and to accept the editorial cuts, the limit on illustrations, and the layout standards involved. Instead they arranged with a publisher— with limited distribution facilities—to publish a book entirely written and assembled by themselves in return for "guaranteed" sale of a specified number of copies. The title page inscribed "Volume I" and the introductory promise "to publish further volumes which shall fully illustrate sculpture models, installed sculpture, completed and installed murals, and all other work in the fine arts created for the decoration of Federal buildings," betrayed the expectations of the authors when they began. Although the obscure work provided the fullest published account of Treasury art 30 years later, the authors lost money on their $6.50 self-praising work. The Carnegie Endowment later advanced Watson $6,000 for a volume on federal sculpture, but it was not forthcoming. Watson's articles about the Section and Sec-

tion artists in the *Magazine of Art* had an easily recognizable tone—uncritical, tenderly egotistical, and suspicion inspiring for readers whose support the project needed most. Bruce fed selected anecdotes, photographs, and statistics to other writers, but never invited scholars or popular writers to move freely in the offices and files for an objective—and more believable—study.

The record of the FAP in attempting to enroll the reading public was worse. Any information or manuscript concerning a local art project destined for publication had to pass the state FAP director, the state Women's and Professional Division director, and if the publication circulated outside the state the material had to clear the Washington office. Parker rebuked violators and lectured them: "We must subordinate our activities and modulate our voices to blend with the long-time plans of Mr. Hopkins and the chorus directed by Mr. [David] Niles" of the Women's and Professional Division. Parker expected workers to inform each state's citizenry "of the worth of the Art Project" and "regardless of special circumstances, contacts, relationships, or inspirations" to refer "any and all inquiries" from nonlocal publications to Washington. When Washington granted local projects permission to write for national distribution, the prose and illustrations crossed Parker's desk before they went to the publisher. Feeling that one of Mrs. McMahon's articles left the administration "open to much criticism," the Washington censors asked for section rewrites and "another conclusion." The writer with the New York City information service who included the comment in his proposed article that the 1937 layoffs left the project "badly shaken and almost completely demoralized" infuriated Parker. Project writers, he ordered, must "remember in the preparation of such articles that they are employees of the Federal government." Information not prepared in a "dignified" manner—a term the assistant chief used synonymously with "laudatory"—"should not be released to the public."[11]

The FAP never completed the one publication which would have portrayed it most accurately and possibly won supporters. In 1938 Cahill and Parker began preparation for a book, *Art for the Millions*. The plan called for about half of the projected

85 Joe Jones (Section of Fine Arts), mural in the post office, Seneca, Kansas

75,000 words to consist of signed 500 to 1,500 word articles by project workers, artists, supervisors, and administrators. The other half would be "editorial comment and factual text" and tables. Embellished with 150 illustrations the book would retail for about $2.50 ($1.00 to project workers). By spring 1939 they had solicited material and signed an agreement with the Guild's Committee for Federal Writers' Publications, one of the front groups which enabled Federal One to escape publishing through the impossible Government Printing Office. The directors assured writers of their freedom from censorship and even asked the often critical artists unions in New York City, Chicago, San Francisco, and Minneapolis to contribute articles. The radical project artist Stuart Davis agreed to write on "Abstract Painting Today," Edward Millman on "Symbolism," while others tackled such essays as "An Approach to Mural Decoration," "The Sculptor's Point of View," and "The Negro Artist Today." The finished anthology would offer pieces on project concerns from children's murals and puppetry to psychographic theory and abstract technique.[12]

The reorganization of 1939 caught the endeavor in mid-course, invalidated many of the statistics, required revised explanations

184

of operations, and repeatedly required the contract publisher, Albert Whitman Company, to set back the publication date. Finally in April 1940 the manuscript was assembled "in final form" and sent to Mrs. Kerr's office to be "cleared." Suddenly, the FAP began emphasizing aid to the war effort and the creative art projects took rank behind poster and model making, and in the commotion of change no one mentioned *Art for the Millions*.[13] The manuscript disappeared.

Besides failure to influence artists and the general public in behalf of continued patronage, the art units failed to win champions in the government. Art agencies irritated some civil servants because somehow they kept requiring exceptions to traditional procedures and controls. The art agencies on occasion used the machinery to gain advantages one over the other, and they never learned how to present a strong case in their own behalf and never offered a united front to win converts among the professionals on matters of procedure or principle.

For all the faith of Bruce's colleagues in his ability to mouth jargon and adopt airs appropriate to the marketplace, the salon, or the anteroom, the Section chief was not convincing to the highest decision makers. He tried too hard, promised too much, and overacted. In the spring of 1939, a time when Europe was virtually falling apart and when American intellectuals were under sharp attack for their social commitments, Bruce managed to get an invitation to show some post office mural designs to the President and the cabinet. Around the walls of the cabinet room Bruce propped sketches submitted in the competition for the Wausau, Wisconsin, Post Office, and he told the nation's top executives that the Section was making America's rural post offices "little cultural centers." These little cultural centers raised the standard of living by bringing into the lives of the people something beautiful and made people realize how much richer was life when it touched something of beauty and good taste. It was the "best panacea," Bruce asserted, "against all the rotten unrest" that tormented the

86 The Cabinet Room, spring 1939, before the President and Cabinet arrived to view entries in a competition run by the Section of Fine Arts for a mural in the post office at Wausau, Wisconsin

world. Moving from panel to panel he asked the cabinet to observe the lack of evidence of defeat and social unrest among Section artists. "I do not believe that one of these artists who painted these pictures likes either Hitler or Mussolini," he said striving to be relevant, "I have a feeling they all know and like the Twenty-Third Psalm."[14]

Bruce feared the attempts to make WPA permanent might succeed. When William I. Sirovich began hearings in 1935 on the possibility of establishing a Department of Science, Art, and Literature, Bruce tried to convince the New York representative that assuring permanency for the Treasury art project would "accomplish the main objective" of the plan. In 1938 when the Coffee-Pepper bill explicitly perpetuated the WPA projects, Bruce privately asked Morgenthau to use his influence to stop its passage. Watson told backers of the bill that "artists and other citizens can be best served by such an organization as the Section." Publicly Bruce and Watson took the position that before any bill went to Congress, Roosevelt should appoint a commission to study "exactly what the WPA has accomplished for art" and the function of arts bureaus in other countries. After Congress rejected the art bureau scheme, Senator Pepper and others urged Roosevelt to appoint the commission Bruce had recommended. Bruce then advised the President: "I am frankly considering the question raised from the point of view of the program of the Section of Fine Arts and I believe the appointment of a committee . . . would have a tendency to divert attention from our main objective." At that juncture Bruce's main objective was construction of the Smithsonian Gallery of Art. And when Roosevelt sent the letters he received championing a permanent bureau of art to Bruce "for preparation of reply," the Section chief always noted in the suggested response that there already existed "a plan for the Smithsonian Gallery of Art which embraces the idea of a great modern museum serving as a national library for the circulation of pictures in various communities."[15]

WPA's opportunity to retaliate against the Section came after the reorganization of 1939 made both components of the Federal Works Agency. When Roosevelt began to divert public building funds into the defense program, Bruce proposed a scheme

185

87 Michael Lantz (Section of Fine Arts), *Man Controlling Work*, one of a pair of limestone sculptures placed at the convergence of Pennsylvania and Constitution Avenues, Washington, D.C.

whereby his Section could maintain its independence but use WPA money, a scheme with inherent problems but one which would force unprecedented cooperation. He wanted to hold competitions for murals and sculpture even though the Public Buildings Administration had no funds. The winning artists would sign the usual contract in the amount announced in the competition. WPA would then put the artist on the nonrelief WPA payroll long enough to receive, in monthly salary, the amount of the Section's contract. Parker protested that the plan gave muralists and sculptors advantages over artists in other creative fields, failed to recognize WPA belief that relief certification had no bearing on ability, but most important constituted a project "in direct conflict and competition with WPA projects." And by exempting the competition winners from "all the procedures and regulations of the WPA," the plan placed the FAP "in an extremely invidious situation." Mrs. Kerr recognized that a combination of high stipend and fast painters might result in "keeping some workers on the payroll, after completion of the job, without duties." Such a plan, she wrote Works Projects administrator Harrington, "does not seem to me necessary." The discussion ceased.[16] With the country becoming more conservative and cost conscious, with defense projects gnawing away the sources of art patronage, with two art units trying to justify existence in the Federal Works Agency, both hastened their impending ends by failing to cooperate to win friends.

Finally, neither the Section nor WPA art program inspired Roosevelt to weave art patronage into government operations. The President carefully avoided pleas to Congress to include art patronage in the appropriation bills, and he refrained from backing any of the art legislation, even though some of his most loyal followers on Capitol Hill supported it. Privately he spoke of "the importance of continuing the projects in some form." At the same time he noted that the action of legislators who opposed the art schemes reflected the views of their constituents who did "not yet appreciate the need of encouraging art, music, and literature."[17] However much Roosevelt may have believed in continuing the cultural programs, other projects received higher priority; and

88 David Smith (FAP, NYC), sculpture

clearly he did not intend to jeopardize them by dissipating his energies and support on Federal One.

Although the projects did not last the question remains: Is this kind of government support for the arts a good idea? For all the feeling that art and artists contribute zest, reflection, and inspiration to life, and for all the evidence that there would have been fewer artists without the depression projects, there were too many problems within the experiments of the 1930s to make them worthy models for the future.

The American government and the American people never decided whether the support of the arts was a legitimate and desirable function of government. They remained divided in opinion about the place of art in American life. They never agreed on such first premises as the compatibility of traditional art with popular democracy or on the definition of the term "professional artist." For Henry Allen Moe, the influential head of the John Simon Guggenheim Foundation, "the plain fact" in the 1930s was that "there never were five thousand artists (in the sense of original creators) in any one country at any time, and there are not anything like that number in the United States now." Holger Cahill thought that under Moe's definition there might be ten in the country.[18] Yet as WPA art chief, Cahill defined an artist as anyone who made his living through the sale of his art or one who, given normal times, could make his living through the sale of his art. And despite the fury attending the federal move to make art a part of daily life, there remained large numbers of artists and laymen who opposed government projects on grounds that they mongrelized art. They retained the view that they had before 1929, namely that good art was something that only an elite group could produce and an elite group could appreciate. No future government subsidy to artists can succeed until these questions are more satisfactorily answered than they were in the 1930s.

A generation after the New Deal projects Americans were no closer to resolution of these questions. Artists like Jackson Pollock, Robert Rauschenberg, and Frank Stella did not much care whether the man on the street understood their art. The important art clientele in New York, Chicago, and Los Angeles were sure he could not and took smug pride in the fact. And there were even more critics than in the 1930s who insisted upon "the movement of the audience up to the best art, not vice versa," and who feared that America's "bourgeois civilization . . . is powerful enough to take over art." The elitists among artists and critics were alarmed especially in the late 1960s by a widely publicized "cultural boom," a phenomenon in which increased quantitites of "things artistic" were discussed, coveted, and consumed by the middle class. Yet the cultural boom did not mean that art was appreciably more integrated with daily life and that Americans were willing to have artistic talent developed as a national resource. William McNeil Lowry of the Ford Foundation, one of the most astute observers of the "cultural boom," branded it "largely an explosion of words." It was a movement characterized by surface involvement; by much activity, and little intensity. The abundance of "culture vultures" notwithstanding, Americans in the 1960s were not much concerned with the arts or the economic livelihood of creative artists.[19] Until artists, critics, and public more nearly reach agreement on what constitutes art and on the place of art in national life, further experiments seem destined for the same divisions that weakened the New Deal effort.

The compatibility of bureaucracy with the creative spirit is at the center of another unresolved issue. A sizable part of the New Deal art story concerns colliding empires, federal-state conflicts, and petty outrages of a thousand sorts. That the bureaucracy of the New Deal was worse than that which came before or after is doubtful. That New Deal art bureaucracy, with its relief requirements, tentative building budgets, fragmented authority, and befogged purposes, failed to develop the full potential of the experiment is certain. Whether another bureaucracy could inspire a stronger allegiance from artists to making art a greater part of American daily life and waste less energy is a question for the generation of Americans and bureaucrats who renew the experiment.

Edward Bruce correctly told artists that his office would be held responsible for the art that went into federal buildings. And being responsible he had no choice but to assure that the art would be acceptable to those who held him responsible. Artists who might have compromised a point for a private patron, where the relationship was more personal, very frequently viewed the same demand from the government as unbearable censorship. Nothing after mid-century indicated that the nature of artists or the federal bureaucracy had changed much. While art historian Lloyd Goodrich considered the New Deal programs free of censorship and propaganda in a degree "almost unparalleled in modern governmental art" and thus acceptable as a framework for other subsidy, the fact that it was government art, others insisted, meant censorship, surveillance, and interference. Without those devices, George Biddle came to see, "no responsible Government agency could operate."

Another important reason the New Deal art programs must be disqualified as a basis upon which future programs might be built is that they were created to do one thing, and then they proceeded to attempt quite another. Harry Hopkins, Henry Morgenthau, and Franklin Roosevelt extended tax money to the PWAP, TRAP, and FAP primarily to maintain skills and feed artists during the depression. Even the Section of Fine Arts, which did not use relief money, probably would not have existed had it not rationalized that needful artists would receive its commissions. Administrators in both art agencies, while fastidiously faithful to the rhetoric of relief, established higher priorities—those of raising the level of national taste and making art a part of daily life (and perhaps of perpetuating their own existence in the process).

WPA Commissioner Howard O. Hunter, in August 1941, asked Librarian of Congress MacLeish to convene officers of the cultural projects and prominent writers, artists, and musicians to evaluate government cultural work. The evaluation, Hunter said, should lead to "a determination as to whether such activities are important enough to retain in our American life." In the ornate Whittall Pavilion of the Library of Congress, Bruce, Cahill, and Mrs. Kerr joined, among others, the museum directors Francis Taylor and John Walker, the writers John Steinbeck, Van Wyck Brooks, Malcolm Cowley, and Freida Kirchway, and the musicians Howard Hanson and Eric de Lamarter. The meeting immediately and permanently bogged down on the questions of whether, relief considerations aside, the product of the government experiments was worth the cost, and who and what the government should subsidize when relief was no longer a necessary consideration. After hours of bickering and restatement of well-known positions, MacLeish asked for agreement on the proposition that "government has a relationship toward, and a useful and necessary activity in . . . the fine arts which is altogether apart from any obligation it may owe to any citizen to eat and work." Turning to the WPA delegation and goading them for a response, the chairman continued, "It seems to me what you people in WPA did, to speak very frankly, was completely hypocritical and wrong. You started certain activities, and being human and alive, you kept telling yourself [sic] you were actually giving people a job, but you were really interested in your program." Florence Kerr, not denying the charge, retorted, "You must admit it is one of the higher types of hypocrisy."[20]

Franklin Roosevelt understood better than cultural enthusiasts of the time and of later times that the New Deal art programs were not models for the future. A few weeks before Pearl Harbor, Edward Bruce offered the President some advice. The world's truly great artists, he wrote, sought perfection, designed their pictures with care, and did not begin painting until the rhythm was complete and every detail made a harmonious whole. Among such artists Bruce placed the President because of his work, the New Deal. Bruce volunteered that Roosevelt's design was complete, and like Leonardo da Vinci when he finished his greatest picture, the President should study it long hours, touching it occasionally, adding a little here and there, and finally offer a masterpiece, a permanent contribution to civilization. Roosevelt replied to "dissent violently over the simile." A great picture was a contribution to civilization for all time, the President agreed. On the other side, he told the well-meaning Section chief, "there 'ain't no sich thing' as a masterpiece of permanence in the art of living or the art of government. That type of art catches a mood, fits the method of expression into the emotions of the day and mingles oils with watercolors, and steel

89 Anton Refregier, *Curtain?* (from *12 Cartoons Defending WPA by Members of the American Artists Congress*, New York, 1939)

engravings with dry point."[21] So it was that New Dealers had caught a mood in the early depression years that permitted them to subsidize art and artists. They mingled relief and construction programs and aesthetics. When the emotions of the Second World War called for change, Roosevelt abandoned the art projects. The mood which enabled government to subsidize art in the 1930s did not recur after the war. Or if it did, there was no Roosevelt to catch it, no New Dealers to mix the metaphors, to mingle expediency and idealism.

[1] *Magazine of Art*, XXIV (Nov. 1941), 488-90; Florence S. Berryman, "Three Years in Art," *American Art Annual*, XXXV (1941), 34.

[2] Frank Getlein, "Federal Aid to Art: Distribution," *New Republic* (Aug. 8, 1960), 21; James Thrall Soby, Jacques Barzun, Douglas Haskell, and Lloyd Goodrich, "A Symposium: Government and Art," *Magazine of Art*, XLII (Nov. 1950), 243-59; Hearings before a Special Subcommittee on the Committee on Labor and Public Welfare on S. 741, S. 785, and S. 1250 (hereafter *Hearings on S. 741, S. 785, and S. 1250*), 87 Cong. 2 Sess. (1962), 181; Hearings before the Special Subcommittee on the Arts of the Committee on Labor and Public Welfare on S. 165 and S. 1316 (hereafter, *Hearings on S. 165 and S. 1316*), 88 Cong. 1 Sess. (1963), 104, 119.

[3] The 1920 census reported over 35,000 artists and art teachers. The 1930 census showed over 57,000, an increase of nearly 62 percent compared to 16 percent total population increase. As shown, artists and total population increased roughly 12 and 7 percent respectively in the 1930s. Census figures showed 83,000 artists and art teachers by 1950, a 26 percent rise while the American population grew 14.5 percent. U.S. Bureau of the Census, *Historical Statistics of the United States: Colonial Times to 1957* (Washington, 1960), 75; O'Connor, *Federal Support for the Visual Arts*, 96.

[4] See oral history interviews with Anton Refregier, Nov. 5, 1964, Peter Hurd, March 28, 1964, Chaim Gross, Sept. 1, 1964, Archives of American Art; Seymour Fogel to Francis O'Connor, May 13, 1968, files of Federal Support of the Visual Arts.

[5] O'Connor, *Federal Support for the Visual Arts*, 96, 97; Isaac Foster to O'Connor [1968], papers relating to Federal Support of the Visual Arts.

[6] Maurice Glickman to O'Connor, July 15, 1968, files of Federal Support of the Visual Arts; oral history interviews with Lee Krasner, Nov. 2, 1964, Adolf Dehn, Feb. 26, 1964, Marion Greenwood, March 12, 1964, in Archives of American Art.

[7] O'Connor, *Federal Support for the Visual Arts*, 95; oral history interview with Ibram Lassaw, Nov. 2, 1964, Archives of American Art.

[8] Mrs. Mary Brittan to Roosevelt, Jan. 27, 1938, W. M. Caleen to Cahill, Nov. 30, 1936, Emerson W. Evans to Roosevelt, April 7, 1937, RG69/651.315; Parker to Harry Knight, April 26, 1939, RG69/FAP.

[9] Raymond O. Richards to Parker, Oct. 25, 1938, RG69/211.5; memorandum by McMahon, March 24, 1937, Parker to Joseph A. Danysh, Dec. 5, 1936, RG69/FAP; Nelson H. Partridge to Cahill, Nov. 18, 1935, WPA Division of Investigation Case Nos. 11-CA-166 and 11-CA-206, RG69/315.

[10] Cahill to Mildred Holzhauer, Feb. 13, 1939, RG69/FAP; C. E. Triggs to National Directors, Nov. 30, 1939, RG69/all; Parker to Morris, April 11, 1939, C. Adolph Glassgold to Richard C. Morrison, April 13, 1938, RG69/211.5; "Progress Report Federal Art Project, Nov. 1937-April 1, 1938," Cahill Papers.

[11] Parker to Samuel H. Friedman, March 3, 1937, RG69/FAP; Parker to McMahon, Nov. 3, 1936, Feb. 20, Sept. 15, 1937, RG69/211.5.

[12] Parker to Morris, March 10, 1939, Benson to Joseph Allen, Aug. 14, 1939, Benson to Grace Clements, Aug. 31, 1939, RG69/211.5.

[13] See correspondence in "Art for the Millions" folder in RG69/211.5. The manuscript has recently been retrieved through the efforts of Professor O'Connor from a storage area used by Holger Cahill. Plans are to publish part or all of the document and to place the original in the Library of the National Collection of Fine Arts.

[14] [Edward Bruce], typed copy of speech before cabinet [spring 1939], RG121/124.

[15] Staff memorandums, July 22, 28, 31, 1939, AAA Reel, NDA/HP1; Bruce to Edwin Fairfax Naulty, Jan. 27, 1936, Pepper to Roosevelt, July 8, 1939, Bruce to Roosevelt, June 22, 1939, Watson to Rowan, Feb. 1, 1938, RG121/124.

[16] Parker to Kerr, April 5, 1940, Kerr to Harrington, April 17, 1940, RG69/211.5.

[17] Roosevelt to Nelson Rockefeller, June 6, 1939, AAA Reel NDA/HP1.

[18] "The Government and the Arts: A Proposal by George Biddle, with Comment and Criticisms by Others," *Harper's*, CLXXXVII (Oct. 1943), 433.

[19] W. McNeil Lowry, "So Much Activity, So Little Intensity," *Chicago Daily News Panorama*, Oct. 9, 1965, 3; *Hearings on S. 165 and S. 1316*, 142, 147; *Hearings on S. 741, S. 785, and S. 1250*, 129, 293; Russel Lynes, "The Case Against Government Aid to the Arts," *New York Times Magazine*, March 25, 1962, 86; Mark Harris, "Government as Patron of the Arts," *New York Times Magazine*, Sept. 13, 1964, 35, 139-40; Stanley Kauffmann, "Can Culture Explode," *Commentary*, XL (Aug. 1965), 19-28; Soby and others, "A Symposium: Government and Art," 257.

[20] "Conference on the Arts Program of the Works Projects Administration, Oct. 8, 1941," typescript, 14, Cahill Papers.

[21] Bruce to Frederic A. Delano, Sept. 26, 1941, Roosevelt to Bruce, Oct. 2, 1941, AAA Reel NDA/HP1.

Note on Sources

Textbooks in American history usually make passing reference to the New Deal cultural projects, sometimes dwelling for a paragraph on the Federal Theatre Project's dramatic fate. The trend toward expensive, illustration-filled textbooks has given exposure to perhaps a dozen federal art works, but the art projects retain low priority among the alphabet agencies traditionally discussed. The general histories of the Roosevelt era offer little more. Arthur M. Schlesinger, Jr.'s third volume of *The Age of Roosevelt, The Politics of Upheaval* (Boston, 1960); Basil Rauch's *The History of the New Deal, 1933-1938* (New York, 1944); and James MacGregor Burns's *Roosevelt: The Lion and the Fox* (New York, 1956) describe the circumstances in which the projects were born but not the projects themselves. William E. Leuchtenburg's one paragraph in *Franklin D. Roosevelt and the New Deal, 1932-1940* (New York, 1963) probably overemphasizes murals and the Mexican influence.

Several more specialized books deal with the art projects in various ways. William F. McDonald, *Federal Relief Administration and the Arts: The Origins and Administrative History of the Arts Projects of the Works Progress Administration* (Columbus, 1969) is a labored tome of more than 850 pages. Under the auspices of the American Council of Learned Societies a team of researchers worked and interviewed through the war years and completed the manuscript for this book in 1946. After its first editing by Macmillan Company in 1949 a feud erupted between the authors and some of the cultural project leaders who felt that the manuscript was unduly critical, stressed bureaucracy, and failed to portray in proper perspective the sacrifices and achievements of the government workers. Neither Macmillan nor McDonald saw fit to explain publicly the pressures which stopped publication. The edition by Ohio State University Press differs little from the original (a microfilm copy of which, entitled "Federal Relief Administration and the Arts: A Study of the Works Progress Administration," is in the Music Division, Library of Congress). Large sections of the book seem gratuitous; it is poorly documented (correspondence is cited to such vague and gargantuan collections as "WPA Files," and some references are cited to the Federal Works Agency Library, which did not exist at the time the book was published); and it is incomplete. Still, the work is impressively detailed, contains the results of surveys and interviews, and offers defensible conclusions about federal patronage.

Francis V. O'Connor, *Federal Support for the Visual Arts: The New Deal and Now* (Greenwich, Conn., 1969) is a report to the National Endowment for the Arts on a research project of the same name. O'Connor offers an accurate and well-ordered accounting of the FAP, TRAP, and Section in New York, a guide to project records, and proffers recommendations for contemporary patronage by government. In the course of his study O'Connor surveyed surviving federal artists in New York and commissioned 10 ex-workers to write "research reports" on various aspects of New Deal programs. These appear in *The New Deal Art Projects: An Anthology of Memoirs* (Washington, 1972). Other materials created and discovered on the project have been deposited for scholarly use in the Library of the National Collection of Fine Arts, Smithsonian Institution. This rich cache includes the original manuscript of *Art for the Millions* which O'Connor, at the time of this writing, is preparing for publication. O'Connor has also written a short but useful account of federal patronage in the form of a catalogue for an exhibition of Treasury and WPA art. His *Federal Art Patronage: 1933 to 1943* (College Park, Md., 1966) includes a helpful bibliography.

Edward Bruce and Forbes Watson, *Art in Federal Buildings: An Illustrated Record of the Treasury's New Program in Painting and Sculpture* (Washington, 1936) displays Treasury taste, provides a brief history, and details Section procedures. Edwin O. Christensen, *The Index of American Design* (New York, 1950) contains more Index plates than any other published work to date and a revealing "Introduction" by Holger Cahill. A two-volume collection of Index plates, *Treasury of American Design* by Clarence P. Hornung, is now (1972) in process of publication. Grace Overmyer, *Government and the Arts* (New York, 1939) offers the kind of information found in press releases on the Treasury and WPA projects. Ralph Purcell, *Government and Art* (Washington, 1956), devotes a chapter to the 1930s. Purcell emphasizes the achievements and lightly dismisses the problems of the projects. The opposite criticism can be directed toward George Biddle's *An American Artist's Story* (Boston, 1939), especially the portions of the book dealing with the Section of Fine Arts. Jane Dehart Mathews, *The Federal Theatre, 1935-1939: Plays, Relief, and Politics* (Princeton,

1967) is a model of organization and includes an excellent account of the Dies committee. See also the introductions to the exhibition catalogues by Holger Cahill, *New Horizons in American Art* (New York, 1936), Thomas C. Parker, *Frontiers of American Art* (San Francisco, 1939), and Richard C. Morrison, *Federal Art in New England, 1933-1937* (np, nd). The social commitment of many New Deal artists is in John Taylor Arms, *Art as a Function of Government* (New York, 1937) and American Artists' Congress Against War and Fascism, *First American Artists' Congress* (New York, 1936). An accessible source for project statistics and reports on activities is *American Art Annual*, XXXII-XXXVI (1935-1945). The state of art at the beginning of the New Deal is the subject of Frederick P. Keppel and R. L. Duffus, *The Arts in American Life* (New York, 1933).

Few art historians have shown a special interest in government art projects, and much of what these specialized historians have written centers on the two dozen or so most recognized artists. Moreover, a certain *ars gratia artis* running through their work usually obscures the relief and social issues. Milton W. Brown, *American Painting from the Armory Show to the Depression* (Princeton, 1955) is excellent background. Oliver W. Larkin, *Art and Life in America* (rev. edn., New York, 1964) contains an accurate account of depression art projects, as does Edgar P. Richardson, *Painting in America: The Story of 450 Years* (New York, 1956). Social themes are treated in John I. H. Baur, *Revolution and Tradition in American Art* (Cambridge, 1951), and in Donald Drew Egbert, *Socialism and American Art* (Princeton, 1967). Lloyd Goodrich and John I. H. Baur, *American Art of Our Century* (New York, 1961), Barbara Rose, *American Art Since 1900: A Critical History* (New York, 1967), and *The Artist in America* (New York, 1967), compiled by the editors of the journal *Art in America*, stress individual artist's achievements and evolution through the 1930s.

Donald S. Howard, *The WPA and Federal Relief Policy* (New York, 1943) and Arthur W. Macmahon et al., *The Administration of Federal Work Relief* (Chicago, 1941) are essential to unraveling the procedural and administrative tangles of WPA. The role of WPA chief Harry Hopkins is the subject of Searle F. Charles, *Minister of Relief: Harry Hopkins and the Depression* (Syracuse, 1963) and the first third of Robert E. Sherwood, *Roosevelt and Hopkins: An Intimate History* (New York, 1948). James T. Patterson, *Congressional Conservatism and the New Deal* (Lexington, 1967), well illustrates the nature and strength of the coalition which all but eliminated the WPA art project in 1939. Walter Goodman, *The Committee: The Extraordinary Career of the House Committee on Un-American Activities* (New York, 1968) is more useful on the early Dies committee than August Raymond Ogden, *The Dies Committee* (Washington, 1945) and Frank J. Donner's unscholarly *The Un-Americans* (New York, 1961).

A number of unpublished manuscripts are pertinent to the New Deal Art projects. Norman Pietan, "Federal Government and the Arts" (Ph.D. dissertation, Columbia University, 1949), used the interviews and basic materials collected by William F. McDonald's ACLS team, but Pietan is less critical. Erica Beckh Rubenstein, "The Tax Payers' Murals" (Ph.D. dissertation, Harvard University, 1944) is a sympathetic and highly competent survey of the content and style of government murals. Not the least valuable part of the work is the bibliography on legislation and attempts at legislation in behalf of the arts. Belisario R. Contreras, "The New Deal

Treasury Department Art Programs and the American Artist: 1933 to 1943" (Ph.D. dissertation, American University, 1967) examines in detail the theories of Edward Bruce and his associates. Contreras further chronicles Section relationships with the most prominent artists and administrators. Eleanor M. Carr, "The New Deal and the Sculptor: A Study of Federal Relief to the Sculptor on the New York City Art Project of the Works Progress Administration, 1935-1943" (Ph.D. dissertation, New York University, 1969) is largely concerned with the questions of which sculptors did what, and where they did it in New York. Gerald M. Monroe, "The Artists Union of New York" (Ed.D. dissertation, New York University, 1971) answers the important questions about the social conscience of artists during the thirties, their motivations to organize, and their collective achievements and failures. Also helpful is Karal Ann Marling, "Federal Patronage and the Woodstock Colony" (Ph.D. dissertation, Bryn Mawr College, 1971).

The most important sources are the working office files of the art projects, now in the National Archives. Record Group 121, records of the Public Building Service, contains over 138 linear feet, exclusive of photographs and card files, of the day-by-day paper accumulated by the Public Works of Art Project, the Section of Fine Arts, and the Treasury Relief Art Project. Material applicable to all the projects is scattered throughout the collection and there is much duplication. Since Edward Bruce frequently was away from the Washington office, his staff conducted extensive and candid correspondence, thus incorporating into the record arguments and decisions that under other circumstances would be matters of interoffice conversation. Moreover, Bruce kept letters from all his important correspondents in office files and, despite the fact that they worked in one suite of offices, his staff seemed given to circulating memorandums.

Record Group 69, records of the Works Progress Administration, is no testimony to WPA administrative efficiency. The records of the Federal Art Project (and the WPA Art Program, as it was called after 1939) came to the National Archives from file cabinets much neglected by the depleted office staff of 1943. One feels that project secretaries made as many copies as the typewriters could accommodate and instructed file clerks to salt several folders with them in order to assure finding any needed copy. Eliminating the duplication and bringing some order to the chaotic arrangement is a task yet facing the National Archives. The present categories imposed by the Archives roughly correspond to divisions in the WPA system. Stories still circulate of raids by departing officials on project records and office references. The most troublesome events are not a matter of record, and there is no complete set of WPA or art project publications. A further frustration of working in this early testimony to the paper revolution is the official tone of the correspondence, especially that from Washington. Certainly the personalities of WPA officials do not project so clearly as those of the Section of Fine Arts.

The art project decimal file and the segregated art project file (cited in this work, RG69/FAP) consume much more archival space than the Treasury art records. Most of the material that exists from the state projects is in the segregated file, although much is duplicated in the state decimal file. Most state project offices forwarded to the Archives little that revealed local personality. In 1943 each state submitted a statistical and narrative art project report as a part of its final WPA report. Holger Cahill prepared a national report, "Record of Program Operation and Accomplishment: Art Program." All are disappointing. Cahill's report never leaves the theme of the ill effects caused by loss of federal technical controls in 1939. The state reports in many cases were written by art project directors appointed after 1939 who knew little of previous achievements and problems, and in other cases by directors embittered by events after the 1939 reorganization. Also important are the records of the Works Progress administrator (unquestionably the most orderly of WPA records), the records of the Women's and Professional Division (little cited in this work and consisting of unmeasured linear feet yet unexamined by scholars), and records of the WPA Division of Information. The latter supported a relief project charged with making a newspaper clipping file on WPA subjects and writing a daily press summary for top administrators. The Audio Visual Division of the National Archives is the custodian of thousands of photographs of government art works.

The papers of Franklin D. Roosevelt and Harry Hopkins in the Roosevelt Library, Hyde Park, applicable to the New Deal art projects are a part of the microfilm collection of the Archives of American Art (AAA) which maintains research facilities in Detroit, New York, and Washington, D.C. The extensive collection of the AAA, the result of a program, "The New Deal and the Arts," underwritten by the Ford Foundation in 1964, includes microfilms of the Treasury art records in Record Group 121 and WPA art records in Record Group 69 of the National Archives. AAA workers also salvaged many art project records which remained in the states and conducted tape recorded interviews with many surviving artists and administrators. Then in 1966 the Ford Foundation grant expired before the work was completed. At the time of writing a considerable part of the AAA collection is closed and will remain so until the organization acquires money and manpower to index the mass of material and arrange it in workable order. The taped interviews which are presently available are uneven in quality, and one wishes that more of the AAA interviewers had approached the successful alumni of federal projects with something more positive and provocative than: "Is there anything you want to say about the government art projects?"

The AAA is also the repository of the Edward Bruce Papers, most of which are duplicated in the records of the Section of Fine Arts. Several artists who worked with the projects have deposited papers. Most will be more useful in studies of individual aesthetic convictions, career, and personal development than in evaluating federal projects. Complete AAA holdings are listed in successive issues of the *Journal of the Archives of American Art*.

Holger Cahill left no extensive body of personal papers. Some miscellaneous items from his personal files are in the files of Federal Support for the Visual Arts: The New Deal and Now, Library of the National Collection of Fine Arts, Smithsonian Institution. A 600-page oral history interview on file with the Columbia University Oral History Collection reveals more about Cahill's personality and background than the official records and other surviving miscellany.

Few of the principles of the New Deal art drama left personal papers. Francis C. Harrington did not. Florence Kerr did not. Thomas C. Parker

did not. The George Biddle Papers (Manuscript Division, Library of Congress) are rewarding—full of correspondence with leading artists, art organization leaders, and all the government project chiefs. The Charles Moore Papers in the Library of Congress have been carefully censored but are still useful in establishing the mood of the Commission of Fine Arts. Congressmen most closely associated with the art project and the move to create a Department of Science, Art, and Literature left little for historians. The records of the House Committee on Patents (William I. Sirovich's committee), the House Committee on Education (John C. Coffee's committee) and the Senate Committee on Education and Labor (Claude Pepper's committee) in the National Archives are useless to the student of federal art subsidy. Even so, there are helpful published hearings of the Patents Committee and the Senate Education and Labor Committee.

Published hearings in addition to those on a federal art bureau or department which tell important parts of the New Deal art story are those of the House Committee on Appropriations, especially those of the 75th Congress, and the first four volumes of the hearings before the House Committee on Un-American Activities.

The American Magazine of Art (after 1939, *Magazine of Art*), *Art Digest*, *Parnassus*, and *Art Front* covered New Deal art better than other periodicals. The Section of Fine Arts enjoyed special standing with the *American Magazine of Art*. Peyton Boswell, editor of the *Art Digest*, generally favored Section work over the WPA, but he faithfully reported events from all the projects. Audrey McMahon of the New York City FAP unit was editor of *Parnassus* until the summer of 1939. *Art Front*, an irregular monthly from 1934 through 1937, was the critical but stimulating organ of the Artists Union. Especially useful articles in the *American Magazine of Art* are: Emanuel M. Benson, "Art on Parole," XXIX (Nov. 1936); George Biddle, "Mural Painting in America," XXVII (July 1934); Edward Bruce, "Implications of the Public Works of Art Project," XXVII (March 1934); two articles by Olin Dows, "Bruce, An Appraisal," XXX (Jan. 1937) and "Art for Housing Tenants," XXXI (Nov. 1938); Edward B. Rowan, "Will Plumber's Wages Turn the Trick?" XXVII (Feb. 1934); Francis H. Taylor, "Pork Barrel Renaissance," XXXI (March 1938); and Forbes Watson, "Steady Job," XXVII (April 1934), "Return to the Facts," XXIX (March 1936), "The Public Works of Art Project: Federal Republican or Democratic?" XXVII (Jan. 1934), "Edward Bruce the Man," XXVII (Nov. 1934). In *Parnassus*, see Audrey McMahon, "The Trend of Government in Art," VIII (Jan. 1936); Emily Genauer, "New Horizons in American Art," VIII (Oct. 1936); Holger Cahill, "American Art Today," XI (May 1939); Forbes Watson, "Art and the Government in 1934," VII (Jan. 1935); and the April 1937 issue containing several short articles on FAP artists.

Other important articles are: Olin Dows, "The New Deal's Treasury Art Programs: A Memoir," *Arts in Society*, II, nd; Erica Beckh, "Government Art in the Roosevelt Era," *Art Journal*, XX (Fall 1960); George Biddle, "The Government and the Arts," *Harper's Magazine*, CLXXXVIII (Oct. 1943), "Art Under Five Years of Federal Patronage," *American Scholar*, IX (Summer 1940); Holger Cahill, "Murals America," *Architectural Record*, LXXXII (Sept. 1937); and Stuart Davis, "What About Modern Art and Democracy?" *Harper's Magazine*, CLXXXIII (Dec. 1943).

Index